Eyewitnesses at the Battle of PERRYVILLE

Compiled and edited by

DAVID R. LOGSDON

Copyright 2007

ISBN 978-0-9798166-0-4

2711 Barclay Drive
Nashville, Tennessee 37206

Other Books in This Series

Eyewitnesses at the Battle of Fort Donelson

Eyewitnesses at the Battle of Franklin

Eyewitnesses at the Battle of Nashville

Eyewitnesses at the Battle of Stones River

Eyewitnesses at the Battle of Shiloh

Sources for Illustrations

Cover: *Official and Illustrated War Record,* by Wright, Bree and Boyd; 1898

Pages vi, vii, 10, 24, 50, 58 and 105: *Battles and Leaders of the Civil War,* Vol. 3; 1888

Pages 2, 6, 8, 26 and 62: *Battles and Leaders of the Civil War, The Century War Book, People's Pictorial Edition;* 1884

Pages 3, 20, 38 and 80: *Campfire and Battlefield an Illustrated History of the Campaigns and Conflicts of the Great Civil War,* by Rossiter Johnson; 1894

Page 12: *Harper's Pictorial History of the Civil War,* Vol. 2; 1894

Pages 15, 46, 70, 75 and 99: *Frank Leslie's The Soldier in Our Civil War,* Vol. 1; MDCCCXC

Page 18: *Harper's Pictorial History of the Civil War,* Vol. 1; 1894

Page 34: *Harper's Weekly,* Nov. 1, 1862

Pages 57, 101 and 114: *Official and Illustrated War Record,* by Wright, Bree and Boyd; 1898

Pages 69 and 119: *Under both Flags, A Panorama of the Great Civil War,* C.R. Graham, editor; 1896

Page 83: Drawing by Studio G, Columbia, Tenn., from a postwar photograph in the Ekstrom Library's Special Collections, University of Louisville

Pagee 85: Drawing by Studio G, Columbia, Tenn., from a photograph, courtesy of Ren and Scott Hankla.

Page 92: *Thirty Years After. An Artist's Memoir of the Civil War,* by Edwin Forbes; 1890

Page 98: *Military Goods Catalogue* (Francis Bannerman Sons); *January 1929*

Contents

Sources for Illustrations ii

Perryville's Significance iv

About this Book. v

Map of the Perryville Battlefield. vii

Map of Bragg's Invasion of Kentucky ix

Chapter 1, Drawn to Perryville. 1

Chapter 2, Duel of the Big Guns 7

Chapter 3, Charging the Federal Batteries 17

Chapter 4, Confederates Advance 33

Chapter 5, Starkweather Stops the Confederates 52

Chapter 6, Darkness Ends the Fighting. 63

Chapter 7, Night on the Battlefield. 77

Chapter 8, Confederates Retreat 93

Chapter 9, The Wounded and Dying 113

Chapter 10, Epilog. 120

Bibliography 121

Eyewitnesses Index 127

General Index 129

Perryville's Significance

Perryville was the biggest Civil War battle fought in Kentucky, and it is important because it kept Kentucky from leaving the Union and joining the Confederacy.

Perryville is also notable because the Federal commander did not seize the chance to inflict a crushing defeat on the South early in the war because he didn't know a battle was going on until after it was over.

Perryville is special, too, for the impression it made on survivors. A number of them, looking back over their experiences in the war, considered the fighting at Perryville the most intense and traumatic.

About This Book

This is the Battle of Perryville told by soldiers and civilians who were there.

They tell the story through excerpts from letters, diaries, memoirs, recollections and books.

The eyewitnesses' grammar and spelling have been corrected only when necessary for clarity. Any words added to the eyewitnesses' accounts are enclosed in parentheses, and ellipses mark any place where eyewitnesses' words have been omitted.

Confederate and Federal soldiers are distinguished by (CS) and (US), respectively, and the men are identified by regiment, brigade and division.

Many people have helped me with this book, but I owe special thanks to:

Kurt Holman and Jonie House at the Perryville Battlefield, for reading the manuscript, providing sources, answering questions and making the battlefield's archives available;

David Fraley at the Carter House in Franklin, Tenn., for making his research files available;

Stuart W. Sanders of the Perryville Battlefield Preservation Association, for making the organization's archives, including copies of Kenneth W. Noe's files, available;

Nashville Library's Interlibrary Loan Department, which consistently provided hard to find books and articles;

Jamie Gillum, for sharing his files on the 16th Tennessee;

And Rita C. Logsdon, for proofreading the final manuscript.

David R. Logsdon
2711 Barclay Drive
Nashville, Tennessee 37206

BATTLEFIELD MAP INDEX

Anderson's division: D4-E4-F4-G4,

Barn (burned): C4,
Beswick (J.) house: E2,
Board house: B5,
Bolding house: F1,
Bottom: D4,
Bottom (G.): D2,
Bottom (H.P.) house: C4,
Bottom (Widow) house: C4,
Bragg's army: B5-C5-D5,
Bragg's headquarters: see Crawford house
Buckner's division: B4-C4-D-4,
Buell's army: B3-C3-D3-E2
Buell's headquarters: see Dorsey house

Caldwell: E4,
Carlin's brigade: E5,
Carpenter (Widow) house: B3,
Cemetery, Carpenter's: B3,
Cemetery, Wilham's: A3,
Chaplin River: A4-A5-B5-B4-B5-B6-C6-C5-D6 -D5-E5-E6-F6-G6,
Chatham house: C4,
Cheatham's division: A4-B4,
College: D6,
Confederate Cemetery: B4,
Crawford house: C6,
Crittenden's division: F3-F2-G2-H2, E3-F3-F2 -G2-H2,

Danville Pike: D6,
Doctor's Branch: F1,
Doctor's Creek: B5-C4-C3-D3-D2-E2-F2-G2-H2,
Dorsey house: E1,
Douglas house: G1,
Dye house: C5,

Gammon house: A4,
Gibson (Widow) house: C4,
Gilbert's corps: D1-E1-E2, C3-D3-E3,
Gooding's brigade: C3,
Goodnight house: B5
Gray (A.) house: H1/I1,
Grain house: G1,

Hardee's wing: D4-E4,
Harmon (J.B.) house: H2,
Harts house: A4,
Harrodsburg Pike: D6-C6,
Hartwell house: F2,
Hazen's brigade: G4,
Hope (Widow) house: F4,

Hope's Creek: E6-F6-F5-F4,

Jackson's division: B4,

Lebanon Pike: I1-H1-H2-G3-G4-F4-F5-E5
Logan house: F2,
Loomis' Battery: C4,

Mackville Pike, Old: A2-B2-B3-C3-C4-D4-D5,
McCook's corps: B3, B4-C4,
McGinnes house: B5,
Middleburg Pike: E6-F6-G6,
Mitchell's division: D3-E3,
Moss house: B3,
Murphy house: C3,

Perryville: D5-D6-E5-E6,
Polk's wing: A4-B4,

Reynolds (Widow) house: C3,
Rousseau's division: C4,
Russell house: E2,
Russell house: B3,

Schoepf's division: D2,
School house: C3,
Sheridan's division: D3, D4,
Smith's division: H2/H3,
Springfield Pike: E1-E2-D2-D3-D4-D5-E5,
Starkweather's brigade: B4,
Steedman's brigade: C3,
Sutherland house: A2,

Terrill's brigade: B4,
Tollgate: H2, D4, F5,

Van Cleve's division: F2/G2, E5/F5

Wagner's brigade: E4,
Waldon house: F5,
Walker house: B5,
Walker's bend: B5
Watkins (B.) house: E3,
Webb house: C5,
Wilkerson house: see Wilkinson house
Wilkinson house: B3,
Wilson's Creek: B3-B4-A4,
Wofert house: C2,
Wood's division: F4,

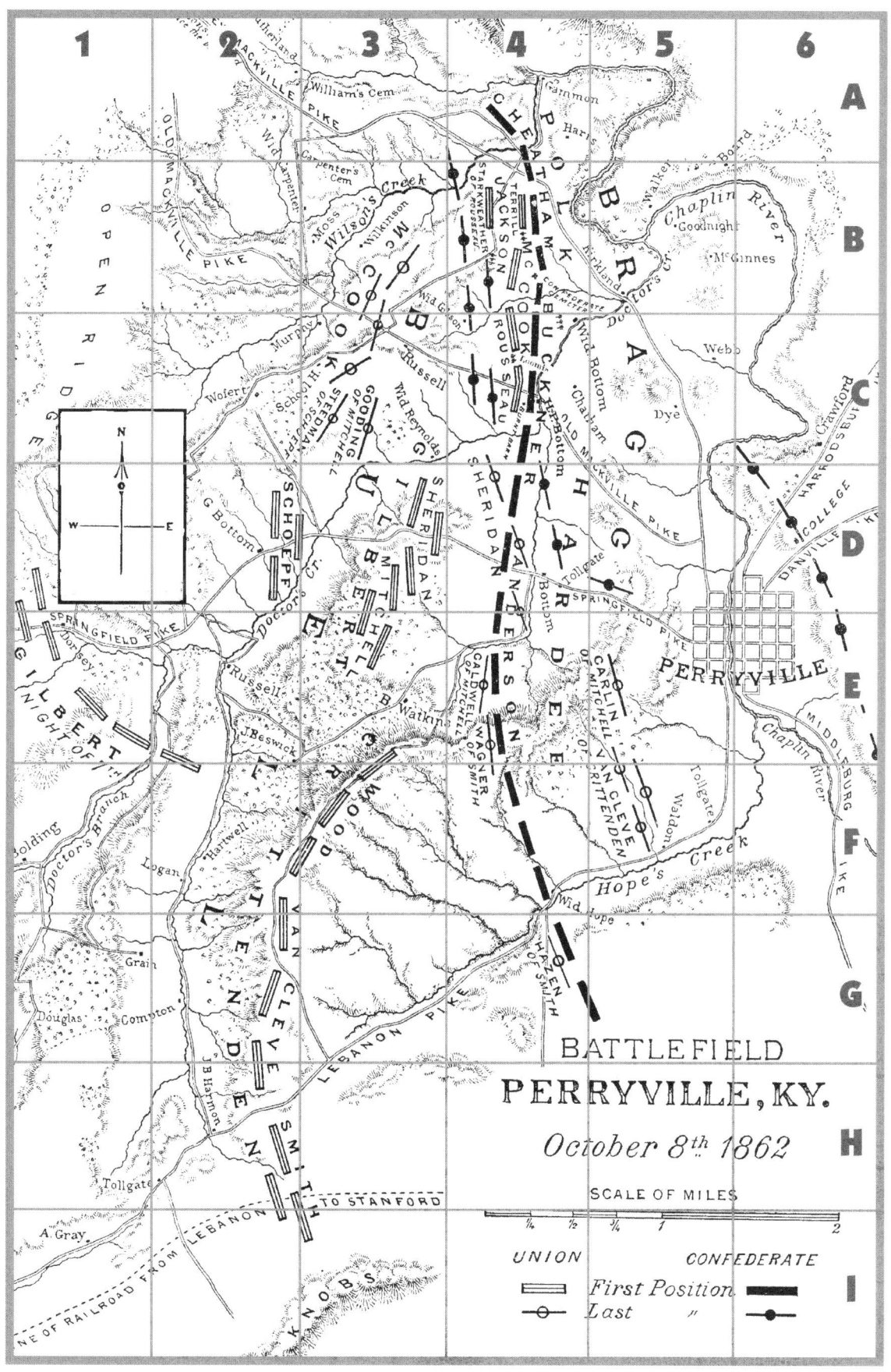

DRAWN TO PERRYVILLE

In October 1862 Confederate and Federal armies are struggling for control of Kentucky. The Confederates have won some victories, but their two armies, under Braxton Bragg and Kirby Smith, are separated. The Federal Army of the Ohio, about 55,000 men under Maj. Gen. Don Carlos Buell, is marching east toward Harrodsburg, Bragg's headquarters for the Army of the Mississippi. The Confederate commander, who has a fighting force of about 16,800 men, doesn't realize danger is approaching, because he expects the showdown with Buell will be to the north. Buell's three corps are pursuing the wing of Bragg's army commanded by Maj. Gen. William J. Hardee as it hurries toward Harrodsburg. As the Federals advance, civilians feel safe to return to their homes. Among them is a businessman who lives about a mile from Springfield:

E.L. Davison, a Springfield merchant:
"We heard Bragg's army had passed through Springfield with Buell's army after them, about 20 miles behind, and that Buell's army would reach Springfield that afternoon. About 12 o'clock (on Oct. 5) . . . I started for Springfield and reached Gen. Crittenden's division encamped within half mile of the town. I had about 50 barrels of old whiskey stored in a brick ware-house near the road, in the town limit of Springfield. As I approached the first big tent, about one-half mile from my ware-house, I smelt my whiskey. I inquired for Gen. Crittenden's camp, rode to it and called to the guards to know where he was or where I could see him. He heard me and halloed out 'Who are you and what do you want?' I . . . told him his soldiers had broken into my warehouse and drank large quantities of whiskey, and were becoming greatly demoralized. He said, 'You do not care for the demoralization of the men, but it is the loss of your whiskey that brought you out this late in the night.' I said, 'All right, good-night.' I then hurried on to the ware-house and met hundreds of soldiers with whiskey in their canteens, tin-cups and everything that would hold it. One man was barefoot and carrying a boot in each hand, full of whiskey. When I got to the ware-house there was a crazed mob of soldiers in front of the door. The doors and windows were broken open and barrels, with their heads knocked out, were on the side-walk. . . . In a short time came an officer with several hundred soldiers. They drove the men up the street . . . but others followed in behind and got into the whiskey. I got the guards to turn their men around and help get them out of the ware-house."

Liquor is also a problem for Confederates marching toward Perryville:

(CS) Sgt. W.C. Gipson, 17th Tennessee, Johnson's Brigade, Buckner's Division:
"I was . . . in charge of the rear guard. Unfortunately the Fifth Confederate, mostly Irish, had got some whiskey, and many of them were drunk, and we had a hard time getting them forward while we tried to keep the enemy back. We had to leave some of them, as they could not travel. We carried their guns for some time, but the enemy pressed us so hard that we hid the guns – twelve in number – under a brush pile."

(CS) Brig. Gen. St. John R. Liddell, brigade commander, Buckner's division:
"We found the roads very dusty and the water very scarce. . . . Buell's column was now fast coming upon our heels and it was getting high time for us to turn upon its head, to avoid being severely pressed. . . . The sound of Artillery reports on the Springfield road behind us evidently indicated the coming of the enemy. . . .

"On the evening of the 6th Oct. whilst preparing to camp after having passed a short distance on the Harrodsburg road from Perryville, Hardee rode near me with his staff and requested me to go with him . . . to look at the ground north of the town, with a view to fixing upon a line of Battle and as he wanted prominent points sketched to bring with me paper and pencils.

"As we rode along together, he remarked that we must fight, since he could not march with the enemy so close at his heels, who must be driven back, or checked at least, to save some supplies we had at Danville. He

Maj. Gen. William J. Hardee

asked my opinion of the position as one from which to give Battle. I unhesitatingly answered that we could hardly have a better one, and that our possession of the water in Chaplin Fork was a decided advantage, as there was none on the road upon which the enemy was advancing . . . and as it was so dusty and dry, the inconvenience . . . would be seriously felt. . . .

"He readily concurred . . . and told me that Genl (Leonidas) Polk had been communicating with Bragg . . . to get his consent and make arrangements for a general engagement here.

"After examining different positions between the Springfield and Mackville roads, he returned to Perryville, and rode to a house on an elevation in a commanding position for a Battery to the south of the place, which we found was owned by a Widow Padlock, having with her a large family of females. The gallant General was quite at home, bandying compliments, particularly with the widow, who . . . expressed her sincere sympathy for the general, that one so advanced in years should be engaged in the dangers and troubles of war. 'Why Madam,' exclaimed the General (47), horrified and touched to the quick, 'how old do you take me to be?' 'Well sir, I am 72 and I think you are about a year younger.' 'How! What! Why Madam, I am not as old as that man!' pointing to (me). . . . But the lady shook her head in utter disbelief and the General now quite concerned fell seriously to work to convince her of her error, and in the eagerness of arguments, appealed now and then to me for confirmation. . . . I was busily engaged in making out my sketch of the localities of the expected Battle ground, and after getting through, . . . I saw clearly that he was making no progress in convincing the lady, and therefore proposed to beat a retreat – insisting that we could not afford to waste any more time upon the subject now; but that I could freely say in his support we were nearly of the same age! But the lady shook her head, not at all satisfied."

Early in the morning of October 7, Polk orders Confederate reinforcements to Perryville. But, he doubts a very large Federal force is approaching the small town of 300 inhabitants, and so informs Bragg. The Federal commander, however, has ordered his three corps (Maj. Gen. Alexander M. McCook, 13,000 men; Maj. Gen. Thomas L. Crittenden, 20,000 men; and Acting Maj. Gen. Charles C. Gilbert, 22,000 men) to converge on Perryville for a coordinated attack in the morning of October 8:

Mrs. J.B. Berkshire, on a farm near Perryville:
"The morning of the Seventh of October dawned, beautiful and bright, under a cloudless sky."

(US) Dr. John Tilford, 79th Indiana, Beatty's brigade, VanCleve's division:
"We took up our line of march about 10 o'clock this morning."

(US) Maj. J. Montgomery Wright, assistant adjutant-general on Buell's staff:
"The country through which Buell's army marched is almost destitute of water."

(US) William G. Putney, bugler, Barnett's battery, Greusel's brigade, Sheridan's division:
"The battery marched in the dust and sun."

(US) Brig. Gen. William P. Carlin, brigade commander, Mitchell's division:
"The march . . . was slow and tedious, the weather being still warm and the country very dry."

(US) Ormond Hupp, 5th Indiana (Simonson's Battery) Light Artillery, Harris' brigade, Rousseau's division:
"It was a hard matter to find water in this vicinity and what our coffee was made of had a green scum over the top a whole inch thick but it was all there was. . . . The way we managed it was to boil it and keep the scum off for some time before putting in the coffee: it would in this way do very well."

(US) Dr. Tilford, 79th Indiana, Beatty's brigade, VanCleve's division:
"Marched quite fast all day; our army suffers terribly for water, it is almost impossible to get any. . . . Our fellows take water out of mud holes, and drink, as if it was the best water they ever tasted."

(US) Hupp, Simonson's Battery, Harris' brigade, Rousseau's division:
"Traveling through rough country all day, but found many Union people on the road greeting as we passed in an encouraging manner."

Mrs. Berkshire, on a farm near Perryville:
"Hurrying to the highway . . . we beheld a sea of blue, Federal soldiers under the command of General Buell were passing. . . . A great phalanx of infantry first greeted our view, then cavalry, commissary wagons, artillery . . . Awed and almost speechless, we watched what seemed to be a never ending parade; but the sight was exciting and thrilling as the fifes and drums were playing, officers galloping up and down the lines giving orders to their men; flags flying; buttons, buckles, epaulets, bayonets all glittering in the bright sunshine. . . .

"Orders were given to halt, and the soldiers had the opportunity to tell of their great suffering for water. Canteens were filled for as many as could be served. Sister and I took what we could manage, and hurriedly filled them from our wonderful spring. . . .

"An old bent, much-wrinkled, colored woman had come from the big house on the hill to find out what it was all about. The excitement was too much for her and in a frenzy she would jump up and down and shout 'Hurrah for the Union.' A soldier . . . told her he would introduce her to President Lincoln. He took her to one of the big wagons and told her the driver was the President. He reached his hand out and gave her a hearty shake, which she responded to in another burst of enthusiasm, crying – 'God bless you, Massa Lincum.' She was told if she was a Union woman, she would take the red ribbon off her cap and change it for blue, which she afterwards did. The lines began to move again."

(US) Robert M. Rogers, 125th Illinois, McCook's brigade, Sheridan's division:
"The dust was terrible, and about the middle of the afternoon a division of cavalry came riding by pressing on to the front. They rode in column of two's, and it seemed to us that they would never get by. The dust raised by their horses was fearful, and we were not in the best of humor. So as they rode along . . . curses flew at their heads. . . . Some of the boys

actually pricked the horses with their bayonets. But at length they passed us, and glad enough we were to get rid of them."

(US) Brig. Gen. Carlin, brigade commander, Mitchell's division:
"Some skirmishing during the day between the cavalry of Capt. Ebenezer Gay . . . and the rebel rear guard, and occasional cannonading between them."

(CS) W.H. Davis, 4th Tennessee Cavalry Battalion, Wharton's brigade:
"On the afternoon of October 7 Capt. J. R. Lester, commanding Company B of the 4th Tennessee Battalion, under Maj. J. R. Davis, with his company, to which I belonged, was sent from our extreme right to find out General Buell's exact position. . . . We met a company of about our number, all dressed in new Confederate uniforms, wearing sabers and regulation brass Yankee spurs. Our respective captains saluted each other, while their horses' necks were lapped. The captain with the new uniform asked our chief, 'To what command to you belong?' and he received the reply: 'To Wheeler's command, Wharton's Brigade.' Our captain then asked him, 'To what command do you belong?' to which an evasive reply was given. During this colloquy the men of the respective companies advanced to the right and left of their respective commanders, their horses' noses touching. Their sabers and spurs gave the little game away, and as quick as thought our captain yelled out" 'Boys, they are d– yankees; turn loose your six-shooters!' . . . We emptied a volley into them, killing and wounding more than half their number. As the sham captain wheeled his horse to escape, Captain Lester shot him in the back, but it did not knock him out of the saddle. The whole troop quickly followed him, with us in hot pursuit. We got eight or ten more before running into a hornets' nest on the main line of Buell's left wing, where we received a baptism of fire and beat a hasty retreat."

(US) Brig. Gen. Carlin, brigade commander, Mitchell's division:
"It was a pleasant afternoon on the 7th of October that Gilbert's corps arrived at a point about one and a half miles north of Perryville. . . . On the right of the road . . . was a ridge with rather a steep side on the East. Gen. Buell and staff had ridden to the top of the ridge and halted. They dismounted. . . . Having here placed my brigade in bivouac, I approached the staff. . . . Gen. Buell was viewing the country to the south, which his position overlooked, through a telescope, and scanned it long and carefully, sweeping it around from west to east . . . . I supposed from his careful observation that Bragg's army occupied the field he was scanning, but I could see nothing but the woods and open fields that were in the lower lands along the creek . . . lying just north of Perryville, and the highlands beyond. . . . Before night fell I took a long walk to the southwest, in search of water, but found hardly enough to afford a drink for a horse. I had understood that (Maj. Gen. George H.) Thomas, with Crittenden's corps. had marched some miles to the southwest . . . in search of water for a camp."

Buell learns Crittenden's and McCook's corps are too far away to be in position for the attack planned for the morning of October 8. He postpones the attack until October 9:

(US) Capt. Allen L. Fahenstock, 86th Illinois, Greusel's brigade, Sheridan's division:
"That Evening there was Skirmishing untill Dark. All Me and the Men had for Supper was tea and Coffee. Our Regiment had Orders To go Out on Picket that knight. We were placed on the Left of the Battle Field on the Extreme front in a Dangerous Position. We arrived there at 1 O clock at knight. My men Weary and hungry. I had My Men stack their Guns and Lay down while Me and My 1st Lieut watched. All was Quite through the knight although I Could Distinctly See the Rebble Picketts."

(US) Putney, bugler, Barnett's battery, Greusel's brigade, Sheridan's division:
"At night (the battery) camped at the right of the Springfield pike, on a hill, west of Doctor's Fork (Creek), a stream nearly dry, but with occasional pools where one, with a spoon, could dip water enough into a canteen to keep down thirst yet possessing sand and mud enough to pave the throats of those who drank."

Dr. Jefferson J. Polk, retired physician and Perryville resident:
"(The Confederates) had possession of two fine springs, the only good fountains of water in the neighborhood, as there had been a drought for many weeks."

(US) Maj. Wright, assistant adjutant-general on Buell's staff:
"At Perryville a stream flowed between the contending armies. . . . Buell accompanied the center corps – Gilbert's –, and the advance reached this stream on the evening of October 7th. From that time until the stream was crossed there was constant fighting for access to it, and the only restriction on this fighting was that it should not bring on an engagement until time for the general attack should arrive. . . . I obtained a canteenful (of water), and about dark on October 7th, after giving myself a good brushing and a couple of dry rubs without feeling much cleaner, my careless announcement that I was about to take a tin-dipper bath brought General Buell out of his tent with a rather mandatory suggestion that I pour the water back into my canteen and save if for an emergency."

(US) Putney, bugler, Barnett's battery, Greusel's brigade, Sheridan's division:
"It was a cool moonlight night, and many a poor boy looked at that pale moon for the last time, as he lay under his blanket with the sky above and the earth for a bed."

(US) Cpl. Alfred Riggs, 36th Illinois, Greusel's brigade, Sheridan's division:
"Our reg't had been up all night on the march until 12 at night. We had got to the front by one AM."

Earlier in the day, the Confederate army commander, Bragg, ordered Polk to take Cheatham's division to reinforce Hardee; after dealing with the Federal force at Perryville, Polk is to gather his forces and join Bragg at Versailles, north of Harrodsburg:

(CS) Thomas R. Hooper, 16th Tennessee, Donelson's brigade, Cheatham's division:
"We remained in camps at Harrodsburg until about dusk but previous to leaving we cooked up about 2 days rations. . . . We got orders to leave our knapsacks, we then knew or thought a fight was close at hand."

(CS) George W. Jones, Stanford's Mississippi Battery, Stewart's brigade, Cheatham's division:
"Left Harrodsburg about sunset."

(CS) Capt. W.W. Carnes, commanding Carnes' Battery, Donelson's brigade, Cheatham's division:
"I was quite ill and our Surgeon . . . wanted to send me off in an ambulance but I refused to go, so the men made a bed on the two rear boxes of a caisson by piling about two dozen blankets together for me, and when the doctor had given me a dose of medicine I fell asleep."

(CS) Jones, Stanford's Mississippi Battery, Stewart's brigade, Cheatham's division:
"Marched 10 miles . . . to Perryville. The ladies are crowding the streets with Confederate aprons and flags. Hurrah for the ladies of Kentucky!"

(CS) Hooper, 16th Tennessee, Donelson's brigade, Cheatham's division:
"We marched out a little beyond Perryville, lay in line of battle. . . . We heard some picket fighting going on in the night. Our batteries taken their positions in the night."

(CS) Orderly Sgt. William A. Brown, Stanford's Mississippi Battery, Stewart's brigade, Cheatham's division:
"We arrived at 10 PM and took position on a hill about a quarter of a mile south of the town, with the expectation of a fight beginning at daylight. "

(CS) Jones, Stanford's Mississippi Battery, Stewart's brigade, Cheatham's division:
"The Yankees seem to be concentrating their forces on our front."

(CS) Hooper, 16th Tennessee, Donelson's brigade, Cheatham's division:
"We expected to be attacked or attacking the enemy in the morning."

(CS) Orderly Sgt. Brown, Stanford's Mississippi Battery, Stewart's brigade, Cheatham's division:
"The hush of a coming battle was all around us, as men spoke to each other only in low tones."

(CS) William E. Bevens, 1st Arkansas, Powell's brigade, Anderson's division:
"We ... camped in the main street of the town. Some of the boys stole a bee-hive and many of them got stung so their faces were swollen and eyes closed. Dr. Arnold was one of the injured ones, but he did not fail to eat his honey. ... I teased him, saying General Hardee would need no further proof; that he carried his guilt on his face. The doctor did not relish this so I turned over to go to sleep when a bee stung me on the cheek. 'Who's the guilty one now?' laughed the doctor and the joke surely was on me. But I knew where the medicine wagon was, and went and got some ammonia. I bathed my face, and the swelling went down at once."

(CS) Orderly Sgt. Brown, Stanford's Mississippi Battery, Stewart's brigade, Cheatham's division:
"I was ordered back into town to find out where 'head quarters' were. The houses were dark and as silent as a church yard. As I rode through the streets there was not even a dog to bark at me. It was a striking picture of a deserted village. All the townspeople had left to get clear of the expected battle."

(CS) Sam Watkins, 1st Tennessee, Maney's brigade, Cheatham's division:
"I stood picket in Perryville the night before the battle. ... During the night, ... (I and another man) made a raid upon a citizen's pantry, where we captured a bucket of honey, a pitcher of sweet milk, and three or four biscuit. The old citizen was not at home – he and his whole household had gone visiting, I believe. In fact, I think all of the citizens of Perryville were taken with a sudden notion of promiscuous visiting about this time; at least they were not at home to callers."

(CS) Luke W. Finlay, 4th Tennessee, Stewart's brigade, Cheatham's division:
"Reaching Perryville about midnight, ... (we) lay in the open field on our arms."

(CS) Jones, Stanford's Mississippi Battery, Stewart's brigade, Cheatham's division:
"Stood by our guns all night."

Perryville, Kentucky

DUEL OF THE BIG GUNS

October 8, 1862, begins early for men in Gilbert's Federal corps:

(US) Cpl. Alfred Riggs, 36th Illinois, Greusel's brigade, Sheridan's division:
"We only got two hours sleep, it was from 3 until 5 AM."

(US) William G. Putney, bugler, Barnett's battery, Greusel's brigade, Sheridan's division:
"At three o'clock in the morning Lieutenant Plant went round to the different guns and roused the men beside their guns and horses. The battery had stood in line of battle all night ready to move at a moment's notice. Not much breakfast was eaten, and soon the battery moved out on the pike before it was hardly light enough to see."

At a camp near Mackville, McCook's Federal corps is stirring:

(US) L.E. Knowles, 1st Wisconsin, Starkweather's brigade, Rousseau's division:
"We got up at about 3 a.m. . . . and had breakfast."

(US) George M. Kirkpatrick, 42nd Indiana, Lytle's brigade, Rousseau's division:
"We expected to fight, and had heard that the Johnies would take all of our grub away from us if they captured us. . . . I ate my two pounds of pickled pork, raw, and chewed up the coffee which I had from fear of its being taken from me."

(US) Knowles, 1st Wisconsin, Starkweather's brigade, Rousseau's division:
"(We) moved out about day light. It was our first chance in regular battle, . . . and the boys were so eager for the fray that the usual order of 'steady on the right' was changed to 'steady on the left,' as there was at all times danger of the line getting doubled up by the left getting ahead."

A sick and medicated Confederate battery commander is asleep on one of the caissons arriving at the lines near Perryville:

(CS) Capt. W.W. Carnes, commanding Carnes' Battery, Donelson's brigade, Cheatham's division:
"(I) did not awake till I was almost turned off the caisson in making a turn on the side of a steep hill on the extreme left of what was afterwards the battlefield. That was very early, about sun-rise."

(US) Putney, bugler, Barnett's battery, Greusel's brigade, Sheridan's division:
"In a short time, from the front, came the sharp crack of the musket, sounding on the early morning air. A quiet order of halt was given to the battery, while the . . . infantrymen cleared the way. Then forward again to a hill beyond just barely lighted by the coming dawn. This hill became famous as the northern name for the coming battle, Chaplin's Hill. There was a quick move by the line of skirmishers, a short sputter or two of musketry, and with a dash the ridge was ours. By early daylight the right section under Lieutenant Plant moved up and took position on its crest, at the right of the Springfield pike."

In Confederate lines:

(CS) Luke W. Finlay, 4th Tennessee, Stewart's brigade, Cheatham's division:
"Aroused early on the 8th by the skirmishing on the front."

(CS) Capt. John M. Taylor, 27th Tennessee, Maney's brigade, Cheatham's division:
"Early in the morning I accompanied Lieut. Albert Andrews, of my company, to the creek, where we washed our hands and faces. He . . . spoke of being killed, and what he wanted me to do in that contingency. I endeavored to shake this presentiment . . . but to no effect."

(CS) Orderly Sgt. William A. Brown, Stanford's Mississippi Battery, Stewart's brigade, Cheatham's division:
"By daylight we were all up and expecting to see the lines of the Federals. At sunrise cannonading began on our right – only occasional shots. There was no sign of the Yankees on our front, though we continued to expect them."

(CS) W.H. Davis, 4th Tennessee Cavalry Battalion, Wharton's cavalry brigade:
"The sun rose bright and clear into a cloudless day."

(CS) Carroll H. Clark, 16th Tennessee, Donelson's brigade, Cheatham's division:
"It took considerable time to get . . . (the) army in the desired position. . . . We were formed in line and awaited the order to march forward. The enemy was about one half mile from us, and the crack of the picket's rifle and the occasional roar of a canon made me feel sad."

(CS) Thomas B. Ellis, 3rd Florida, Brown's brigade, Anderson's division:
"Knowing that a battle was on hand and my brother would be in it, I now deserted my position as wagon guard and set out to find my Company, and did find it in line of battle. . . . With one or two more men I was detailed to take all the canteens of the Company and go to a spring not very far off, and fill and bring back."

(CS) William R. Talley, Palmer's Battery, Brown's brigade, Anderson's division:
"Our brigade was held in reserve. The infantry had camped in this wood and left a lot of old clothing that they had thrown away and our boys found the first body lice that we had ever seen."

While Federal and Confederate troops at Perryville wait for the battle to begin, more units of Buell's army are approaching. The heat, lack of water and strenuous march are taking their toll on a soldier who had eaten his pickled pork and coffee beans so they wouldn't be taken from him if captured:

(US) Kirkpatrick, 42nd Indiana, Lytle's brigade, Rousseau's division:
"Water was very scarce and the salt meat took effect with a vengeance. . . . With this, and the dry weather . . . , we were sorely in fear and distress."

(US) Sgt. Mead Holmes Jr., 21st Wisconsin, Starkweather's brigade, Rousseau's division:
"We marched on. Such roads, — so hilly and stony."

(US) Kirkpatrick, 42nd Indiana, Lytle's brigade, Rousseau's division:
"While still four miles from the scene of battle, we could hear cannonading in front."

Gen. Braxton Bragg

(US) 1st Lt. George W. Landrum, signal officer, 2nd Ohio, Harris' brigade, Rousseau's division:
"We had seen several small parties of the enemy at different points on the road, and some skirmishing was going on at these points, and by this we knew they were near us."

(US) Erastus Winters, 50th Ohio, Webster's brigade, Jackson's division:
"Presently we came in sight of the Signal Corps, busy at work, sending their messages to different parts of the field; batteries were hurrying past us."

(US) Lt. Spillard F. Horrall, 42nd Indiana, Lytle's brigade, Rousseau's division:
"The 42d Regiment moved on the 'double-quick' for more than a mile. . . . Before the command took position, it was drawn up into line, as if on dress-parade, and an order was read to the men, to the effect that under no conditions would a soldier be allowed, under penalty, to assist a comrade off the battle field who was unfortunate enough to be wounded. . . . Reading of that kind does not always act as a nerve tonic."

(US) Col. John Beatty, commanding 3rd Ohio, Lytle's brigade, Rousseau's division:
"At ten o'clock we were hastened forward and placed in battle line on the left of the Maxwell and Perryville road; the cavalry in our front appeared to be seriously engaged. . . . In a little while the firing ceased, and with a feeling of disappointment the boys lounged about on the ground and logs awaiting further orders."

Federal commanders assume the Confederates are continuing to retreat. Confederate Gen. Polk, however, has orders to rout what Bragg assumes is a small Federal force approaching Perryville. But Polk is beginning to suspect he is facing a much stronger Federal force, and he delays the attack. He is, in fact, confronting McCook's corps. In Harrodsburg, Bragg is listening for sounds of battle. Hearing none, he decides he had better go to Perryville and find out why. He arrives shortly before 10 a.m., rides to the front and examines the terrain. He makes the Crawford house his headquarters, and just before 11 a.m. he meets with Generals Polk and Hardee, commanding the two wings of his army.

Bragg's Confederate and McCook's Federal lines run roughly north and south and are generally parallel. Bragg's plan is to mass Cheatham's division on his right, have it crush the north end of the McCook's line and then roll it up while Buckner's and Anderson's divisions hit the Federal's front. Cheatham's division is ordered to march north, cross the nearly dry Chaplin River and extend the Confederate line; Polk will be in command of this wing of the Confederate army. The hilly terrain conceals the Confederate divisions as they move into position to strike McCook's corps:

(CS) Capt. Carnes, commanding Carnes' Battery, Donelson's brigade, Cheatham's division:
"Cheatham's Division was . . . ordered (north) to the right flank, marching through fields in rear of other commands in line on higher, timber-covered ground to our left. . . . An officer hastily rode up and told Gen. Leonidas Polk . . . that General Wood had urgently asked for a battery of artillery on his line as he could see Federal artillery ready to open on him from the woods across open fields between them. . . . General Polk directed me to follow the officer . . . and report to General Wood."

Confederate commanders are not aware of the arrival of more troops and artillery on the north end of the Federal line:

(US) Albion W. Tourgee, 105th Ohio, Terrill's brigade, Jackson's division:
"About eleven o'clock we halted in column by division on the right side of the pike, a half mile in the rear of the Russell House. . . . Our battery (Parsons') came up and halted near us on the left of the pike."

(US) A.D. Cleaver, 123rd Illinois, Terrill's brigade, Jackson's division:

"Tired and worn out – not even halting to rest – us not having eaten nothing that day except 1 biscuit – that a lady on the way gave me. . . . We were all suffering with thirst, too, for few of us have water in our cantines."

(US) Col. Beatty, commanding 3rd Ohio, Lytle's brigade, Rousseau's division:

"At 11 a.m. the Third was directed to take the head of the column and move forward. We anticipated no danger, for Rousseau and his staff were in advance of us, followed by Lytle and his staff."

Y.S., newspaper correspondent with Rousseau's federal division:

"At about eleven o'clock a.m., artillery-firing commenced. Upon the left where Jackson's division was stationed was one of our batteries feeling for the enemy. No response was elicited, however, nor did a battery connected with Mitchell's division, which came up about this time and took position upon the right of Sheridan's, meet with any better success."

(US) Ormond Hupp, Simonson's Battery, Harris' brigade, Rousseau's division:

"By the time our battery got up Capt. Loomis had . . . his guns at work. . . . Here within eighty rods (440 yards) of where they were firing, we stopped and fed our horses, awaiting orders as the firing that was going on was merely trying their position. At 11 a. m. we were ordered forward and in a corn field about 40 rods (220 yards) from the (old Mackville) road."

(US) Daniel H. Chandler, Simonson's Battery, Harris' brigade, Rousseau's division:

"The . . . (battery) went into position in an open field. The 38th Ind on our right, 10th Wis. on left."

(US) D.D. Holm, Simonson's Battery, Harris' brigade, Rousseau's division:

"The 2nd Ohio (was) in reserve immediately in rear of the Battery."

Y.S., news correspondent with Rousseau's federal division:

"Captain Loomis's Michigan battery, posted on a hill which overlooked the whole space between our advance bodies and the wooded hills where the enemy's legions lay massed, also threw a few shells toward these heights, and Captain Simonson did the same. But the enemy gave no sign."

(US) 1st Lt. Landrum, signal officer, 2nd Ohio, Harris' brigade, Rousseau's division:

"A company of the 10th Ohio were sent out to skirmish the hills. They returned in about an hour, after exchanging a few shots with the Rebel skirmishers. We all supposed they were leaving, as we could see

Looking northeast from Loomis' Battery position, in the center of Rousseau's line.

nothing of them, and all was quiet for about two hours; and orders were issued to all the Brigades to be brought in and advance on Perryville by the road leading down a steep hill to the river, a very rough road, and completely commanded by the hills on the opposite side. We had advanced to the front, and Gen. Rousseau, ... (Capt.) Gay, Gen. Jackson, Col. Lytle, Col. Chapin of the 10th Wisconsin, and many other officers, some fifty or sixty, were standing – with the Signal Corps – around the guns of Loomis' Battery looking over on the hills on the opposite side."

Y.S., newspaper correspondent with Rousseau's federal division:
"The position occupied by ... (Loomis' and Simonson's) batteries was peculiarly favorable for operating against the enemy should he endeavor to cross the open space in front of them, but it was at the same time exposed and dangerous if the enemy should, previous to charging, open fire with his artillery from his position upon the hills. ... At the foot of the hill just behind the batteries, was stationed Rousseau's division, the Seventeenth brigade, Colonel Lytle, ... The Ninth brigade, Col. Harris ... , and ... the Twenty-eighth brigade, Col. Starkweather ."

More Confederate batteries are moving into position, and Cheatham's division is on the march. Federal Gen. Rousseau notices the dust raised by Cheatham's troops, but he assumes the Confederates are continuing to retreat. Rousseau sees no prospect for battle and decides to let his thirsty troops seek water in Doctor's Creek, which is below Squire Bottom's house:

(US) Maj. James M. Shanklin, 42nd Indiana, Lytle's brigade, Rousseau's division:
"We were first ordered to support one battery, Loomis', which had been thrown rapidly forward. ... Scarcely had we taken this position, when one of Rousseau's aids rode up, ... ordering Colonel Jones to take the regiment down into a ravine in front of Loomis' battery to get water."

(US) Lt. Horrall, 42nd Indiana, Lytle's brigade, Rousseau's division:
"The day was very hot, and few of the men had water in their canteens. ... The 42d was ordered to take position in a dry creek, at the foot of a rugged hill, about three hundred yards in advance, and one hundred to the right of Loomis' battery."

(US) Kirkpatrick, 42nd Indiana, Lytle's brigade, Rousseau's division:
"(The) creek near the ... Bottom's farm house ... was dry except for a few puddles of water with green scum over it. But in our desperate need, we skimmed the water, and put it into a pot and boiled it, making ourselves some coffee."

(US) Maj. Shanklin, 42nd Indiana, Lytle's brigade, Rousseau's division:
"In front of the creek, that is facing the enemy, the bank rose gradually towards the woods, ... the space between the creek and the woods, about a quarter of a mile, being an open field. All back of us, excepting the road down which we came, and which had been cut out, was a precipitous rocky bluff, from twenty-five to fifty feet high, up which it was impossible to ride a horse, and only possible for a man to climb. This bluff extended down the creek about a quarter of a mile, where the bank gradually ascended again to the place where Loomis had his guns."

At Loomis' two guns, above the 42nd Indiana:

(US) 1st Lt. Landrum, signal officer, 2nd Ohio, Harris' brigade, Rousseau's division:
"I was using my glass, when suddenly I saw a man pop out of the woods, and then another, and another, etc., etc. I called the General's attention to it, and told him they were Rebel skirmishers. ... (Gen. Rousseau) took the glass and said, 'No, they are our own men.' I replied, 'If so, they were dressed in "Butternut" clothes.' After looking a long time, I was perfectly satisfied of it, but could not convince anyone else of the fact. Suddenly there was considerable ... dust raised at the point where I saw the men. I wanted the Gen. to let them have a few shells, but he, still thinking they were our men, would not give the order."

On the Confederate side of Doctor's Creek:

(CS) Capt. Carnes, commanding Carnes' Battery, Donelson's brigade, Cheatham's division:
"When we reached the position . . . the guns were unlimbered and formed in battery in front for action just in the edge of heavy timber, with an open valley in front, across which, in the edge of the woods opposite, our field glasses showed the battery (Loomis') that had caused the call for us; . . . We were ordered to open fire. We first took full time to estimate the distance and instruct the gunners about cutting the time fuses of our shell and shrapnell shot."

Gunners in other Confederate batteries also have their sights on Rousseau's position. Their orders are to open fire at 12:30 p.m.:

(US) 1st Lt. Landrum, signal officer, 2nd Ohio, Harris' brigade, Rousseau's division:
"I looked over again and saw the wheels of some kind of carriage, and spoke of it; but before I could get the attention of the party on the spot, the report of a gun was heard, a shell came whizzing over to us, and struck within thirty or forty feet of us. All were then convinced that they were Rebels, and such a skedaddling to get out of range I never saw before – Gens., Cols., Capts., Lieuts., Signal Officers and men – all scattered in every direction. I could not help laughing; at the same time I felt as though I would be safer a littler farther off."

Y.S., newspaper correspondent with Rousseau's federal division:
"Captain Simonson was in the very midst of a vivid description . . . of the operations about Stevenson, Alabama, . . . when a spherical shot buried itself deep in the side of the hill, just below where we were standing, and a half dozen more whistled fiercely over our heads, and raised great clouds of dust as they struck in the dried-up fields beyond. At this time but two pieces of Loomis's battery were in position upon the hill, the remainder being stationed upon another eminence some distance in the rear.

"These were at once ordered up, the shot and shell of the enemy's guns meantime continuing to plough up the ground in our vicinity and to crash through the branches of some half-dozen trees, which were grouped together on the hill immediately to the right of Loomis's position. 'Captain Loomis,' said I, as he was riding back toward the main portion of his battery upon the hill behind, 'don't you intend to reply to that fire?' 'Yes,' said he, 'I'll fetch 'em!' Simonson's battery had opened in the mean time, and another away off to the right of the road."

(US) 1st Lt. Landrum, signal officer, 2nd Ohio, Harris' brigade, Rousseau's division:
"I checked my horse after the first jump or two, and moved off to the right of . . . (Loomis') Battery in company with Capt. Grover, Adjt. Gen. to Col. Lytle . . . , and one of my men, and took position near a barn almost fifty yards from the Battery. . . . Our Battery opened on them."

(US) Chandler, Simonson's Battery, Harris' brigade, Rousseau's division:
"Firing rapidly extended along the line and soon became very hot."

(US) Holm, Simonson's Battery, Harris' brigade, Rousseau's division:
"The Confederate artillery . . . was . . . in the thickly wooded hills beyond the creek."

(CS) Capt. Carnes, commanding Carnes' Battery, Donelson's brigade, Cheatham's division:
"Our attack brought a fearful response . . . , for within a few minutes we were under the fire of four 6-gun batteries at different points opposite. All seemed to be using rifled guns, as, though the distance was extreme for us, none of their shots fell short, but, fortunately . . . most of them went high overhead, cutting off limbs of trees that fell on us. The infantry back of us could only hug the ground and wait. . . . Other batteries opened on our side to divert a part of the enemy's fire from our battery."

(CS) James T. Searcy, Semples' Battery, Wood's brigade, Buckner's division:
"We went into the fight while the enemy were firing upon us – One of their shells killing one of our horses before we got into position."

(CS) Orderly Sgt. George Little, Lumsden's Battery, Jones' brigade, Anderson's division:
"After we had gotten the guns in position and put the horses in the rear, I got behind a big poplar tree a little to one side; while I was there my friend Lanneau got tired of working his gun and came over behind my tree to rest. He said that this looked like such a good safe place he would just stay there until the fight was over; just then a shell broke right over our heads, and he decided to go back to the battery."

Y.S., newspaper correspondent with Rousseau's federal division:
"All Loomis's pieces were now in position and thundering away with the sharp, quick, deadly report which rifled Parrotts always make. To the extreme left, another battery immediately opened and the enemy replied from at least half a dozen different positions, and shot and shell of every description flew in all directions. . . . While I was watching with intense interest the effect of our fire on the enemy, a shell came hurtling through the air and exploded in the very midst of Captain Simonson's battery, killing two of his horses and wounding a couple of his men The next moment a case-shot tore away the head of another horse, entered his fore-shoulder and ranged through the entire length of his body."

(US) 1st Lt. Landrum, signal officer, 2nd Ohio, Harris' brigade, Rousseau's division:
"We sat on our horses looking on for about fifteen minutes, when suddenly a shell came whizzing over us, fell, and exploded almost under our horses' feet. Then another came so near Capt. Grover's head that he could feel the wind rush by, and a third took off the corner of the roof of the barn over our heads. They were evidently directly firing at us, and had the range perfectly. Our horses were jumping and plunging about almost uncontrollable. . . . We skedaddled again. I do not know whether I was scared or not; I was anxious to get out of range, but with it all, I could not help laughing. There was an excitement new to me about it; at first a sort of cold chill ran down my back, my hair seemed to be raising my hat off my head. We changed our position to another where we could see just as well, and kept changing around, not giving them time to get the range of us again, but not leaving the field. The Batteries blazed away at one another . . . and occasionally a musket ball whistled over us."

(US) Holm, Simonson's Battery, Harris' brigade, Rousseau's division:
"Shot and shells from the Confederate batteries . . . were now coming 'thick and fast,' shrieking over and around. Solid shot plowing deep furrows in the dry earth in close proximity to men, guns and teams, then 'richochetting' and with a wild defiant shriek, go spinning over the ground."

(US) 1st Lt. Landrum, signal officer, 2nd Ohio, Harris' brigade, Rousseau's division:
"For about an hour there was a fine artillery duel."

In the dry bed of Doctor's Creek is the 42nd Indiana, caught in the middle of the artillery duel:

(US) Maj. Shanklin, 42nd Indiana, Lytle's brigade, Rousseau's division:
"Loomis' shells passed over our heads, and although the Rebels did not see us, their shells occasionally dropped in among us."

(US) Lt. Horrall, 42nd Indiana, Lytle's brigade, Rousseau's division:
"Many of the enemy's shells burst over the heads of our men."

Another Confederate battery is about to enter the fray:

(CS) John Euclid Magee, Stanford's Battery, Stewart's brigade, Cheatham's division:
"Went through an old meadow into a cornfield and formed in position under the enemy's fire. Their batteries were on a hill about one and a half miles distant – a very advantageous position."

(CS) Orderly Sgt. Brown, Stanford's Battery, Stewart's brigade, Cheatham's division:
"The infantry was thrown into line under cover of the hills, and, as a few introductory shells exploded above their heads, we were ordered to load. While the ramrods rattled in the guns, we could feel the blood recede to the heart and the knees shake. We felt our faces grow a shade paler. . . . Not far from us Gen. Cheatham sat on his horse in the midst of his staff calmly smoking his pipe. Couriers were constantly coming and going. Nearly half a mile to our left Capt. William W. Carnes' Tennessee battery was warmly engaged with the Federals. Capt. Carnes reported to Gen. Cheatham that the other battery was beyond his range and was using him up badly with long-range guns. . . . We had a battery of brass rifles, and so Gen. Cheatham at once ordered us to relieve Carnes' battery."

(CS) Magee, Stanford's Battery, Stewart's brigade, Cheatham's division:
"General Cheatham ordered us a few hundred yards to the left. . . . We immediately limbered up and proceeded to the place under a terrible hot fire."

(CS) George W. Jones, Stanford's Battery, Stewart's brigade, Cheatham's division:
"We took position as Carnes withdrew."

(CS) Orderly Sgt. Brown, Stanford's Battery, Stewart's brigade, Cheatham's division:
"We opened up on the Yankees with our rifles. The battery we were fighting was in position something over a mile distant. The smoke from their guns was all we could see. . . . They already had our range, and every shot was well aimed."

(CS) Magee, Stanford's Battery, Stewart's brigade, Cheatham's division:
"They . . . were showering the balls around us, when we very deliberately opened on them."

(CS) Orderly Sgt. Brown, Stanford's Battery, Stewart's brigade, Cheatham's division:
"As I was orderly sergeant I had nothing to do with the actual management of the battery, my duties being to keep up with the captain and carry out his orders. . . . My first mission after the battery opened was to have the sponge buckets filled with water. By the time I returned to the battery a brigade of infantry had formed in line and lay down . . . in rear of our guns to support us. The firing was going on slowly and steadily between our battery and the other battery, with both groups trying to keep their guns cool and make very shot count. . . . I found myself 'in line' behind a large red oak, which stood close by."

(CS) Jones, Stanford's Battery, Stewart's brigade, Cheatham's division:
"The fire was just awful, had one of our ammunition chests to explode."

(CS) Orderly Sgt. Brown, Stanford's Battery, Stewart's brigade, Cheatham's division:
"An unlucky shell stretched out three of our boys on the ground. . . . Pvt. J.C. Roycroft, was killed instantly, and . . . mortally wounded . . . were Pvt. Calvin P. McCall and Pvt. John W. Wakefield. Capt. Stanford ordered me to the rear for an ambulance. . . . The Federals seemed to redouble their fire. Shells exploded all through the woods, but I was soon clear of them. . . . I soon found an ambulance and returned to the battery. The wounded boys were quickly placed in the ambulance, and I returned with them to the field hospital, getting them out of the ambulance and as comfortable as possible. . . . Pvt. McCall . . . said that he was dying and did not want the surgeon to examine his wound. The doctor only looked at (it) for a minute and then turned away to the other cases, knowing that death alone could relieve the suffering."

On the firing line, as the artillery duel continues:

(CS) Orderly Sgt. Little, Lumsden's Battery, Jones' brigade, Anderson's division:
"I left my horse under the tree and went back to the battery . . . , and while I was talking to one of the drivers, who had charge of two horses, a shell . . . struck one of the horses, went entirely through its body and struck the other horse and knocked it down; the driver who was leaning against the second horse, fell with the horse but was not hurt. Then of one of our guns was shot in two, and the equipment that hangs under the other one was shot all to pieces. . . . I found one member of our company who was a wild character named Sainty Cummins, crouched behind a tree and tried to get him to go back to the battery; but he said he was too scared, so I let him alone. Another member of our company passed by me going to the rear. I thought he was wounded. . . . He had deserted."

(CS) Searcy, Semples' Battery, Wood's brigade, Buckner's division:
"We carried on this duel, half a mile distant perhaps. . . . Our Battery fired about two hundred rounds. . . . Every once in a while we could see quite a commotion among the enemy. They dismounted one of our guns – Killed three of our horses and wounded two of our men seriously one on the head and one on the leg. Several were scratched and bruised. Shivers had his toes mashed- Charlie had the Port fire Stock cut off close to his hand, as he was about to touch off the gun. Every one had escapes."

On the Federal side, Loomis has run out of long-range ammunition. He pulls his guns out of line and takes them west on the Mackville Road to the Russell house, where his caissons are waiting. The 10th Ohio in Lytle's brigade moves up to take the battery's place in line on the hill overlooking Squire Bottom's house:

(US) Chandler, Simonson's Battery, Harris' brigade, Rousseau's division:
"The supporting Regts were lying flat on the ground on either side & far behind the guns. Shot & shell from Rebel Batteries howled and shrieked over & around, now tearing up the dry earth and again 'richocheting' with a wild unearthly shriek again (to) strike or explode with terrible effect. This was our first real battle and we soon ... lost our anxiety for a fight."

Confederate gunners, expecting the infantry to begin moving out, start reducing their fire. Gen. Polk, however has delayed the attack because of reports more Federal troops are arriving at the north end of the Federal line, the target of the Confederate assault. Down in the dry bed of Doctor's Creek:

(US) Maj. Shanklin, 42nd Indiana, Lytle's brigade, Rousseau's division:
"Captain Bryant and I were lying under a tree eating a sweet potato, when the Captain remarked, 'Loomis must have dismounted some of their guns, they have quit firing.' I said, jokingly, 'Suppose a couple of regiments of cavalry should come down on us through this ravine, wouldn't we be in a nice fix?' ... The Rebel guns had really ceased, but our cannoniers kept blazing away at the place where they had been."

The Federal corps commander, Gen. McCook, arrives at the front. He looks for Confederate infantry, and, seeing none, orders an end to the artillery firing. The shooting begins to peter out after 1 p.m., with the batteries on each side confident they have won the duel:

(CS) Jones, Stanford's Battery, Stewart's brigade, Cheatham's division:
"We ... finally silenced the battery."

(US) Hupp, Simonson's Battery, Harris' brigade, Rousseau's division:
"Their batteries were silenced and a shout rung out along our line."

(US) 1st Lt. Landrum, signal officer, 2nd Ohio, Harris' brigade, Rousseau's division:
"I supposed they had brought the Battery there to cover their retreat, as I had lost all faith in their fighting us. When the firing ceased I left the field and established a station, about a quarter of a mile in the rear of the Battery, to communicate with the other Division, and succeeded in sending messages to Sheridan's Division, some two miles off to our right."

CHARGING THE FEDERAL BATTERIES

Federal Brig. Gen. James Jackson is extending McCook's line to the left with his infantry and artillery. Parsons' Battery is ordered to occupy a cleared area that will become known as Open Hill or Open Knob:

(US) Albion W. Tourgee, 105th Ohio, Terrill's brigade, Jackson's division:
"The eager comrades . . . swung themselves into their saddles and dashed forward at a sharp trot! The sun was hot and the horses' flanks were covered with sweat from the day's march. . . . The guns . . . took their way along a narrow country road toward the front."

(US) Lt. Henry Harrison Cumings, Parsons' Battery, Terrill's brigade, Jackson's division:
"Our battery was thrown forward to the extreme left of the line. . . . I commanded one section composed of two twelve-pounders, and . . . my section had the right of the battery and went into position at the right of the line."

Parsons' Battery is on the crest of Open Hill, and is to the front and left of the 123rd Illinois. Confederate commanders, however, do not realize Terrill's brigade is extending the end of the Federal line. Cheatham's Confederate division is at Walkers Bend and forming for the attack. Cheatham is to open the battle by crossing the almost dry river bed, climbing the bluff and turning what Confederate commanders think is the north end of the Federal line. Though Federal officers are watching for any sign of Confederates, the woods and rolling terrain hide Donelson's, Stewart's and Maney's brigades as they gather for the attack. About 1:30 p.m. Wharton's cavalry regiments move out to cross Chaplin River and clear bluffs over Walkers Bend for Cheatham's attack.

(CS) A.B. Briscoe, 8th Texas Cavalry, Wharton's brigade:
"Each squadron formed left front into line, which made us present five lines, one behind the other, and in this order we charged up the hill, into the woods and among the Yankees. This whole movement was made in a sweeping gallop and as if on parade."

Wharton's cavalry runs into skirmishers from the 33rd Ohio on the bluff:

(CS) Briscoe, 8th Texas Cavalry, Wharton's brigade:
"The Yankees were brushed back from the hill and woods."

The Federal skirmishers scurry back to the main line of the 33rd Ohio:

(CS) Gilbert L. Macmurphy, 8th Texas Cavalry, Wharton's brigade:
"We could not sustain ourselves against the numbers brought to bear on us."

(CS) Briscoe, 8th Texas Cavalry, Wharton's brigade:
"The bugle sounded the recall and we returned . . . But . . . our commander, . . . (Capt.) Mark Evans, . . . fell mortally wounded."

(CS) Lt. Frank Batchelor, 8th Texas Cavalry, Wharton's brigade:
"He was struck by a large-sized musket ball just above the right temple and ranged over the skull, tearing the flesh out some four inches and a half in length by one in width and leaving the skull bare and slightly fractured."

With the bluffs cleared of Federal troops, Cheatham's division moves forward:

(CS) Col. John H. Savage, commanding 16th Tennessee, Donelson's brigade, Cheatham's division:
"The Sixteenth was ordered by General Donelson to ascend the bluff, through the timber and undergrowth, which was steep and difficult to get up. The path led along the foot of the bluff some fifty or sixty yards to a dug road, up which I rode into an open field and saw a (Federal) battery of artillery (Harris') some two hundred yards out in the field."

(CS) James R. Thompson, 16th Tennessee, Donelson's brigade, Cheatham's division:
"We went up an old road, and the 15th Tennessee reached the top about the time we did."

(CS) Col. Savage, commanding 16th Tennessee, Donelson's brigade, Cheatham's division:
"Riding to where the men were getting up the hill into the edge of the field, I formed the regiment into line on the edge of the bluff directly fronting . . . (Harris') battery."

(CS) Capt. J.J. Womack, 16th Tennessee, Donelson's brigade, Cheatham's division:
"We . . . quietly formed in line of battle behind the top of the hill, lying, till the whole line would have time to cross over and form."

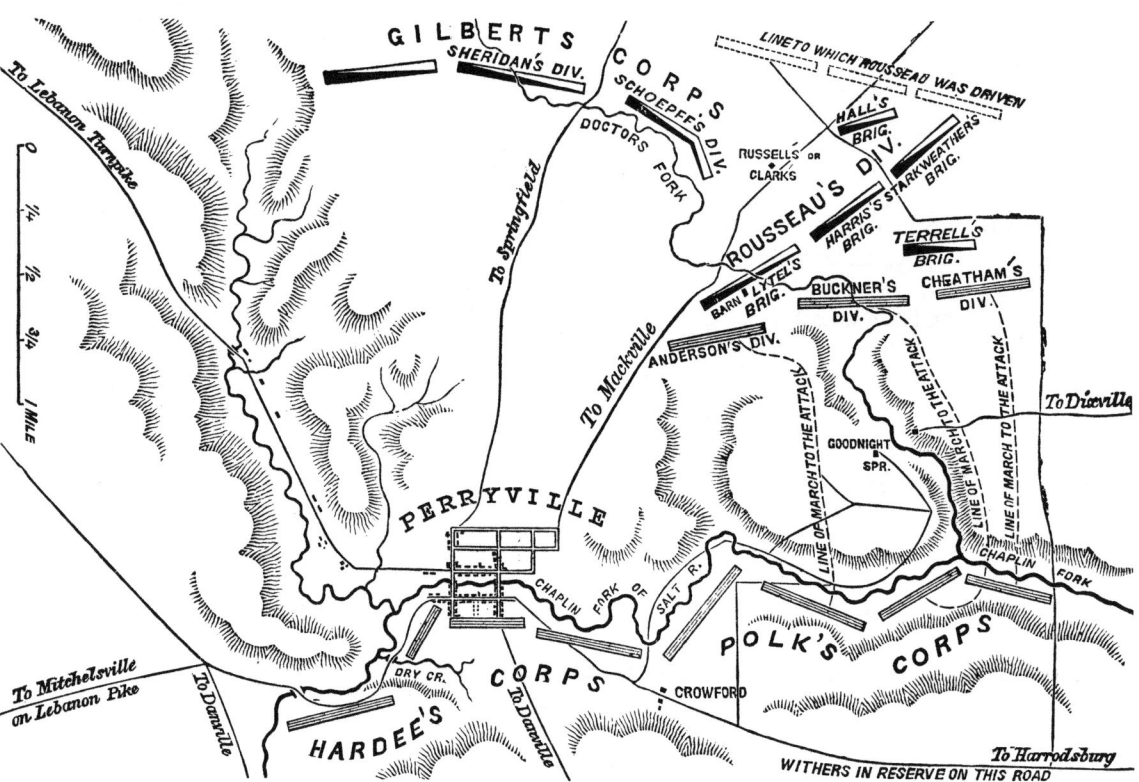

(CS) Thompson, 16th Tennessee, Donelson's brigade, Cheatham's division:
"We were given a few minutes rest."

Troops from another Confederate brigade move into line on the bluff:

(CS) Lt. Edwin H. Rennolds, 5th Tennessee, Stewart's brigade, Cheatham's division:
"We were . . . ordered to lie down in the timber of small growth, in support of Donelson's Brigade."

It is about 2 p.m. Bragg's plan is for the brigades all along his line to attack in sequence, starting with Donelson's brigade, at the north end of the Confederate position. Donelson, with about a thousand men, is facing Harris' battery, which Confederate commanders assume is anchoring the end of the Federal line. Donelson's plan is for the 15th and 16th Tennessee to attack the battery from the side while the 38th Tennessee attacks the front.

(CS) Thomas A. Head, 16th Tennessee, Donelson's brigade, Cheatham's division:
"There was some confusion in commands, and Col. Savage . . . thought best to await the arrival of the other regiments before advancing any further. General Donelson came along about this time, and, thinking the other troops were up the hill, ordered Col. Savage to advance."

(CS) Col. Savage, commanding 16th Tennessee, Donelson's brigade, Cheatham's division:
"General Donelson rode up and said, 'Colonel, I am ordered to attack,' to which I made no reply. . . . I believed that the battery was supported by a strong line of infantry concealed by a fence, and a forest not more than eighty yards in its rear, and that it had been placed in the field . . . to invite a charge. I believed that a charge would end in my death and the death and ruin of my regiment, and while I had often disobeyed Donelson's orders, for which he had court-martialed me, I could think of no military principles that would authorize me to disobey such an order in the face of the enemy and at the beginning of such a battle. . . .

"He repeated a second time, 'Colonel, I am ordered to attack.' I again made no reply.

"He repeated for a third time, 'Colonel I am ordered to attack the enemy!' I then said: 'General, I see no enemy to attack except that battery over there in the field. Do you mean, sir, that you want the Sixteenth to charge that battery?' He said, 'Yes.' I replied, 'General, I will obey your orders but if the Sixteenth is to charge that battery you must give the order.' He raised his voice in a rather loud and excited tone and said, 'Charge.' . . . There was running up from Chaplain Creek a long hollow about half way between the battery and where the regiment was in line. I thought as soon as I moved into that hollow I would be out of reach of the battery and that I could come up on the other side within sixty or seventy yards of the battery. I was in no hurry; got in front of my regiment and said, 'Forward, march!' "

(CS) Thompson, 16th Tennessee, Donelson's brigade, Cheatham's division:
"We were then ordered forward, which was obeyed with a loud 'Hurrah!' "

When the Confederates reach the top of the bluff they are confronting a Federal line that is stronger than expected. Off to the left is Harris' brigade, with Simonson's Battery; in the middle is Webster's brigade, with Harris' Battery; and to the left is Terrill's brigade, with Parsons' Battery:

(CS) Carroll H. Clark, 16th Tennessee, Donelson's brigade, Cheatham's division:
"We . . . (were) ordered to halt and reform. We were in sight of the enemy, and it looked to me like the whole face of the earth was covered with Yankees."

Among the Federal regiments supporting Harris' Battery are the 80th Indiana and 98th Ohio, whose soldiers are lying face down and holding loaded rifles:

(US) Joseph P. Glezen, 80th Indiana, Webster's brigade, Jackson's division:
"The position we in the 80th occupied was in an open field. Harris' battery about 20 paces in front and a little to our right, on the top of a ridge descending considerable . . . to the front and rear. About 200 yards in front of us was a piece of woodland where the enemy were concealed, and . . . to the right of our front . . . there was a cornfield."

(CS) Clark, 16th Tennessee, Donelson's brigade, Cheatham's division:
"The whole line of battle was expected to keep in line on the forward movement, but some of the boys . . . raised the yell and rushed forward which caused our regiment to get far in advance of our main line."

As the 16th Tennessee advances toward Harris' Battery, it pushes back skirmishers from the 33rd Ohio:

(US) 1st Lt. George W. Landrum, signal officer, 2nd Ohio, Harris' brigade, Jackson's division:
"Suddenly there emerged from the wood the head of a column of men, and as they came out, their bayonets glistened in the sun."

CHARGING THE FEDERAL BATTERIES

(US) Wesley S. Poulson, 98th Ohio, Webster's brigade, Jackson's division:
"We saw . . . a swarm of rebels come out of the woods about half a mile in front of us. When they got into open land and lines dressed they started on double quick shouting and hollering like wild men, . . . but it . . . only made us grasp our rifles more firmly."

(US) 1st Lt. Landrum, signal officer, 2nd Ohio, Harris' brigade, Jackson's division:
"I knew they were coming for us. I immediately called the attention of the Commander of the Battery, and he gave the command to load canister. Directly the head of the column was in full sight. They advanced at 'double quick' and formed in line of battle under cover of a small knoll. I notified the Col. of the 10th Wisconsin Regt. of their advance, and he moved his men to meet them."

Simonson's and Harris' batteries begin firing into Donelson's men. Parsons' Battery, surprised to see Confederates to its right, begins swinging its guns to fight off the threat. Soon the 15th Tennessee joins the 16th in the hollow, where both are blasted by Harris', Parsons' and Simonson's batteries:

(CS) Clark, 16th Tennessee, Donelson's brigade, Cheatham's division:
"Three batteries of cannon and a brigade of the enemy were directed at our regiment, and the boys were falling dead and wounded all around me, and I thought all would be killed. Some of my school and playmates, neighbors and friends lost their lives there. . . . I had no hope of getting out alive. . . . I was scared before we got in the thickest of the fight."

(CS) Robert C. Carden, 16th Tennessee, Donelson's brigade, Cheatham's division:
"There was a battery on our left that was giving us grape and canister and the bullets were singing around us. A man was standing just in front of me while I was loading my gun and I happened to have my eyes on him just as a canister struck him in the breast and I saw the white flesh before it bled. He was a dead man."

(US) 1st Lt. Landrum, signal officer, 2nd Ohio, Harris' brigade, Jackson's division:
"(Simonson's) Battery poured in a charge of Cannister. The line wavered an instant, but again advanced in fine order. Another charge of Cannister and the line was broken, but they immediately reformed, and on they came."

(US) Poulson, 98th Ohio, Webster's brigade, Jackson's division:
"Musketry was brought into action by both sides by regiments that were coming into contact."

Donelson realizes Savage is facing too much opposition and sends word for him to halt while he sends support; then, Savage gets orders from Cheatham to keep moving toward Harris' Battery. Cheatham is sending Stewart's brigade to bolster the attack while Maney's brigade will attack Parsons' Battery, to the right:

(CS) Col. Savage, commanding 16th Tennessee, Donelson's brigade, Cheatham's division:
"I . . . ordered my color bearers to the front and ordered the regiment to dress on them so as to march in the . . . direction indicated by Cheatham's order."

Donelson's troops are moving in two lines. In the first is the 16th Tennessee, with the 15th Tennessee slightly behind and to its left; the second line is the 38th Tennessee:

(CS) Thompson, 16th Tennessee, Donelson's brigade, Cheatham's division:
"We were perhaps two hundred yards from the enemy when we were ordered to open fire."

(US) 1st Lt. Landrum, signal officer, 2nd Ohio, Harris' brigade, Jackson's division:
"The rattle of the musketry was terrible. The bullets whistled around us, and I was . . .astonished that I was not hit. . . . (Simonson's) Battery continued to pour in the Cannister, and I could see them fall, and waver, and fall back, only to come on again, yelling and cheering like so many devils."

(CS) Thompson, 16th Tennessee, Donelson's brigade, Cheatham's division:
"Colonel Savage, who was in front of our line, rode around to our side and his horse got wounded."

(CS) Col. Savage, commanding 16th Tennessee, Donelson's brigade, Cheatham's division:
"I was riding in front of the regiment; a grape shot passed through the head of my horse below the eyes. . . . I threw the bridle . . . over a snag, took a Remington pistol from the holsters, and ordered the regiment forward to get out of range of the battery."

(CS) Thompson, 16th Tennessee, Donelson's brigade, Cheatham's division:
"I ran forward to a little stump six or eight inches through and about two feet through and rested my gun on top and took deliberate aim. Before I could fire, some of our men shot a ball into the stump, which barely missed me. I stormed at them that if any of them shot me, I would come back there and kill him."

(CS) Col. Savage, commanding 16th Tennessee, Donelson's brigade, Cheatham's division:
"Descending the hill some forty or fifty yards, we were fired on by the . . . (33rd Ohio), not more than fifty or sixty yards distant, concealed behind a rail fence, which was a prolongation of the fence enclosing the field in which the battery was situated. There was a fence and a field on my right running up to two cabins at the line of the enemy's forces. There were skirmish lines along this fence which fired on our rear as we advanced. The Sixteenth had no protection except a few trees in the forest. I ordered a charge."

(CS) Thompson, 16th Tennessee, Donelson's brigade, Cheatham's division:
"We went forward with a rush. The enemy fell back and we crossed the fence they were behind, amid . . . their slain."

(CS) Col. Savage, commanding 16th Tennessee, Donelson's brigade, Cheatham's division:
"We drove the enemy from behind the fences, killing many of them as they fled."

(US) Maj. George T. Simonson, 80th Indiana, Webster's Brigade, Jackson's division, McCook's corps:
"The rebels . . . advanced directly in our front for the purpose of (capturing) Harris' Battery."

On the Federal side, McCook sends the 2nd Ohio to the Widow Gibson's cornfield to help the 33rd Ohio. Fire from the 2nd Ohio drives the 15th Tennessee back; then the 2nd Ohio shifts fire to the 16th Tennessee. Donelson's attack stalls. To Donelson's right, Maney prepares to enter the fight by splitting his brigade, making his first line the 6th and 9th Tennessee and the 41st Georgia. His second line is the 1st and 27th Tennessee.

(CS) Capt. John W. Carroll, 27th Tennessee, Maney's brigade, Cheatham's division:
"William Rhodes of Lexington, Tenn., one of the nicest young men of the regiment and . . . brave . . . ; and Frank Buck, a mere boy, both . . . came to me when we were in line of battle and told me they were going to be killed that day. Their pale features, their calm demeanor, their determined looks impressed me much. While I had no authority to offer such thing, yet I did offer that they . . . drop out, which they refused to do and were both killed in less than two hours."

Off to Donelson's left, Jones' Confederate brigade of three Mississippi regiments advances toward Simonson's Battery and the 10th Wisconsin of Harris' brigade and the 10th Ohio of Lytle's brigade:

CHARGING THE FEDERAL BATTERIES

(US) Ormond Hupp, Simonson's Battery, Harris' brigade, Rousseau's division:

"The enemy could be seen at a mile distant with their bayonets glistening in the sun – for it was a beautiful day – and advancing toward us. . . . Their batteries opened a cross fire which seemed to make the earth quake, this fire from the enemy (artillery) was doing much damage but we could only stand as best we could, our line reserving their fire until their infantry got within thirty rods (165 yards), we then opened on them and finally after about fifteen minutes they fell back."

While Jones' brigade rallies for another attack, action shifts to the Confederate far right as Maney's first line, about 900 men, moves through woods to hit the flank of Parsons' Battery and the 123rd Illinois, about 770 men:

(CS) Lt. James Iredell Hall, 9th Tennessee, Maney's brigade, Cheatham's division:

"Our advance . . . came upon a large body of Federal troops strongly posted on a hill top. Directly on top of the hill was stationed a battery of six guns."

(US) William T. Hunt, 123rd Illinois, Terrill's brigade, Jackson's division:

"Just six weeks from our enlistment we . . . formed at the edge of a woods and loaded our muskets. To do that we put the stock of the gun on the ground. With one hand we held the muzzle, and with the other, took from our belts a small package of powder done up in paper, just enough for one load. With our teeth we tore the paper open and put the powder and ball in. Then the wads went on top and it was all tamped down with our ramrods. We could shoot once and it was all to do over again. Our guns ready, we came out of the woods, crossed a small meadow, climbed over a rail fence and started down a small hill. There was a small stream at the bottom, small shrubs here and there, and also a few trees, but no sign of a Gray uniform anywhere."

(US) Lt. Cumings, Parson's Battery, Terrill's brigade, Jackson's division:

"A short distance in front of us and extending to our left was a dense woods which . . . was full of the enemy. They charged us at once."

(US) Hunt, 123rd Illinois, Terrill's brigade, Jackson's division:

"The whole valley at the bottom erupted into a mass of Johnny Rebs. They came charging up that slope with their terrible rebel yell. Guns blazing. It looked like a million of them."

(US) A.D. Cleaver, 123rd Illinois, Terrill's brigade, Jackson's division:

"We were ordered to fall down at the first fire of the rebels which we did. So heavy was the fire that we could see their bullets in the air."

Terrill sees Parsons' Battery in danger of being overrun and orders the green 123rd Illinois to stop Maney's Confederates with a charge down toward a fence between the woods and the open hillside. Heavy fire from Maney's veterans drives the 123rd Illinois back:

(US) Hunt, 123rd Illinois, Terrill's brigade, Jackson's division:

"We lost no time starting back. . . . Some fired their guns, but most of us had but one thought and that was to get out of there but fast. When we reached the fence. I threw one leg over, and just as I started to jump down the wind blew my cap off. Of course it fell on the side I did not want to be on just then. I gave one look at that cap, then at the Johnnys getting so close and my comrades getting so far ahead of me, and decided who needs a cap anyway."

As the 123rd Illinois rushes back up the hill toward Parsons' Battery, the 105th Ohio is approaching the guns from the rear:

(US) Lester D. Taylor, 105th Ohio, Terrill's brigade, Jackson's division:
"We were ordered to support . . . (Parsons') battery and double quicked it, up one hill, down, part way up another."

(US) Second Lt. John Calvin Hartzell, 105th Ohio, Terrill's brigade, Jackson's division:
"We were on the side of a hill; our fine, new battery (Parsons') on a crest some five hundred feet in front of our line. . . . In our rear was a double rail fence, or two fences, from two to four feet apart and running parallel to our line – called a 'Devil's Lane.'"

(US) Tourgee, 105th Ohio, Terrill's brigade, Jackson's division:
"The battery was firing with frenzied rapidity. . . . Shells from the enemy's battery flew over our heads and cut the limbs of the trees by which we stood, sending down a shower of acorns. Bullets pattered about us. We could see the artillery men dashing back and forth as the smoke lifted from the guns. Men were coming back from the hell which the crest hid from our view, some wounded, some stragglers. Somebody suggested that the guns were empty, and the order to load was given in some of the companies. . . . A mounted aide pointed out our position and rode beside our adjutant at the head of the column as we advanced. A caisson, the horses . . . unmanageable, dashed through our line to the rear."

(US) Stephen J. Hutchinson, 105th Ohio, Terrill's brigade, Jackson's division:
"We were led in on the run at the same time the order being given to load."

The 105th Ohio passes behind Parson's Battery and goes into line to the battery's left:

(US) Tourgee, 105th Ohio, Terrill's brigade, Jackson's division:
"Our division and brigade generals were standing . . . just in the rear of the battery."

(US) Lt. Cumings, Parsons' Battery, Terrill's brigade, Jackson's division:
"General Terrill was with us, directing the working of the guns."

(US) Charles K. Radcliffe, 105th Ohio, Terrill's brigade, Jackson's division:
"We were rushed . . . up into that tornado of lead and iron sweeping that knoll to save Parsons' Battery – planted in advance – when nearly every man in the battery had been killed or wounded."

Brig. Gen. James S. Jackson

(US) Lt. Cumings, Parsons' Battery, Terrill's brigade, Jackson's division:
"General (James S.) Jackson passed me and spoke to me but a moment before he fell."

(US) Tourgee, 105th Ohio, Terrill's brigade, Jackson's division:
"General (James S.) Jackson fell just as we advanced."

(US) Maj. James A. Connolly, 123rd Illinois, Terrill's brigade, Jackson's division:
"General Jackson commanding our Division was killed by a musket ball within a few feet of me. He was on foot and had just advised me to dismount when he fell. . . . Bullets went over our heads and sounded like a swarm of bees running away in the hot summer air overhead."

(US) Hutchinson, 105th Ohio, Terrill's brigade, Jackson's division:
"As soon as we arrived . . . on the top of the hill where our battery was at were ordered to advance & fire over the brow of the hill."

CHARGING THE FEDERAL BATTERIES

(US) Tourgee, 105th Ohio, Terrill's brigade, Jackson's division:
"There we first saw the enemy; two lines of gray in the edge of the brown woods scarce ninety yards away. Puffs of smoke and jets of flame shot out from the undergrowth and along the fence."

(US) Hutchinson, 105th Ohio, Terrill's brigade, Jackson's division:
"The enemy were close upon us & judging from the continuous firing & whistling of bullet there must at least have been 3 or 4 regts opposed to us."

(US) Radcliffe, 105th Ohio, Terrill's brigade, Jackson's division:
"Jackson, our division commander, lying dead near the guns – and Cheatham's Confederate veterans, in overwhelming numbers, charging up the slope, firing as they came."

(US) Josiah Ayre, 105th Ohio, Terrill's brigade, Jackson's division:
"We could not form into proper line and after going through several maneuvers in order to do so we became mixed and confused."

(US) Bliss Morse, 105th Ohio, Terrill's brigade, Jackson's division:
"The rebels had the start on us by two rounds while we were forming and loading our pieces."

(US) Ayre, 105th Ohio, Terrill's brigade, Jackson's division:
"Finally we were ordered to load and fire the best we could although I could not see a rebel at the time on account of the shape of the ground. Some of (our men) . . . commenced firing however, and I with some others marched forwards in front of the regiment so that we could get sight at them and let drive, falling back to load."

(US) Tourgee, 105th Ohio, Terrill's brigade, Jackson's division:
"It was slow work loading and firing with the . . . muzzle-loaders. The air seemed full of flashing ramrods."

(US) Taylor, 105th Ohio, Terrill's brigade, Jackson's division:
"The enemy . . . opened cross fires on us, but as we worked on our knees, the balls passed over us. I never knew hail to fall faster than the bullets did."

(US) Tourgee, 105th Ohio, Terrill's brigade, Jackson's division:
"Men fell, sometimes with a groan, sometimes without a sound. . . . One and another staggered wounded to the rear. The line officers went back and forth encouraging, directing. We stood alone, a thin line of blue, in the open field. The enemy were mostly under cover."

(CS) Col. George C. Porter, 6th Tennessee, Maney's brigade, Cheatham's division:
"One of the most deadly and destructive fires . . . was poured in . . . (our) whole line by the enemy, who occupied a strong and well-chosen position on an eminence in an open field about 300 yards to the front. Here . . . (was) a battery of eight guns, strongly supported by infantry. This command still pressing steadily forward, all the time . . . (into) grape, canister, and shell, together with the small-arms of the strong supporting force, it came to a high fence . . . at the edge of the wood."

(CS) J.N. Lennard, 41st Georgia, Maney's brigade, Cheatham's division:
"(Capt. John C. Curtright) was wounded. . . . The ball entering his right side and passing through, resting on the left side of his spine. Not once did he complain of his wound or fall, but took it calmly and peacefully & requested that I should notify . . . (his wife), his Father & Mother how he died & that I should save & send . . . (his wife) his Sword."

(CS) Lt. Hall, 9th Tennessee, Maney's brigade, Cheatham's division:
"Our advance up the hill was hindered by a worm fence, the corners of which were grown up thick with bushes and briars. The fence had to be let down in some places to enable out officers to ride through. We lost a good many men here."

(CS) Col. Porter, 6th Tennessee, Maney's brigade, Cheatham's division:
"It seemed impossible for humanity to go farther. . . . A temporary halt was the inevitable result."

A businessman from nearby Springfield on his way to see the battle comes upon Gen. Buell's headquarters, about three miles behind Sheridan's division:

E.L. Davison, Springfield merchant:
"I saw a tent. In going by I saw a man lying on a cot with his feet elevated on a stool; his foot was bandaged up. I recognized him as Gen. Buel, commander of the entire army. I asked the guards what was the matter and they said his horse had fallen with him and injured his foot and ankle."

(US) Brig. Gen. William P. Carlin, brigade commander, Mitchell's division:
"He had been thrown from his horse the day before . . . , being compelled, consequently, to keep to his tent."

Davison, Springfield merchant:
"He was reading a book. Knowing he was a very grum man I did not speak to him. Some four or five men guarding him were all I saw then, but on riding a few yards farther I soon found myself among thousands of soldiers, some of whom I knew well. I told them there must be a big battle going on as I heard the noise for an hour or so, but they laughed at me and said it was only a skirmish."

(US) Brig. Gen. Carlin, brigade commander, Mitchell's division, Gilbert's corps:
"Buell's headquarters were in a hollow; the sound from McCook's battle passed over the ridges on either side of his headquarters without being distinctly heard there. . . . McCook had brought on the fight under the plea of getting water for his troops, and had neglected to notify Buell that he was engaged in a life and death struggle."

Because the sound of battle does not reach Buell's area, reports of fighting are dismissed as minor clashes as his three corps gather for tomorrow's attack on Bragg's Confederates. Besides, his generals have orders not to get into a full-blown battle until the attack. Behind the Confederate battle line:

(CS) Charles Quintard, surgeon and chaplain, 1st Tennessee, Maney's brigade, Cheatham's division:
"When the wounded were brought to the rear, . . . I took my place as a surgeon on Chaplain's Creek, and throughout the rest of the day and until half past five the next morning, without food of any sort, I was incessantly occupied with the wounded. . . . The Rev. Dr. Joseph Cross . . . assisted me."

(CS) Chaplain Joseph Cross, Donelson's Brigade, Cheatham's division:
"The first sight I see there makes me sick at heart; a poor fellow from one of the batteries, with both legs crushed by a cannon-ball. Another has a hole through his body which would admit a man's arm; yet, . . . he lives a

Maj. Gen. Don Carlos Buell

full hour. A third, smeared with blood and brains. . . . Some are shot through the breast, through the lungs; others through the arm, the hand, the shoulder. One has lost a little finger or a big toe; another is minus a nose, or has had one of his ears cut away; while a third will need a new set of teeth, and has parted perhaps with a piece of his tongue."

Elsewhere, comrades take charge of Capt. Mark L. Evans, a Confederate cavalry officer mortally wounded in the sweep of the bluff over Walkers Bend:

(CS) Lt. Batchelor, 8th Texas Cavalry:
"I sent his brother Clay with two others to see that everything was done that could be and not to leave him. . . . They . . . got an ambulance and took him to Harrodsburg, . . . , to the house of a Mrs. Mills."

Behind Webster's brigade in the Federal line, at the Wilkerson farm house:

(US) Dr. S.K. Crawford, regimental surgeon, 50th Ohio, Webster's brigade, Jackson's division:
"Surgeon McMeans, 3d Oho, was our Acting Brigade Surgeon . . . , and assisted by . . . several other Surgeons and myself (had) selected a small farm-house, with its barn and other outbuildings, as the best we could do in the way of hospital. The improvements stood in a . . . little valley, between two high hills, and immediately surrounding the dwelling was a beautiful greensward. . . . After the first arrival of wounded, all the space in and out of doors . . . was occupied. This location was . . . considered a safe one, and thither stragglers were wont to gather. The sward made a nice place where we could spread blankets for a temporary resting place for wounded upon their arrival, and it was soon thickly covered with them."

A Federal regiment awaiting orders in a cornfield watches wounded being brought to a field hospital:

(US) Sgt. A. Lanson Gierhart, 17th Ohio, Walker's brigade, Schoepf's division:
"Ambulances strung along the road from the battle line to where we lay, hauling the wounded to a large white house, on the road down a little ways from where we were halted. We went down to see the wounded. The yard layed full and the house was full. The Surgeons were busy amputating legs and arms and hands and feet, until there was a small stack of legs and arms lying by the amputation table, with wounded soldiers lying around . . . shot in every conceivable way."

A civilian sightseer approaches a Federal field hospital after leaving Buell's headquarters area:

Davison, Springfield merchant:
"I rode on to . . . (a) house where they were carrying the wounded and saw them lying on the ground. I saw two tables near the houses that the surgeon used in cutting off their legs and arms. I then noticed how they were using chloroform and taking off my coat I offered my assistance. Supposing I was a country doctor they asked me to give the chloroform, which I used on those brought on the table. Only those wounded in legs and arms could be placed upon the table.

"When they were on the table, I cut off the clothes with a pair of scissors exposing the wound. There was a large Confederate soldier, suffering very much, on the ground behind me and he begged me to take him next. He was so large I could not lift him on the table.

"A new surgeon appeared at this time and from his instruments I supposed he was the head surgeon. All stopped for a moment and the man caught my leg and begged me to take him next. I got some help, put him on the table and before long had him ready for the operation. He begged me not to give him chloroform and said he would not flinch or move during the operation. The surgeon ordered me to give him chloroform. I did so but not enough to make him insensible. He had been shot through the knee and was the gamest man I ever saw; he helped me to hold his leg steady. About this time my preacher, Rev. Miles Sanders appeared and I asked him to help me. The bone was sawed off and naturally flew up – it not being held tight enough – spinning the blood over everything; Sanders fell over in a faint.

"When I took the man off the table; we could not find a shady spot and had to put him in the hot sun. I cut a limb off an apple tree and dug a hole with my pen-knife and stuck it in the ground so as to shade his face. I had only one bottle of spirits left in my saddle-bag and that was black-berry cordial. I gave it to him and told him to keep it by him as he would need more of it. I also gave him a sandwich. He was the most grateful man I ever saw. He told me he was from Arkansas and that his name was Timothy Burns."

On the battlefield, about the time Maney's first line is trying to capture Parsons' Battery on the far left of the Federal line, Johnson's Confederate brigade is coming up to the left of Jones' brigade, struggling against troops supporting Simonson's Federal battery. Johnson's regiments are moving toward Doctor's Creek near the H.P. Bottom house. The six regiments soon lose coordination, but Johnson allows their disjointed advance to continue. The 37th Tennessee finds itself alone as it pushes toward the crossing of the creek below the Bottom house. The 42nd Indiana is still in the dry creek bed, unaware of the approaching Confederates:

(US) Lt. Spillard F. Horrall, 42nd Indiana, Lytle's brigade, Rousseau's division:
"All were engaged in cooking and eating dinner."

(US) Maj. James M. Shanklin, 42nd Indiana, Lytle's brigade, Rousseau's division:
"Captain Bryant . . . said, 'Listen! Do you hear that?' We could plainly hear the command given by the Colonel of some regiment up in the woods marching towards us by the flank, 'By company, into line! March!' and immediately afterwards, 'Forward into line by company, left half wheel!' to form the regiment into line of battle. So confident was I, even then, that there was no enemy up there, that I said, 'That is one of our regiments taking position on our right.' The men were lying round with their guns stacked, when suddenly a few stray shots . . . came whizzing by us."

To the south, skirmishers in Adams' Confederate brigade also are approaching the 42nd Indiana's position in the dry creek bed:

(CS) W.L. Trask, adjutant, Austin's Sharpshooters, 14th Louisiana Battalion, Adams' brigade, Anderson's division:
"We advanced cautiously through a skirt of woods. Directly in front of us the enemy was discovered drawn up behind a stone fence along (the creek). . . . On top of a sloping hill beyond a long line of battle could be plainly seen. At first General Adams would not believe it was the enemy, and contended it was our own men. He ordered Austin's Sharpshooters who had been placed in front, as skirmishers, not to fire. Our men knew better . . . and . . . would fire a few shots at a party getting water from the (creek) . . . , killing five of them at the first volley. This excited a reply in the shape of a tremendous volley from behind the stone wall, completely filling the air with bullets. Their artillery followed suit at once and General Adams who was standing by Captain' Slocomb's side in the act of aiming one of our (Washington Artillery) pieces, when the enemy's shot came crashing through the woods near his head, exclaimed suddenly: 'By God, they are Yankees - Fire!' Slocomb opened up on them."

(US) Lt. Horrall, 42nd Indiana, Lytle's brigade, Rousseau's division:
"The first intimation we had of the immediate presence of the rebels was a shot from their cannon, which passed over the heads of the field and staff officers, cutting limbs and branches away, which fell with a crash upon 'headquarters' mess.' The next one was aimed lower, which knocked away a stack of guns."

(US) Maj. Shanklin, 42nd Indiana, Lytle's brigade, Rousseau's division:
"Colonel Jones immediately called attention, and the men sprang to their arms."

(US) Lt. Horrall, 42nd Indiana, Lytle's brigade, Rousseau's division:
"Then, in quick succession, the rebel infantry uncovered from the woods, and began firing into our right flank."

Darden's Battery joins Slocomb's gunners in shelling the Federals:

(US) Maj. Shanklin, 42nd Indiana, Lytle's brigade, Rousseau's division:
"The enemy poured down a volley of musketry, and commenced sweeping the ravine with the artillery which we had thought silenced. The first three or four rounds they did not get our range, consequently few were struck. . . . I mounted my horse, a young stray colt . . . I had picked up on the road. He became unmanageable at once; the saddle turned with me, and I dismounted, holding him by the bridle. Colonel Jones swung the right wing round, and gave orders to fire; but the enemy was completely hidden by the woods and the fire was quite ineffectual."

(US) Lt. Horrall, 42nd Indiana, Lytle's brigade, Rousseau's division:
"A staff officer from . . . (Col.) Lytle dashed down the hill, and gave orders for the regiment to break by companies to the rear, and re-form on the top of the hill to the left of the 10th Ohio."

(US) Maj. Shanklin, 42nd Indiana, Lytle's brigade, Rousseau's division:
"Colonel Jones . . . told Colonel Denby to take the right wing out, and he would accompany the left. I remained in my position, and saw Colonel Jones come down past me. I could not hear what he said, but seeing the right wing give way, I supposed the intention was to take the regiment out of the ravine, if possible. It was a terrible position. In front a concealed enemy firing volley after volley; on our right a battery throwing grape, with little accuracy . . . but all the time getting nearer the range; behind, a steep precipice, up which the men must climb, exposed to the fire of sharpshooters. Colonel Jones rode down the ravine to the place where the bluff ceased, and managed to get out; Colonel Denby and a part of two companies succeeded in getting back up the road that we came down; but the main body was compelled to clamber up the bluff the best way it could. I started up the bluff, climbing rock by rock, grape-shot striking all round. I did not know what the orders were, or whether there were any, and when, on looking back, I saw Captain French's and a part of Captain . . . (Eigenman's) companies still down in the ravine, firing from behind a little island in the bed of the creek, I turned round and went back, thinking it best for all of us to stay with them. I had been there but a few minutes, when Lieutenant St. John, of Lytle's staff, rode down to the edge of the bluff and waved his hand. His words I could not hear, but I supposed that we were ordered to leave the ravine. Captain Eigenman ran up ahead, and shouted back to me, 'Major, they are flanking us; they are coming down the ravine.' We all then started up the bluff."

(US) William H. McCleary, 42nd Indiana, Lytle's brigade, Rousseau's division:
"Formed behind a stone fence and fired some two or three rounds on them and was over powered by a large number of rebels on three sides of us and had to fall back to keep ourselves out of the rebels hands."

The 42nd Indiana is ordered to retreat and reform in an open field to the left of the 10th Ohio:

(CS) Sgt. W.C. Gipson, 17th Tennessee, Johnson's Brigade, Buckner's Division:
"We crossed a creek, then bounded over the wall."

(US) Lt. Horrall, 42nd Indiana, Lytle's brigade, Rousseau's division:
"Three or four of our men were hurt, and twenty-one taken prisoners, including Capt. Myler."

(US) Maj. Shanklin, 42nd Indiana, Lytle's brigade, Rousseau's division:
"I thought we never could get the regiment together again . . . ; but the men proved themselves true metal, coming up slowly over the hill in line of battle, and looking desperate and determined."

(US) McCleary, 42nd Indiana, Lytle's brigade, Rousseau's division:
"Fell back fireing."

(US) George M. Kirkpatrick, 42nd Indiana, Lytle's brigade, Rousseau's division:
"We had two sergeants, Jack Jones and Nath Matheney. . . . Both of those men had been in service in the Mexican War, and we young fellows looked to them for information. . . . The former had told us what to do if we heard a cannon shot. He had said, 'don't dodge as when you hear it, it is past.' Jack was running right ahead of me, and every time a cannon ball or shell would go over, he would duck to the ground."

(US) McCleary, 42nd Indiana, Lytle's brigade, Rousseau's division:
"We went some 2 or 3 hundred yards and formed a line in rear of the 10 Ohio."

Friendly artillery fire and confusing orders hinder Johnson's attack on Lytle's Federal brigade. Two of Johnson's regiments, the 25th and 44th Tennessee, get separated, leaving the 5th Confederate, 17th, 23rd and 37th Tennessee to press the assault on Lytle's brigade, holding the ridge above the H.P. Bottom house. Just on the other side of the ridge crest is the 3rd Ohio, supported by the 15th Kentucky. To the north is the 10th Ohio:

(US) Col. Curran Pope, commanding the 15th Kentucky, Lytle's brigade, Rousseau's division:
"The 3d Ohio and 15th Kentucky were . . . on the right of the road leading from Mackville to Perryville. The 3d was placed on the brow of the same hill where the batteries were all placed, along a rail fence. A little to the right of their centre was a large barn filled with hay. . . . A cornfield extended from the fence about a hundred and fifty yards, down to a stone fence, and further over to the right was . . . (H.P. Bottom's) farm house."

(US) Col. John Beatty, commanding 3rd Ohio, Lytle's brigade, Rousseau's division:
"The rebel infantry was seen advancing across the valley, and I ordered the Third to . . . take position on the crest. The enemy's batteries now reopened with redoubled fury, and the air seemed filled with shot and exploding shells. Finding the rebels were still too far away to make out muskets effective, I ordered the boys to lie down. . . . There was a universal cry from the boys that I should lie down also; but I continued to walk up and down the line, watching the approaching enemy. . . . They advanced under cover of . . . (H.P. Bottom's) house on the side hill, and having reached a point one hundred and fifty yards distant, deployed behind a stone fence which was hidden from us by standing corn. . . . The left of my regiment rested on the Maxville and Perryville road; the line extending along the crest of the hill, and the right passing somewhat behind a barn filled with hay. . . . With the enemy's batteries pouring upon us a most destructive fire, the Third arose and delivered its first volley."

(CS) Capt. C.W. Frazer, 5th Confederate, Johnson's brigade, Buckner's division:
"Our Colonel, with some three hundred men then in the regiment, was moving alone by the left flank, a stone fence on the right and a rail fence on the left, . . . when . . . a volley . . . was fired into us without note or warning. The shock was terrific - the line swayed as one body, leaving a track of dead and wounded."

The 10th Ohio, to the Confederate right, opens fire on Johnson's men, too:

(CS) Sgt. Gipson, 17th Tennessee, Johnson's Brigade, Buckner's Division:
"Our colonel, A. S. Marks, proposed to Gen. Bushrod Johnson, our brigade commander, to charge the stone wall, which was about four hundred yards in our front, but Gen. Johnson thought it too perilous. Col. Marks replied: 'It can't be worse than this; we shall all be killed if we stay here.' The charge was then ordered."

(CS) Capt. Frazer, 5th Confederate, Johnson's brigade, Buckner's division:
"A yell . . . burst almost simultaneously from officers and men."

(CS) Sgt. Gipson, 17th Tennessee, Johnson's Brigade, Buckner's Division:
"We went double-quick right for the stone wall under a heavy fire of both grapeshots and musketry."

(CS) Capt. Frazer, 5th Confederate, Johnson's brigade, Buckner's division:
"(We) charged over dead and dying and drove the enemy from the fence."

(CS) Sgt. Gipson, 17th Tennessee, Johnson's Brigade, Buckner's Division:
"The Yankees fell back through a sorghum patch, and formed behind a rail fence, some two hundred yards distant."

(CS) Capt. Frazer, 5th Confederate, Johnson's brigade, Buckner's division:
"All along our front a solid line of (Federal) dead and wounded lay, in some places three deep, extending to the right from the barn, which served for a temporary hospital for the wounded enemy."

(US) Col. Beatty, commanding 3rd Ohio, Lytle's brigade, Rousseau's division:
"The air was filled with hissing balls; shells were exploding continuously, and the noise of the guns was deafening."

Though Johnson's regiments cannot advance and are running out of ammunition, their rifles and shelling from supporting batteries are wearing the Federals down:

(CS) Capt. Frazer, 5th Confederate, Johnson's brigade, Buckner's division:
"One of our batteries in our rear . . . exploded a shell into . . . (the) barn."

(US) Col. Beatty, commanding 3rd Ohio, Lytle's brigade, Rousseau's division:
"The barn . . . took fire."

(CS) Capt. Frazer, 5th Confederate, Johnson's brigade, Buckner's division, Hardee's corps:
"We heard the shrieks of the wounded as they burned. . . . The barn was on their side, and the fight went on."

(US) Col. Beatty, commanding 3rd Ohio, Lytle's brigade, Rousseau's division:
"Flames bursting from the roof, windows, doors, and interstices between the logs, threw the right of the regiment into disorder. . . . The boys closed up to the left, (and) steadied themselves on the colors."

(CS) Sgt. Gipson, 17th Tennessee, Johnson's Brigade, Buckner's Division:
"At first we could only see their colors, but before what few of them who were not shot down left we could see them very plainly as the cane patch was mowed down. Three or four times the colors would fall, but were no sooner down than they were raised again, by other hands."

(US) Col. Beatty, commanding 3rd Ohio, Lytle's brigade, Rousseau's division:
"Our colors changed hands seven times during the engagement. Six of our color bearers were either killed or wounded, and as the sixth man was falling, a soldier of Company C, named David C. Walker, a boyish fellow . . . who had lost his hat in the fight, sprang forward, caught the falling flag, then stepping out in front of the regiment, waved it triumphantly, and carried it to the end of the battle. . . . Nearly two hundred of my five hundred men now lay dead and wounded on the little strip of ground over which we fought. . . . Colonel Curren Pope, of the Fifteenth Kentucky, whose regiment was being held in reserve at the bottom of the hill, had . . . twice requested me to retire my men and allow him to take the position. Finding now that our ammunition was exhausted, I sent him notice, and as his regiment marched to the crest the Third was withdrawn."

(US) Col. Pope, commanding the 15th Kentucky, Lytle's brigade, Rousseau's division:
"The 15th went forward with fixed bayonets and relieved the 3d (Ohio)."

(US) William P. McDowell, adjutant, 15th Kentucky, Lytle's brigade, Rousseau's division:
"The Fifteenth Kentucky was lying . . . in the rear of a rail-fence, and . . . on the line of the rail-fence, was a barn built of logs and boards."

(US) Col. Pope, commanding the 15th Kentucky, Lytle's brigade, Rousseau's division:
"My horse was killed under me as soon as I reached the line, and, after stepping from him, I received the wound in the fleshy part of my arm."

(US) McDowell, adjutant, 15th Kentucky, Lytle's brigade, Rousseau's division:
"The Colonel immediately approached the line, and moving from man to man, patting them on the back, cheering and encouraging them to fight to the end."

(US) Col. Pope, commanding the 15th Kentucky, Lytle's brigade, Rousseau's division:
"Lieut. Col. Jouett was shot in the leg, and Lieut. McGrath went to his assistance. After raising him, he was himself shot dead through the head. Major Campbell was shot through the body about the same time, and was borne from the field to a house, where he died immediately afterwards. . . . The firing of the regiment . . . was kept up with overwhelming effect, and we had succeeded in driving the enemy entirely behind the stone fence."

(CS) Sgt. Gipson, 17th Tennessee, Johnson's Brigade, Buckner's Division:
"Myself and three others were trying to shoot through . . . a hole in the (stone) wall . . . , and we were in each other's way. So I told them to do the loading and I would do the shooting, and thus we continued. . . . I felt quite safe behind that wall."

(US) McDowell, adjutant, 15th Kentucky, Lytle's brigade, Rousseau's division:
"The rail-fence was almost entirely demolished by the enemy's artillery . . . The color-guard, consisting of nine sergeants, was cut to pieces. As each successive color-bearer was shot down his companion took the standard. . . . The colors were . . . riddled with shot-holes, and the flag staff cut in two. As the staff was severed, and the colors fell, Captain James B. Forman, of Company C, grasped them, and as the staff had been shot off so short that they could not be made visible he mounted the remains of the rail-fence, waving them, cheering the men to continued resistance."

CONFEDERATES ADVANCE

On the Widow Gibson's farm, between Johnson's and Maney's Confederate brigades, Donelson's troops are soon locked in a firefight with Webster's brigade:

(US) Maj. George T. Simonson, 80th Indiana, Webster's Brigade, Jackson's division:
"The rebel devils had filed into line in our front and taken their respective tree to fight behind."

(CS) Col. John H. Savage, commanding 16th Tennessee, Donelson's brigade, Cheatham's division:
"The right of the regiment was at the two cabins. There was a (Federal) battery (Harris') in the line of battle to the right, about thirty or forty yards from these cabins, between which cabins there was an entry, or space, of ten or fifteen feet. The battery opened fire upon us, killing many men, and at the same time a fire of small arms from the line of battle was directed upon these cabins. The battery fired obliquely into this space. I stood between the cabins, would watch the gunner ram home the charge, and say, 'Lie low, boys; he is going to fire,' and step for protection close to the cabin nearest the battery. The battle was furious, the men loading and firing as rapidly as possible, falling back and again charging up to the fence."

(CS) Thomas R. Hooper, 16th Tennessee, Donelson's brigade, Cheatham's division:
"We were . . . about fifty to one hundred yards of a battery of 6 or 9 pieces on our right and our left wing with enfiladed firing down our center, all heavily supported by Infantry."

(US) Joseph P. Glezen, 80th Indiana, Webster's brigade, Jackson's division:
"We were ordered to (rise and fire). . . . Bullets were whistling over me with such fury it seemed as if no man could stand erect and live. But at the word of command, we all bounded to our feet . . . determined to pour the contents of our muskets into the ranks of our ungodly opposers. . . . It was necessary to advance about two rods (33 feet) to the top of the hill in order to bring our arms to bear against the enemy. . . . They kept so well concealed behind trees that only a few could be seen. . . . As we advanced to give the first fire I did not . . . relish the music of the relics as they whistled around my ears. . . . At the word fire we all pulled triggers together and then were directed to load and fire at will. Many of our guns were defective and when I rammed down my second cartridge I discovered my gun contained two loads. I reprimed . . . and thought I would 'double the dose' by firing two balls at once; but my gun again refused to fire. I retired down the hill, took off the tube (nipple), picked the powder in the touch hole, primed, advanced and made a third effort to fire, but in vain. I then threw down my gun in disgust, picked up another, tried it with a ramrod and found it like mine - containing two loads. (I) picked up the second and it was in the same condition - the third ditto - the fourth had lead just about one foot from the muzzle. I then concluded to get out of the way myself, as I did not like to be a target for traitors without at least an equal chance at them. So I went down about four rods (66 feet) and laid down behind a stump with a couple of wounded from my company."

(CS) Col. Savage, commanding 16th Tennessee, Donelson's brigade, Cheatham's division:
"A private, Andrew Dow Mercer, said, 'Boys, let's take the battery,' and started in that direction. At this time I saw a force to my right and in my rear. I countermanded Mercer's order, but he had gone some five or six steps towards the battery to a tree. Seeing that he was not supported, he hugged the tree closely for a short space of time and returned to the cabin without being wounded."

A Federal soldier who has taken cover behind the line because he couldn't find a rifle that would fire bestirs himself:

(US) Glezen, 80th Indiana, Webster's brigade, Jackson's division:
"Thought it was a poor place for a soldier - got up and renewed my search for a gun that would fire - picked up two more near the stump with loads half way down the barrel; found a musket on the fighting ground of Company C that was empty, loaded her, and when I pulled the trigger the . . . gun (fired)."

(US) Erastus Winters, 50th Ohio, Webster's brigade, Jackson's division:
"We move forward, and take our place in line of battle behind the Eightieth Indiana Regiment, who were supporting a battery, and are heavily engaged with the enemy. We were ordered to lie down in supporting distance. . . . They were on higher ground than we were, and on the firing line. While we were in no great danger where we lay, . . . it was more trying on the nerves than being up in front, for the reason we could do nothing where we were . . . , while the Indianians had a chance to get back at them. . . . I began to think we were up against the real thing this time. . . . To say it was demoralizing would be putting it very mild indeed. . . . Had I been given my choices just then, I would have preferred being back at Louisville or Cincinnati."

(US) Wesley S. Poulson, 98th Ohio, Webster's brigade, Jackson's division:
"Our battery kept them back from us for a considerable while."

(US) Sgt. Maj. Duncan C. Milner, 98th Ohio, Webster's brigade, Jackson's division:
"I had the pleasure of seeing the rebels run, who were under fire of . . . (Harris') battery near us. . . . I . . . got some of our men to assist the artillerymen roll back their guns, as they were almost exhausted. The guns were right on top of the hill when they were fired, then would bound back, and it was hard to roll them up again. . . . The air was filled with smoke, and the roaring of the cannons and the rattle of the musketry was almost deafening."

(US) Poulson, 98th Ohio, Webster's brigade, Jackson's division:
"Shells, solid shot, and rifle balls were flying over us. Some high up in the air and some so low as to occasionally make us strike the ground with our noses. One shell burst in the air I suppose some 30 feet above us and a piece of it or some of its contents went into the ground about 15 inches from my head. A cannonball passed over my back which I'm quite sure would have struck me had I been standing up. I thought

when I heard it coming that it would strike my head. I shut my eyes expecting to feel it, but had the pleasure of hearing it whistle over me and afterwards saw the dust fly to the rear of our company some distance. Some of the boys were sleeping not withstanding all the noise that was being made. For my part I could not sleep. There was too much to be seen and the prospect of too much to be done for sleep to bother me.

"To our right was the regiment which was engaged and I could see their men fall, some to rise no more, and others to be carried away by their comrades. I could plainly see the blood on some of them as they were carried back to the surgeon. I could see the rebel's flag on the next hill and occasionally the heads of the rebels when they would rise to shoot at the regiment mentioned. They however took good care to hide their bodies and their heads are so little that they are rather difficult to hit.

"I saw horses without riders running for life. I saw hogs, pigs, and rabbits, all running towards our line scared to insensibility almost by the advancing rebels. To our right a few hundred yards was a barn that had been fired by a shell from the rebels. . . .

"The 10th Ohio Regiment was partly on each side of the barn and . . . maintained their position until their faces were scorched by the heat of the ascending flames, then were forced to fall back some distance. During this time the 98th Regiment was lying on the ground watching the movement of the rebels in front of us."

(CS) Col. Savage, commanding 16th Tennessee, Donelson's brigade, Cheatham's division:
"During the hottest of the battle my lieutenant-colonel, (David M.) Donnell, came to me and said; 'Colonel, order a retreat. We are losing all our men and are not supported.' I replied: 'Protect your men by those trees and fence and I will protect this wing by these cabins. We were ordered to fight. To order a retreat at the beginning of a great battle is not war. We must hold this position until supported, and it is the duty of our commanding officers to bring us support.' The regiment could not then retreat without being brought again under the fire of the battery in the field."

(CS) Carroll H. Clark, 16th Tennessee, Donelson's brigade, Cheatham's division:
"We were in 40 yards of the enemy."

(CS) John H. Nichols, 16th Tennessee, Donelson's brigade, Cheatham's division:
"My brother fell at my side with a broken arm and a broken leg. His arm was lost, but his leg was saved. My clothes were cut in five different places and the long hair from my right temple was furrowed with a shot which burned the side of my head, but I was not seriously hurt."

(CS) Col. Savage, commanding 16th Tennessee, Donelson's brigade, Cheatham's division:
"While standing between the cabins a minie ball passed through my leg without breaking the bone, and the wood off of a canister shot struck the opposite cabin, and glancing knocked me down, paralyzing me for a time."

(CS) James R. Thompson, 16th Tennessee, Donelson's brigade, Cheatham's division:
"Just at this time Colonel Savage got wounded. I was right by him, and he said to me, 'I am wounded. Where is (Lt.) Colonel (Donnell) . . . ? He will have to take charge of the Regiment.' (Lt.) Colonel (Donnell) . . . appeared on the right where I was."

The brigade commander, Donelson, brings the 38th Tennessee up to bolster Savage's position, but he quickly decides his mounting casualties are too much and the Federal line too strong to break; he orders his regiments to fall back. Donelson's troops are low on ammunition and search for it among the dead and wounded. To Donelson's right, Maney's first line is still behind the fence, firing up at the 105th Ohio and Parsons' Battery on Open Hill. Maney realizes he must get his men moving again:

(CS) Col. George C. Porter, 6th Tennessee, Maney's brigade, Cheatham's division:
"General Maney passed along the line from the right of the Georgia regiment to the left of the Ninth Tennessee, ordering and encouraging us to press forward, as it was our last and only chance of safety and success. His presence and manner . . . imparted fresh vigor and courage among the troops."

(US) Albion W. Tourgee, 105th Ohio, Terrill's brigade, Jackson's division:
"Then we first heard the rebel yell. . . . The gray line burst from the wood and rushed up the slope."

(CS) Lt. Hall, 9th Tennessee, Maney's brigade, Cheatham's division:
"After crossing the fence, our advance was up a steep incline until we reached a point where we could look down the muzzles of the enemy's guns, which were . . . just over the crest of the hill. Col. Buford had been severely wounded at the fence and was compelled to retire from the field. The command then devolved upon Major Kelso, whose horse was shot in attempting to cross this same fence. It was a very valuable horse. Had cost him five hundred dollars a few days before, and Kelso thought it would be prudent for him to take the horse to the rear for treatment."

(US) Tourgee, 105th Ohio, Terrill's brigade, Jackson's division:
" 'Forward!' cried Terrill.' Do not let them get the guns!' 'Charge!' commanded the major, whose horse having been shot, was on foot with the left companies. There was a clang of bayonets. The left companies surged forward to the front of the battery."

(US) Lt. Cumings, Parsons' Battery, Terrill's brigade, Jackson's division:
"We gave the enemy canister as fast as we could fire . . . The last gun fired . . . was my right gun, which I fired with my own hands."

(US) Tourgee, 105th Ohio, Terrill's brigade, Jackson's division:
"Cumings . . . fired the two right guns, double-shotted with canister, full into the faces of the enemy, then almost at the muzzles of the pieces, and with his few remaining men dashed through our ranks to the rear under cover of the smoke. . . . When it lifted, the enemy had faltered, half-way down the slope. Our fire was too hot for them to stand. They fell slowly back and began firing again."

The 80th Illinois, about 660 men, and Garrard's battalion, about 195 men, arrive to shore up Terrill's position.

(US) Capt. Robert B. Taylor, Garrard's battalion, Terrill's brigade, Jackson's division:
"Just as we charge the ascent, Col. Garrard ordered 'fix bayonets' and as we went up . . . our dead and wounded, on the ground, far outnumbered the living in the ranks."

Garrard's Battalion goes into line to the right of Parsons' Battery; the 80th Illinois takes a position to the right of Garrard. The new Federal troops are soon feeling the effects of shells from Turner's Confederate battery:

(US) Capt. Taylor, Garrard's battalion, Terrill's brigade, Jackson's division:
"We endured a fearful storm of balls, round shot, and bursting shell."

The 27th Tennessee, about 200 men, advances from Maney's second line without orders and joins the firing uphill at Parsons' Battery and its supporting troops:

(US) Lt. Cumings, Parson's Battery, Terrill's brigade, Jackson's division:
"Their line extending far beyond and wrapping around our left poured down our line an enfilading fire. . . . It was the hottest fire I ever experienced."

CONFEDERATES ADVANCE

Maney turns command of the first line over to the 1st Tennessee's colonel, Hume Feild, and sets off to bring his second line, the 1st and 27th Tennessee, into the fight. Maney is looking for 27th Tennessee when he learns General Polk has ordered Lt. Col. John Patterson to lead the 1st Tennessee against Parsons' Battery. Maney returns to the first line:

(CS) Capt. Thomas H. Malone, staff of Maney's brigade, Cheatham's division:
"I found . . . (Gen. Maney) standing under a great white oak tree at the edge of the field, and in the field I saw the 41st Georgia and the 6th and 9th Tennessee regiments lying on the ground, engaged in a bitter fight with the line of the enemy on the edge of the hill in their front, which line was supported by Parsons' battery of eight 12-pound Napoleon guns. It seemed to me that our men could not have maintained our position at all but for the fact that old Turner - the best artilleryman, but the poorest drilled man in the army - was imperatively demanding the attention of Parsons' guns. He thundered with his little 6-pound howitzers right over the heads of our men, and with grape was making it very hot for Parsons and his infantry supports."

In the Federal line, Terrill decides his line cannot long hold against the Confederate pressure and orders Parsons' Battery to withdraw, but most of the horses are dead or wounded, and few of the artillerymen are at the guns. From the Confederate side, the fighting looks equally desperate:

(CS) Capt. Malone, staff of Maney's brigade, Cheatham's division:
"After looking at the battle for a few minutes Gen. Maney asked me what I thought of it. I told him I didn't think our position could be maintained; that there were seven or eight guns of the enemy against Turner's four, and that the enemy's line of infantry was longer and stronger than ours. He asked what I thought should be done, and I told him I believed our only chance was to take those guns. He asked if I thought it was possible for our men to do it. I said, 'I think so.' He then said, 'Go, direct the men to go forward, if possible.'

"I rode out into the field, in the rear of the line, and, passing the whole length of our line of battle, told the field officers of each regiment what was expected. I was repeatedly assured by officers and privates as I rode along that if it were possible to make a simultaneous movement, they believed they could take the guns, but in the great uproar of bursting shells and crashing of incessant musketry a man could hardly be heard even speaking his loudest. I was discussing this with Capt. Harrison of the 9th Tennessee, when a private of the 9th looked up and called out to me: 'Captain, the 9th will follow you anywhere.' Thereupon I rode up and down the line again, telling the men to look to the centre of the line, and when I rode out and raised my hat that should be the signal for a simultaneous charge."

At the other end of the Confederate battle line, Jones' brigade makes another attempt to storm Simonson's Battery:

(US) Ormond Hupp, Simonson's Battery, Harris' brigade, Rousseau's division:
"They came within twenty yards, but were forced to fall back."

Jones' Brigade is so battered it will not return to the fighting, but Confederate artillery and Jones' infantry have inflicted worrisome casualties on Simonson's Battery. McCook orders the 38th Indiana forward to help protect Simonson's guns:

(US) Henry F. Perry, 38th Indiana, Harris' brigade, Rousseau's division:
"In a hollow between two ridges the regiment was halted, and Col. Scribner gave the command to move forward to the crest of the ridge and fire at will."

(US) Col. B.F. Scribner, commanding 38th Indiana, Harris' brigade, Rousseau's division:
"Our own battery under Capt. Simmonson . . . was ordered away by the chief of artillery."

(US) Hupp, Simonson's Battery, Harris' brigade, Rousseau's division:
"Our battery . . . left one man killed and four horses, also four men wounded. We fell back on the opposite side of the road about fifty rods (275 yards) from our former position."

(US) Col. Scribner, commanding 38th Indiana, Harris' brigade, Rousseau's division:
"We were moved forward to a slight elevation or ridge, where we were partially protected."

As Jones' Confederate brigade falls back, Brown's brigade is coming up to take its place against the Federal line anchored by Simonson's Battery. About the same time, Cleburne's Confederate brigade is moving up to relieve Johnson's brigade in front of Lytle's position. At the far right of the Confederate line, Maney's 6th, 9th, 27th Tennessee and 41st Georgia are poised for a third attempt to storm the ridge held by Parsons' Federal battery and the troops of Terrill's brigade on Open Hill:

(CS) Capt. Malone, staff of Maney's brigade, Cheatham's division:
"I went back to the 9th, rode out about three horse-lengths in front, laughingly charging the fellows not to shoot me in the back, raised my hat and gave a yell. Every man was instantly on his feet."

CONFEDERATES ADVANCE

(CS) A.J. West, 41st Georgia, Maney's brigade, Cheatham's division:
"The commands of Captain Curtright (were) . . . 'Keep cool, my boys! Keep cool!!! Shoot low.' "

Coming up behind Donelson's and Maney's brigades are the five regiments of Stewart's brigade.

(CS) Sgt. Maj. Louis B. McFarland, 9th Tennessee, Maney's brigade:
"Captain Malone, mounted on George, . . . a handsome gray, . . . dashed out to our front, and with drawn sword, ordered: 'Up and charge that battery.' We sprang to the attack, he leading, and we charged."

(CS) Capt. Malone, staff of Maney's brigade, Cheatham's division:
"The 27th (Tennessee) lost its grip, couldn't stand still, and despite orders went with us to a man. The little regiment had been nearly wiped out at Shiloh, but the men that remained were still . . . game."

(CS) Col. Porter, 6th Tennessee, Maney's brigade, Cheatham's division:
"It was near the fence on entering the field that Captain Thomas B. Rains, Company C, and First Lieutenant Ed. Seabrook were killed . . . at the head of their . . . companies. . . . The color-bearer, John Andrews, was here too badly wounded to proceed farther and had to be carried from the field. . . . (The colors) were then seized by John Ayeres, one of the color guard, who carried them . . . for a short distance and was killed."

(CS) West, 41st Georgia, Maney's brigade, Cheatham's division:
"Two batteries were playing upon the 41st Georgia in front and a heavy enfilading fire from the flanks, and, when within one hundred and fifty yards of the enemy, they opened on us with grape and canister."

(CS) Capt. Malone, staff of Maney's brigade, Cheatham's division:
"We suffered terribly while we were charging. . . . I saw . . . a fellow who had become panicky and thrown himself into a ditch, three feet or more deep, where no ball direct from the front could possibly have reached him. I was shaming him for his cowardice, when a ball, coming from Lord knows where, struck him and killed him while I was talking to him."

(CS) West, 41st Georgia, Maney's brigade, Cheatham's division:
"When within fifty yards, they opened on us with musketry, and now the fight became general and looked like the whole world had been converted into blue coats, whistling balls, bursting shells and brass cannon."

(CS) Capt. Malone, staff of Maney's brigade, Cheatham's division:
"One gun pointed at the right company of the 41st Georgia was said to have killed twelve or thirteen men and desperately wounded, as I myself know, the colonel of that company and its captain."

(CS) Martin V. Gribble; 6th Tennessee, Maney's brigade, Cheatham's division:
"I was wounded . . . , and Bob Waire was . . . shot through the mouth and the jaw bone bursted open and the ball passed through, lodging under the skin in the back of the neck."

(CS) James D. Jordan, 9th Tennessee, Maney's brigade, Cheatham's division:
"My brother, Samuel Jordan, was killed by my side and I was shot in the face which resulted in permanent partial deafness."

(CS) West, 41st Georgia, Maney's brigade, Cheatham's division:
"It seemed impossible for mortal men to stand up in the face of such a rain of lead and our lines wavered . . . , and as I cast my eyes down the lines, with my young heart in my throat and my knees growing weak, I saw . . . Bob Duglas, with his sword brandished above his head, urging the boys to stand! At the same moment the clear voice of . . . Frank McWhorter rang out, 'Die, my comrades, rather than give it up.' "

(CS) Lt. Hall, 9th Tennessee, Maney's brigade, Cheatham's division:
"We reached a point where we could look down the muzzles of the enemy's guns, which were stationed just over the crest of the hill. . . . Without Regimental officers . . . command devolved upon the company officers. My position was at the left of the Co. Capt. Irby, who commanded the company next to ours on the left, was the first to discover the position of the Battery and a heavy line of Infantry in its rear. . . . We were brought under the fire of the Battery not fifty feet in front of us and of the infantry lines in the rear. Their fire was terrific and we were losing men rapidly, so much that it caused our line to falter in its advance. Just here I heard Capt. Irby's ringing voice, 'Lieut. Hall, here's the battery in our front. Pass the order down the line let us make a charge and take it.' . . . We went forward with a yell."

(CS) W.J. McDill, 9th Tennessee, Maney's brigade, Cheatham's division:
"The Yankees stood to their batteries until we got to within 30 or 40 yards of them. . . . I got a hole shot in the skirt of my coat."

(CS) Capt. John M. Taylor, 27th Tennessee, Maney's brigade, Cheatham's division:
"Our concentrated fire played havoc in the enemy's lines, almost mowing them down."

(CS) Col. Porter, 6th Tennessee, Maney's brigade, Cheatham's division:
"A.M. Pegues . . . carried (the colors) . . . to the summit where the first battery was placed, where he was badly wounded, being shot in three places."

(CS) Robert Gates, 6th Tennessee, Maney's brigade, Cheatham's division:
"The Color-bearer fell; . . . and for a moment it lay on the ground . . . when Ed. Quinn, private in Co. H, threw down his gun and grasped the fallen banner, and running about fifteen paces in front waved it furiously, and shouted: 'Come on. . . . ; follow your flag!' . . . The line rushed forward . . . and drove the enemy."

Parsons' artillerymen manage to pull off one gun as the 6th and 9th Tennessee charge:

(US) Capt. Taylor, Garrard's battalion, Terrill's brigade, Jackson's division:
"When our ranks began to waver, and give way, Col. Garrard ordered us to fall back to the bottom of the hill."

(CS) Sgt. Maj. McFarland, 9th Tennessee, Maney's brigade:
"The 6th and 9th (Tennessee) went directly through Parsons's Battery."

(CS) Lt. Hall, 9th Tennessee, Maney's brigade, Cheatham's division:
"As we advanced past the guns in pursuit of the Infantry two of our men, Gladney McCreight & Will Carnes were wounded while firing at the retreating enemy from the shelter of the gun carriages, our company passing right over the ground occupied by the guns."

(CS) Capt. Malone, staff of Maney's brigade, Cheatham's division:
"Several of the enemy's guns were loaded and fired while we were making the charge, and it seems to me that the one pointed at the 41st Georgia was fired after George and I passed the battery. Old George wasn't afraid of anything . . . except a wagon. He had been injured, when a colt, by a runaway wagon. . . . Just as the 9th and I were passing through the guns George spied a caisson, and suddenly wheeling and rearing, nearly unseated me. Several of the 9th rushed out of line, calling out: 'The captain's killed,' and seized old George. . . . Neither George nor I received a scratch."

(CS) Sgt. Maj. McFarland, 9th Tennessee, Maney's brigade:
"One of the officers of my company, A, picked up a gauntlet glove of General Jackson, whose body lay among the guns."

CONFEDERATES ADVANCE

The 80th Illinois begins to fall back, and the center of the 105th Ohio is giving way:

(US) Tourgee, 105th Ohio, Terrill's brigade, Jackson's division:
"Terrill gave the order to retire to a fence which ran along the edge of a wood in our rear."

(US) Josiah Ayre, 105th Ohio, Terrill's brigade, Jackson's division:
"Every man seemed to be looking out for himself as we were all broken up. . . . I could not tell whether we had any regiment or not."

(US) Capt. Taylor, Garrard's battalion, Terrill's brigade, Jackson's division:
"As the lines fell back gradually, I saw Thomas Hutchinson, my 2nd Lieutenant, on the ground . . . with his face all bloody. I ran to him. . . . He had been struck in the head with the fragment of a shell and the blood flowed from his face in streams. He looked worse hurt than he really was. He told me he thought he was mortally wounded, and not to stay behind on his account, but I told him not to think of giving up so soon, and seized hold of him, and carried him down the hill."

(CS) Capt. Malone, staff of Maney's brigade, Cheatham's division:
"(With) the enemy's whole line of battle . . . in flight, the butchery was something awful. . . . I could walk upon dead bodies from where the enemy's line was established until it reached the woods, some three hundred yards away. . . . It seemed to me that one-third of them were lying dead on the line . . . they had been holding."

Terrill tries to rally his troops at the farm lane behind his position:

(US) Ayre, 105th Ohio, Terrill's brigade, Jackson's division:
"After falling back 15 or 20 rods we came to a kind of grove."

(US) Tourgee, 105th Ohio, Terrill's brigade, Jackson's division:
"We rallied at the fence."

(US) Lt. John C. Hartzell, 105th Ohio, Terrill's brigade, Jackson's division:
"In crossing this fence many of our men were killed and fell between. . . . Behind this lane was quite a handful of our fellows."

(US) Stephen J. Hutchinson, 105th Ohio, Terrill's brigade, Jackson's division:
"We formed in squads as best we could behind trees. . . . Our line of battle was not formed at all."

(US) Tourgee, 105th Ohio, Terrill's brigade, Jackson's division:
"When the enemy showed above the crest of the hill, (we) renewed the fight. . . . Our adjutant, who rode a chunky, serviceable but not showy stallion, having tarried to see that all the men got the order to retire, found himself face to face with the Confederate line. Turning, he charged down the little slope to the fence, not stopping to hunt any of the numerous gaps. . . . His head was down. . . . The adjutant . . . was no fence-jumping cavalier, but .. with a lift on the reins he plunged his spurs into the side of the old bay, who rose to the occasion and would have bolted to the rear, if one of the men had not hooked on to his rein. Thereupon, the adjutant dismounted, being then the only mounted officer left with us, the brigadier being on foot and his staff either dismounted or on duty elsewhere. Putting up a wounded man in his place, with another clinging to the stirrup, the adjutant sent his . . . steed to the rear and took orders . . . from Gen. Terrill and Col. Hall, both likewise dismounted."

(US) Ayre, 105th Ohio, Terrill's brigade, Jackson's division:
"Getting behind the first tree I saw . . . I gave them a few more rounds."

(US) Lester D. Taylor, 105th Ohio, Terrill's brigade, Jackson's division:
"I kept (to) the fence rising to fire & dropping to load."

(US) Lt. Hartzell, 105th Ohio, Terrill's brigade, Jackson's division:
"I got a gun and banged away. . . . Captain Canfield fell by my side. After a bit he got up, pale as a ghost. A buckshot had hit him true in the center of the forehead at the hair line, plowed its way under the scalp of his crown and passed out. A stream of blood ran down his nose, there parted and trickled down in a little rill on either side. I said: 'Captain, you are done for, get away if you can.' 'Not by a d...n sight,' said he. Hathaway, his Orderly-Sergeant, was nearby, working away industriously, and the Captain roared out, 'Hathaway, give 'em hell!' Hathaway turned his face for a second, and in a hurt voice replied: 'Captain, ain't I givin' 'em hell?' and banged away again."

(US) Hutchinson, 105th Ohio, Terrill's brigade, Jackson's division:
"The air above our heads seemed to be alive with screeching and hissing of the death dealing missiles & after the enemy had gained the hill the shot fell thick & fast around us. It was a wonder that so many of us escaped."

While Terrill's men try to hold their new position, an officer gets a wounded comrade to safety farther down the hill:

(US) Capt. Taylor, Garrard's battalion, Terrill's brigade, Jackson's division:
"When I got (Lt. Hutchinson) . . . down into the bed of Doctor's Fork . . . he moaned and groaned, and made me very miserable. . . . We were laying close in under the bank to protect ourselves from the shower of iron hail that was raining over us, when a cannon ball struck within a few feet of where we were sitting, and raised an immense cloud of dust about us. He asked what that was. I told him it was a 'round shot', and indicated that our position was unsafe. . . . I hurried him off to the (field) hospital."

Back uphill, the Confederate 4th and 5th Tennessee from Stewart's brigade arrive to help Maney's first line against Terrill's new position:

(CS) Lt. Edwin H. Rennolds, 5th Tennessee, Stewart's brigade, Cheatham's division:
"We . . . came into full view of the conflict our comrades were engaged in at a lane about 150 yards down the slope. . . . Breaking into a double-quick, we covered the intervening space in the shortest possible time. . . . Corporal Bob Harris fell to rise no more, and Lieut. G.C. Camp of Company 'H' fell dangerously wounded. At the lane were the limbers and caissons of . . . (Parsons') Battery. All the horses had been killed except one, which Sergeant Kennerly, Company 'D,' who was wounded just then, cut loose and rode to the rear."

(US) Hutchinson, 105th Ohio, Terrill's brigade, Jackson's division:
"My friend Geltz . . . fell mortally wounded at my side. He boldly stepped out . . . aside of the tree behind which 3 or 4 of us were partially (hidden) . . . took aim & fired & immediately not 2 feet from me was struck. Another of our group was wounded."

(US) Charles K. Radcliffe, 105th Ohio, Terrill's brigade, Jackson's division:
"Gen. Terrill . . . again gave the order to fall back."

(US) Lt. Hartzell, 105th Ohio, Terrill's brigade, Jackson's division:
"The bullets were coming like hail against the old fences, when finally an Orderly came on the run with an order from the Colonel to get out of there."

(US) Taylor, 105th Ohio, Terrill's brigade, Jackson's division:
"We were ordered to retreat to the gully six rods to the rear. I did not hear the order, & kept at work."

CONFEDERATES ADVANCE

(US) Ayre, 105th Ohio, Terrill's brigade, Jackson's division:
"I finished loading my gun and started off. . . . I did not go far before a musket or rifle ball struck me in my left leg just below the calf breaking it and passing clear through. I . . . fell and that finished my fighting."

(US) Lt. Hartzell, 105th Ohio, Terrill's brigade, Jackson's division:
"As we left, the Johnnies began to pour over the fences. . . . The bullets were coming like angry bees, so I got an oak tree behind my back and in line with the firing, turned on the juice and ran true, turning neither to the right nor left."

(CS) Lt. Rennolds, 5th Tennessee, Stewart's brigade, Cheatham's division:
"The . . . Federals . . . broke and fled . . . , keeping up a desultory firing as they retired."

(US) Taylor, 105th Ohio, Terrill's brigade, Jackson's division:
"Turning my head a little when sending a bullet home I saw but one man in sight - Charley Hitchcock, turned my head the other way, & saw three men. I delivered that fire, & fell back to the Reg. We did not see Charley alive again."

(US) Tourgee, 105th Ohio, Terrill's brigade, Jackson's division:
"The three right companies, not hearing the order to retire, were cut off . . . under command of . . . Edwards, the senior captain, now thrice wounded, (and) fell back farther to the left, and rallied behind the stone fence that marked the roadway. The left and center, now mere shattered fragments, retired under the command of General Terrill, by whose side marched our colonel."

(US) Radcliffe, 105th Ohio, Terrill's brigade, Jackson's division:
"(I) was . . . just behind Terrill - who, with an Aid, had lost their horses, and were also on foot."

At the other end of the Federal line, Cleburne's Confederate brigade is moving down Chatham hill, overlooking Doctor's Creek, to relieve Johnson's men. Cleburne's troops can see the Federal defenders above the Bottom house:

(CS) Lt. W. E. Yeatman, 2nd Tennessee, Cleburne's brigade, Buckner's division:
"For a mile we could see them, their splendid looking lines. Flags flying, bands playing, and cannons playing on us as we moved to attack them. They were . . . posted in two lines, one at the foot the other at the open ridge."

(CS) Capt. C. W. Frazer, 5th Confederate, Johnson's brigade, Buckner's division:
"After being twice supplied with ammunition, and losing all hope of relief, the Thirty-seventh Tennessee joined us, under Moses White, and his Adjutant, Harvey Mathes. But soon after, we saw a long line of blue-coats, coming down the hill at our rear. Col. Smith, standing near me, said: 'Captain, have you a white handkerchief? I am afraid we will need one.' . . . I answered: 'There's not one in the regiment; and you have on the only "biled shirt," the lower end of which will answer if occasion requires.' Just then they raised a yell - Federals always cheered; it was our own brigade, under . . . Cleburne - the blue (coats) being one of the results of the victory at Richmond."

About the same time Cleburne moves forward, Brown's brigade begins its advance toward the position once anchored by Simonson's Federal battery:

(CS) Col. William Miller, 1st Florida, Brown's brigade, Anderson's division:
"Owing to the fact that some of the men were virtually barefooted, and that there were black locust thickets, some of the first regiment could not go into the battle."

(CS) Thomas B. Ellis, 3rd Florida, Brown's brigade, Anderson's division:
"When I got back with the water (detail) was ordered to charge and me without a gun! ... I had left my gun in the wagon."

(CS) Lt. John L. Inglis, 3rd Florida, Brown's brigade, Anderson's division:
" 'Attention' rang along our line, up jumped the 1st Brigade. Genl. B. lined us up as if on drill, drew his sword and with the command 'forward,' 'guide right, march,' we started from a march to a trot, and yelling like others we were soon at a run, cut into the brambles, high as our heads, and in terrible bad order. Genl. Brown stopped whole line to get 3 Fla. in line cussed us for being too quick, dress up or you 'will be cut to pieces in such order,' men & officers soon were in line, and as bal of brigade was now OK, we again started."

(CS) William R. Talley, Palmer's Battery, Brown's brigade, Anderson's division:
"We ... came to a dry creek and the bluff on the other side was about ten feet high."

(CS) Capt. Joseph Palmer, commanding Palmer's Battery, Brown's brigade, Anderson's division:
"I was brought to a halt on account of a precipice in front, but in a few moments General B. ordered me to leave one section (two guns) of my battery there and move around the hill with the other and take my position in line, and open upon the enemy."

(CS) Talley, Palmer's Battery, Brown's brigade, Anderson's division:
"There was not enough room on the battle line for all of our guns so the 1st section filed to the right, went up the hill and filed to the left and went into action. I belonged to the 2nd section and we were left in the bed of the dry creek."

(CS) Lt. Col. W.C. Hearn, 41st Mississippi, Brown's brigade, Anderson's division:
"Because of a precipitous bank, I was compelled to dismount and go forward on foot with the command."

(CS) Talley, Palmer's Battery, Brown's brigade, Anderson's division:
"Our brigade had to file to the right and go up where the bluff had given out."

(CS) Lt. Col. Hearn, 41st Mississippi, Brown's brigade, Anderson's division:
"Leaving my sword - which I never saw afterward - strapped to my saddle when I was compelled to dismount, I found myself in battle without arms. ... Reaching the top of the creek-bank, we found ourselves on a piece of table-land of a few acres."

(US) Perry, 38th Indiana, Harris' brigade, Rousseau's division:
"The advancing line of rebels had reached a ridge about 200 yards in front of the one occupied by the Thirty-eighth Indiana. The corn which had grown upon the ground during the summer, with the exception of perhaps an acre in a sinkhole between the two lines of battle, had been cut, thus leaving an open field for the terrific contest which was to be waged here for two long hours."

Brown's brigade, supported by Darden's and Palmer's batteries, is soon under fire from the 10th Wisconsin and 38th Indiana of Harris' brigade:

(CS) Talley, Palmer's Battery, Brown's brigade, Anderson's division:
"The two lines were not over three hundred yards apart."

(CS) Capt. Palmer, commanding Palmer's Battery, Brown's brigade, Anderson's division:
"Great God how the balls did whistle! I had one killed and one of my cannoneers wounded before I could unlimber, but when I got in battery I gave them h-ll with canister."

(CS) Lt. Col. Hearn, 41st Mississippi, Brown's brigade, Anderson's division:
"We were held under a most disastrous fire from the enemy behind a fence on the hill."

(CS) Lt. Inglis, 3rd Florida, Brown's brigade, Anderson's division:
"There was a terrible din. We now lay down engaging the enemy firing steady."

(CS) Capt. Palmer, commanding Palmer's Battery, Brown's brigade, Anderson's division:
"We stood within 200 yards of each other, without either line waving a particle! And in an incessant roar of artillery and musketry. I had in my gun detachment only seventeen men. . . . I had one killed and seven wounded; also, twelve horses, out of eighteen, killed or disabled."

(CS) Talley, Palmer's Battery, Brown's brigade, Anderson's division:
"In a few minutes out of twelve horses to the two guns only three were left, and out of sixteen men of the two guns only four were left unhurt - only one was killed. . . . Capt. Palmer ordered Sgt. Sam Giles to go down to our guns and have Lt. Duncan send up one of our horses to pull one of the guns down. Lt. Duncan ordered Tom Skinner to take one of his horses. He took a roan horse and mounted him and said to Sgt. Giles to come on but Giles said 'Go on. I am not going up there anymore.' Skinner rode his horse up and reported to the captain who ordered him to turn the horse over to Tom Marshal, a driver of one of the other guns, and for Skinner to get back to his guns, but Skinner wanted to see the fight. The Captain saw him and ordered him to leave so Skinner came and slid down the bluff where we were."

(US) Col. Scribner, commanding 38th Indiana, Harris' brigade, Rousseau's division:
"Three batteries of the enemy concentrated their fire upon us."

(US) Perry, 38th Indiana, Harris' brigade, Rousseau's division:
"In addition to the deafening roll of musketry, the roar of artillery was incessant. Most of the shells from rebel guns passed over our line before exploding, but some of them created great havoc in our ranks."

Simonson's Battery, which had been ordered to move back and let the 38th Indiana take its place in line, halts about 275 yards behind the Indiana regiment:

(US) Hupp, Simonson's Battery, Harris' brigade, Rousseau's division:
"We had but just got in battery and ordered to lay on the ground, holding our fire for close action, as our ammunition was near gone, when I had to help take one of the lead horses out that had been shot with a minie ball. The bullets and shells came thicker and faster here. . . . We had just got this horse out when one of mine was shot with a minie ball . . . , killing him instantly. . . . When my horse got shot I was lying close by him on the same side. I immediately called one of the boys to help me take him out and run around to the near side . . . to unbuckle the breast strap. I had it but half unbuckled when a shell from the enemy struck me on the left arm and passing on, struck the ammunition chest, exploded and caused the cartridges in the chest to explode. It . . . resulted in the death of F. Erick who was struck in the head with a piece of shell and the wounding of four others, C. Miller, burnt, A Farg, arm broken and badly burnt on head and face; A Pettit, lip cut and wounded slightly in the head and myself cut in the left arm, right arm, and face.

"When the chest blew up it took me in the air about ten feet. I . . . concluded I was torn to pieces, but after striking the ground and lying there about three minutes, I jumped up and saw that I was badly wounded, my clothes all torn off, and the burn from the powder set me near crazy. The smoke of the explosion was so thick I could see nothing and as I remember(ed) the head surgeon passed us before the battle and told us where the hospital would be found and to come there if we got wounded, I thought it . . . best . . . for me to reach them as soon as possible for fear the loss of blood would weaken me so I would be unable to walk off. Leaving everything - for I was in such pain I cared for nothing - I started in their direction. The balls flew around me like hail. . . . A twelve pound shell exploded within a few feet of me, tearing up the ground, . . . and I had not gone more than a quarter of a mile when I felt so exhausted I could hardly stand. Here a young man gave me a canteen of water which revived me and I again started and soon reached the first hospital which was a small log house. . . .

"Shell and shot were passing all around the house. . . . I went in and tried to have my wounds dressed, but the surgeon was so frightened . . . he wanted to take my arm off when there was no bone injured. I left him at once and found another hospital but a short distance in a farm house: here there were about 300 wounded. . . . I saw there was no chance here and as I felt as though I could get a little farther, concluded to find another place; the loss of blood by this time had made me so weak I could hardly stand."

On the battle line:

(CS) Lt. Inglis, 3rd Florida, Brown's brigade, Anderson's division:
"The groans of dying & the cries for water of the wounded was terrible."

(CS) Lt. Col. Hearn, 41st Mississippi, Brown's brigade, Anderson's division:
"Gen. J.C. Brown, commanding the brigade, fell from his horse with a shot through the thigh, and was soon followed by Co. W.F. Tucker, with a shot through the right arm, from which he fainted, and was carried by his adjutant off the field."

(CS) Col. Miller, 1st Florida, Brown's brigade, Anderson's division:
"A staff officer rode up and said, 'Colonel Miller, you are in command of the brigade.' By this time many had exhausted their ammunition. The Ordnance Officer, a nephew of general Brown was drunk, and supplies of ammunition had not arrived. Our officers passed along the line, cutting the cartridge boxes from the bodies of the dead and receiving them from the . . . wounded. Here were wounded Captain Capen Byrd, Captain Wm. G. Poole and a host of others. Major Grover A. Ball was shot in the neck.

"Passing along the line . . . (I) saw a boy sitting on the ground looking at a trickle of blood which came through his pants. . . . (I) asked him if he could walk. 'Yes, Colonel.' 'Then go to the rear.' The . . . little fellow said, with some surprise in his eyes, 'Colonel, I am not going to quit for that,' and he went to his place and was again wounded."

(CS) Lt. Inglis, 3rd Florida, Brown's brigade, Anderson's division:
"Hit in shoulder collar bone broken. . . . Shell passed so close I bled at nose & mouth."

(CS) William A. Bryant, 3rd Florida, Brown's brigade, Anderson's division:
"Men shot down on every side of me, balls striking near me & once as I lay on the ground taking aim a ball so filled my eyes with dirt as to blind me for some time."

(US) Col. Scribner, commanding 38th Indiana, Harris' brigade, Rousseau's division:
"Of the nine men who composed the color guard, five were killed, the color-bearer wounded in two places, two had their clothes penetrated by bullets, thus leaving but one unscathed. The flag was riddled almost into shreds, the top of the staff being shot away and two balls struck the staff, causing it to break, after the battle. . . . I was struck near the knee-joint by a spent ball, which only broke the skin, and my horse was shot in the neck."

(US) Capt. Robert J. Kohlsdorf, 10th Wisconsin, Harris' brigade, Rousseau's division:
"I was struck twice, once by a spent ball, and again by a piece of shell, which struck on my sword down on my leg, and the good sword, the gift of my fellow citizens, saved my leg."

Though both sides are running out of ammunition, neither Brown's Confederate brigade
nor the 10th Wisconsin and 38th Indiana will retreat:

(US) Capt. Kohlsdorf, 10th Wisconsin, Harris' brigade, Rousseau's division:
"Our cartridges were expended, even those of the killed and wounded, when we received orders to march back for ammunition."

(US) Col. Scribner, commanding 38th Indiana, Harris' brigade, Rousseau's division:
"Having exhausted their forty rounds of cartridges, . . . (the men) proceeded to use those in the boxes of the killed and wounded, and when none were left they fixed bayonets and awaited orders. It was of vital importance that our line should be held, for the flank of Gen. Lytle on our right would have been turned had the enemy passed on through a gap made by our withdrawal."

About the time Brown's brigade crossed Doctor's Creek to attack Harris' Federal
position, Cleburne was moving into action on Brown's right. Cleburne advances to relieve
Johnson's stalled brigade, which is low on ammunition.

(CS) Lt. Yeatman, 2nd Tennessee, Cleburne's brigade, Buckner's division:
"We moved up in two lines. In our front was a dry branch, on the opposite bank a breast-high rock fence, behind the fence their advance line. It was carried by our regiment and the 3rd Tennessee regiment where we attacked jointly after an almost hand to hand fight, and in the face of their fire from both lines. As their line broke, we had them, and gave it to them in the back. . . . A great many Federals were killed here - more as they ran up the hill, than at the rock wall."

The Confederate attack gains momentum as Adams' brigade comes up on Cleburne's left
to join the fight:

(CS) John W. Headley, Austin's Sharpshooters, 14th Louisiana Battalion, Adam's brigade, Anderson's division:
"Our own artillery was now pouring a continuous storm of shot and shell on the enemy's infantry line and now the battle was hot from end to end. Major Austin, galloping to our left, ordered us to double-quick

straight down to the left and right face to the enemy. Then he yelled 'Charge!' It was a clean spot of ground outside of the farm between the creek and the enemy. We went yelling about half way, aiming to flank the enemy at a large barn. Major Austin was right along on my horse. . . . The fire in front of us and from both flanks was too hot and Major Austin ordered us back behind the rock fence. A number of our men fell in the five minutes we were out there. But in a moment General Adams, with four regiments, crossed the creek to the left, and we were ordered to go out to the same spot again, and did, when Adams brought his line even with us. . . .

"The large barn across the orchard had been set on fire by the shells from our cannon. We went forward in Adams's line, all walking and firing as we went. The enemy broke on the left of the (burning) barn from us and General Adams pushed his men forward. We pressed the enemy back. Their line was still standing from the barn on to the dwelling-house, but our whole line was right up against them. Major Austin turned us to the right, in the rear of the line behind the orchard."

(US) Col. Curran Pope, commanding the 15th Kentucky, Lytle's brigade, Rousseau's division:
"We saw them beginning to file around our right, but our ammunition was exhausted, and the sun was down, and the enemy had passed to our rear in the fields on our left."

Pope and Beatty send a few companies to blunt Adams' attack, but they are quickly overwhelmed. Lytle forms a new defensive line with the 3rd Ohio, 15th Kentucky and 10th Ohio, respectively, along the Mackville Road. When he learns that Harris' brigade cannot support him, Lytle realizes he must pull his regiments back and sends an aide with orders just as Cleburne and Adams' Confederate brigades launch another push which drives the 10th Ohio back:

(US) Col. John Beatty, commanding 3rd Ohio, Lytle's brigade, Rousseau's division:
"After consultation with Colonel Pope, it was determined to move our regiments to the left, and form line perpendicular to the one originally taken, and thus give protection to the rear and right of the troops on our left. The enemy . . . advanced rapidly toward us, when I about faced my regiment, and ordered the men to fix bayonets and move forward to meet him; but before we had proceeded many yards, I was overtaken by Lieutenant Grover, of Colonel Lytle's staff, with an order to retire."

(CS) Headley, Austin's Sharpshooters, 14th Louisiana Battalion, Adam's brigade, Anderson's division:
"The enemy gave way in a disorderly retreat, as did the line down to our left. We were in a large cornfield, but the cornstalks were cut and shocked. A ridge ran about the middle, parallel with the creek or front. There was about the same slope from the crest of the ridge to the rear as to the creek. We got to the top of the ridge about the time the enemy got over the back fence of the field and squatted behind it. Many of them went on that the officers could not rally. We were about seventy-five yards from the fence in the open, General Adams's whole brigade being in line. We had been firing all the time at thirty to fifty yards' range, but the losses were all on their side after we passed the barn. General Adams now ordered us to lie down and shoot. He and Major Austin were riding up and down our line while we exchanged volley after volley with the enemy. But our whole army was driving the enemy to the right and left and General Adams ordered a charge. Austin rode with us bareheaded and waving his hat."

(CS) Lt. Edmund E. O'Neill, 2nd Tennessee, Cleburne's brigade, Buckner's division:
"The brigade . . . rushed onto the crest of the rise, gave the yell, and the enemy's lines broke before we had a chance to fire on them. There I captured . . . (Col.) Lytle who was wounded and left on the field. I had him carried off the field when the line of battle came up."

(CS) Headley, Austin's Sharpshooters, 14th Louisiana Battalion, Adam's brigade, Anderson's division:
"The enemy gave way in disorder, going down for fifty yards and then up a hill in a clean woods pasture. They were in a drove now like a flock of sheep. The poor fellows fell like leaves from trees in the fall of the year. It seemed to me that half of them were left on the ground in that pasture."

CONFEDERATES ADVANCE

(CS) Capt. Frazer, 5th Confederate, Johnson's brigade, Buckner's division:
"Being presently joined by the remainder of Johnston's brigade, we scaled the fence, and drove the enemy to the woods beyond."

(CS) Sgt. W.C. Gipson, 17th Tennessee, Johnson's Brigade, Buckner's Division:
"After the enemy retreated, I counted thirteen of their dead in the corner of the fence, where we had seen the flag fall so often."

Buckner sends the 5th Confederate, 23rd and 37th Tennessee to the ridge crest above the Bottom house. The captured position is bolstered by Slocomb's Washington Artillery, Darden's Battery and a section of Calvert's Battery. About the time Cleburne and Adams are forcing the 15th Kentucky and 3rd Ohio to retreat, ammunition arrives for Brown's stalled brigade, and Wood's brigade is moving up in support:

(CS) Lt. Col. Hearn, 41st Mississippi, Brown's brigade, Anderson's division:
"The only way out of the difficulty was up that hill and over the fence."

(CS) Col. Miller, 1st Florida, commanding Brown's brigade, Anderson's division:
"The brigade moved forward over open ground towards the enemy behind a stone fence. As we went towards the fence, a young fellow, almost a boy, tried to shout. His excitement was so great that he only brought out a squeak. The effect was electric. The shout commencing on the left welled along the line until it became a great roar. At the command, the brigade broke into a double quick for the fence."

(CS) Ellis, 3rd Florida, Brown's brigade, Anderson's division:
"(I) joined in the charge up the red clay hill. My brother . . . carried the flag. I was near him, but we had not gotten far up the hill before I was struck in the left elbow. I had my gun up leveled for shooting when the ball struck me. My arm dropped, but I kept on loading and shooting with my right arm. About this time, Frank Saxon, my Captain's brother, was badly wounded in the leg and instep. Then came Captain Saxon to me and said, 'Benton, Frank is badly wounded and as you are in no fix to proceed in the fight, won't you please stop with Frank?' I could not but promise him, however, I hated to leave my brother, - but he went through the battle safely."

(CS) Col. Miller, 1st Florida, Brown's brigade, Anderson's division:
"The enemy, after one volley, fled. The brigade continued to advance, the enemy falling back before our excited boys."

(CS) Lt. Col. Hearn, 41st Mississippi, Brown's brigade, Anderson's division:
"We found the enemy in an open field beyond and in full force, stubbornly contending for every inch of ground, but falling back slowly and in good order. . . . There were many swords on the field, and I picked up a fine blade . . . and carried it to the end of my service. There was a little blood on the hilt and the regulation 'U.S.' on the guard, but I could find no name or mark by which it could be identified."

(CS) Lt. Inglis, 3rd Florida, Brown's brigade, Anderson's division:
"Enemy giving way on all sides. We crawled through corn field, on hands & knees. . . . Came to fence brushed it down, and was right at a battery. . . . (They) are the 10th Ohio. Here it was close to each other, in among the guns. We jumped on them down the gunners. Are chasing the 10 Ohio as they fell back but few of them left."

(US) Col. Scribner, commanding 38th Indiana, Harris' brigade, Rousseau's division:
"Lytle . . . was soon forced to fall back. This exposed our right, which the enemy took advantage of, and had moved up a battery to enfilade us and, therefore, being without ammunition, we were . . . ordered back out of range of the enemy's missiles, where we lay to await the wagon with ammunition."

(CS) Orderly Sgt. George Little, Lumsden's Battery Jones' brigade, Anderson's division:
"When the enemy retreated, I went to see how the battery that we had been fighting had fared; I found all of their horses dead and piled up on each other, and six pieces of artillery so disabled that they could not be carried off. The Federal infantry had taken off their knapsacks and overcoats and laid them out in a row just behind the line of battle, but their retreat was so hasty that this equipment fell into our hands, and our men secured a good supply of Yankee overcoats."

While McCook's corps struggles desperately to hold back Bragg's Confederates, thousands of Federal soldiers who could quickly turn the battle are idle nearby:

(US) Brig. Gen. William P. Carlin, brigade commander, Mitchell's division:
"We could see the smoke of the battle in and through the woods and at the outer edges, but could not see the lines of troops actually engaged. . . . Yet no orders came for us to go in. I saw Gen. Mitchell, my division commander, several times, and asked him to send my brigade into action. He replied that he had spoken to Gen. Gilbert about it, and was told by him that he could not move his troops without orders from Gen. Buell. It was all a mystery to me."

(US) Brig. Gen. Philip H. Sheridan, division commander:
"The Second Corps, under General Thomas L. Crittenden, accompanied by General George H. Thomas, lay idle the whole day for want of orders, although it was near enough to the field to take an active part in the fight; and, moreover, a large part of Gilbert's corps was unengaged during the pressure on McCook. Had these troops been put in on the enemy's left at any time after he assaulted McCook, success would have been beyond question; but there was no one on the ground authorized to take advantage of the situation."

Ridge defended by Stone's Federal battery, seen from the Benton Road. From a photograph in 1885.

CONFEDERATES ADVANCE

(US) Col. John M. Harlan, commanding the 10th Kentucky, Fry's brigade, Schoepf's division:

"Buell was not far from the battle field . . . , and still he did not know that any battle was going on. . . . It was not strange that he did not know of the battle. He anticipated that a meeting might possibly occur that day. But he had given orders to the effect that the direct attack on the enemy should not be made until the next morning, when all would be ready. His headquarters during the afternoon were behind the centre of his army - about five miles in the rear. . . . The battle took place in a small valley, and . . . the wind was blowing heavily from the locality of Buell's headquarters, towards the battle. . . . This accounts for Buell's not being able to hear the sound of musketry or cannon. . . . I was within one hundred yards of Buell's Headquarters during the whole time of the battle. . . . I was in command of a Brigade, and being about to march with my men . . . , Buell sent me an order to stay where I was until further orders, by holding my command ready for action. . . . Later in the afternoon a soldier came from the direction of McCook's corps and gave notice that a great battle had been fought in the early afternoon . . . several miles distant. This was the first intimation that I had had of any battle having been fought. I heard no firing from the direction of the battlefield, and if I did not hear it, Buell could not have done so."

On the battlefield, a wounded Federal artilleryman continues his search for medical attention:

(US) Hupp, Simonson's Battery, Harris' brigade, Rousseau's division:

"When I reached the road - . . . I fell and could go no farther. . . . I had given up to die and cared for nothing - I was almost crazy through pain. . . . J. Countz who had been sent after water for the boys in the battery came along, recognized me at once, got off and poured some water on my head and face, gave me a drink and with some help got me on his horse and started for the hospital a half mile distant. . . . We came to a man that has a tub full of whiskey poured out of a barrel and was giving it to the wounded. Countz handed me a quart basin full and I would have drunk every bit of it had they not taken it away from me; . . . It gave me a new spirit. We pressed on and soon came to a hospital which was a farmhouse. I was there but a short time when Countz brought a surgeon who dressed my arm. I felt but little easier as the greater share of the pain was from the burns, but in about a half an hour I got some sweet oil on my face which eased the pain. Countz got me a quilt from the lady of the house which I put around me and lay down under a tree: he then left me and returned to the battery."

FEDERALS HOLD THE LINE

About the time Cleburne's Confederate brigade is attacking Lytle's troops near Squire Bottom's house, on the Confederate left, Maney's first line, on the far right, is pushing Terrill's retreating Federal troops from Open Hill:

(CS) Lt. Edwin H. Rennolds, 5th Tennessee, Stewart's brigade, Cheatham's division:
"The pursuit led through a narrow strip of woodland and then up a long ascent through a cornfield."

(US) Albion W. Tourgee, 105th Ohio, Terrill's brigade, Jackson's division:
"After the belt of woods was passed, we entered a corn-field; the enemy followed sharply and their bullets cut stalk and leaf and rattled the kernels from the drooping ears beside us, every now and then claiming victim."

(US) Michael H. Fitch, 21st Wisconsin, Starkweather's brigade, Rousseau's division:
"Soon the broken and bleeding troops of Jackson's division . . . came pouring back upon the line of the twenty-first in crowds, and several hundred of them halted just in front of the twenty-first, but without any formation. . . . General William R. Terrill, who commanded a brigade in Jackson's division, dismounted, and apparently almost overcome with vexation and exhaustion, passed to the rear by the right of the twenty-first. He said to the adjutant as he passed, that the rebels were advancing in terrible force. . . . The adjutant hurried to . . . the colonel, who was opposite the centre of the line, but found him wounded."

(CS) Col. Hume R. Feild, commanding the first line of Maney's brigade, Cheatham's division:
"The brigade was ordered immediately formed to take . . . (Stone's) battery about a half mile in advance, planted on a very steep hill, commanding a large corn field, through which we had to advance."

(CS) Lt. James Iredell Hall, 9th Tennessee, Maney's brigade, Cheatham's division:
"While we were forming the lines for a second charge . . . a minie ball . . . came with such force as to knock me down. It was . . . about five o'clock in the evening. . . . Some of the boys lifted me and placed me under the shade of a tree. . . . Jas. Lemmon, John William Calhoun and other boys of my company offered to carry me off the field, but I felt that there were others who needed assistance more than I did."

Maney's 1st Tennessee is sent to the right to attack Bush's battery while Maney's first line, with Stewart's 4th and 5th Tennessee, is sent straight ahead. Pursuit of Terrill's men leads the 9th and 27th Tennessee and 41st Georgia toward the 21st Wisconsin, whose men are prone in the cornfield:

(US) Tourgee, 105th Ohio, Terrill's brigade, Jackson's division:
"Terrill ordered a march by the flank to unmask Starkweather's regiments which lay upon the crest of the hill above us. Some did not hear the order and were still facing the enemy when a magnificent volley-fire by companies, rang out . . . while Stone's and Bush's batteries opened on the pursuing enemy. . . . We flung ourselves upon our faces and crept around the flank of this maelstrom of fire."

(US) Lt. James M. Randall, 21st Wisconsin, Starkweather's brigade, Rousseau's division:
"We were surrounded by a very heavy growth of corn which prevented us from seeing the Confederate charging lines, until they were within twenty feet of us. Our gunners upon the hill in our rear could see this line, and in order to break its force, were unavoidably cutting gaps in our line with grape and canister."

(US) Fitch, 21st Wisconsin, Starkweather's brigade, Rousseau's division:
"The firing had become terrific, and . . . all the firing from the Federal troops, came from the rear of the twenty-first. Reports came from the captains along the line that the men of the twenty-first were being killed by shots from a battery in the rear, and that there were no supports on our flanks. A frightful rush of the disorganized troops who had gathered in the front of the twenty-first, was made to the rear through the ranks of the regiment, followed so closely by the rebel lines that it was impossible for the excessively timid ones to resist going back with the rush, and before the remainder could again close up the line thus broken, the enemy had lapped both flanks and were in addition to firing in front, enfilading the lines."

(US) James Pillar, 21st Wisconsin, Starkweather's brigade, Rousseau's division:
"They came up very near before any comands came but some one gave the comand to fire and so we up and let fly. My gun did not go off. So I was bound to give them a shot so I put on another cap and fired."

(CS) Lt. Rennolds, 5th Tennessee, Stewart's brigade, Cheatham's division:
"Lieutenant J.B. Milam fell, with a severe wound in the leg, and about the same time Ensign J.B. Jones had his thigh-bone broken, but did not loose his hold on the colors. . . . Lieutenant F.M. Clark took the colors, but soon handed them to Color Guard A.A. Dinwiddie. . . . Andrew Thompson of Company 'B' fell mortally wounded, and said to his captain, A.W. Caldwell: 'Tell my mother where I fell,' and drawing the . . . captain down, kissed his cheek and died. By this time all semblance of a line had disappeared, but the officers urged the men forward, and they continued to advance, loading and firing as they went. In this field . . . (I) received a wound in the arm, disabling . . . (me) from using . . . (my) gun, and . . . (I) retired to the rear. Captain John W. Harris was dangerously wounded in passing through the woodland, and Captain John T. Irion and John R. Peeples placed him behind a large whiteoak tree. J.W. Crutchfield was knocked senseless by the explosion of a bomb. Captain Gillett, acting major, was killed. Colonel Venable was partially disabled by a ball which mashed his sword scabbard, tearing off his belt and breaking his horse's leg."

(CS) Capt. John T. Irion, 5th Tennessee, Stewart's brigade, Cheatham's division:
"Col. Venable was thrown from his horse, and though seriously crippled, he continued in the fight, being carried by two of his men. Maj. Lamb was also unhorsed."

(CS) Lt. Rennolds, 5th Tennessee, Stewart's brigade, Cheatham's division:
"Lieutenant-Colonel Swor had his horse killed under him, and his son, G. Wash Swor, lost an arm."

(CS) Benjamin A. Haguewood, 5th Tennessee, Stewart's brigade, Cheatham's division:
"Was struck by something. . . . Was rendered unconscious. . . . I discovered the butt end of a steel rammer sticking out of my left breast which was immediately extracted by my own hand. . . . Was caught between the crossfire of my own men and the enemy. . . . Laid down in a little washout."

(CS) Capt. Irion, 5th Tennessee, Stewart's brigade, Cheatham's division:
"Tip Allen, of Company I, was shot in the neck by a Minie-ball, which he in a short time coughed up."

(US) Fitch, 21st Wisconsin, Starkweather's brigade, Rousseau's division:
"The firing of the regiment checked for a time the rebel advance. . . . Firing had become so terrific, that orders could not be heard though given to retire."

(US) Pillar, 21st Wisconsin, Starkweather's brigade, Rousseau's division:
"I see they had retreated so turned and ran back to where the major was and he said don't run boys. Nelson Rice and I stood still. I was going to load when the major said retreat boys. So we run."

(US) Fitch, 21st Wisconsin, Starkweather's brigade, Rousseau's division:
"The twenty-first was compelled here to retreat over a high fence, through a ravine and then up the face of a bare hill, which the fire of the enemy could sweep with terrific effect."

(US) Pillar, 21st Wisconsin, Starkweather's brigade, Rousseau's division:

"N Rice was wounded. I went down in the holow and loaded again and looked for my chance but I could not fire with out endangering a few of our men. I see they were going up the hill, so I did the same and found N Rice groning very much. So we cared him."

(US) Sgt. Elias H. Hoover, 1st Wisconsin, Starkweather's brigade, Rousseau's division:

"The 21st Wis. . . . occupied the ravine in front of us, and when the rebels made a charge on the battery they broke through our ranks in disorder."

(US) Sgt. Edward Ferguson, 1st Wisconsin, Starkweather's brigade, Rousseau's division:

"Many of them rallied on our line and fought well with our regiment, while many of them . . . lost their lives in the shower of grape and canister now being poured out by the batteries of the rapidly advancing enemy."

At the far right of the Confederate line, the 1st Tennessee drives toward the 1st Wisconsin and the remnants of the 21st Wisconsin defending Bush's Battery:

(CS) Sam Watkins, 1st Tennessee, Maney's brigade, Cheatham's division:

"In our immediate front was their . . . line of battle from which four Napoleon guns poured their deadly fire."

(CS) John A. Bruce, 1st Tennessee, Maney's brigade, Cheatham's division:

"We had nearly reached a battery we were charging."

(US) Sgt. Hoover, 1st Wisconsin, Starkweather's brigade, Rousseau's division:

"We were ordered to rise and fire."

(US) L. E. Knowles, 1st Wisconsin, Starkweather's brigade, Rousseau's division:

"About the time we rose to our feet I was struck in the head by a piece of shell."

(CS) Watkins, 1st Tennessee, Maney's brigade, Cheatham's division:

"Our line was fairly hurled back by the leaden hail that was poured into our very faces."

(CS) Bruce, 1st Tennessee, Maney's brigade, Cheatham's division:

"One ball struck my clothes lightly, one went through my coat sleeve, one through my coat pocket, one took off my cartridge box, one went through my haversack, and the next one brought me down while in the act of loading. It struck me in the thigh and I dropped my gun and walked about twenty yards and then commenced to crawl."

(CS) Watkins, 1st Tennessee, Maney's brigade, Cheatham's division:

"Eight color-bearers (fell) . . . at one discharge of their cannon."

(CS) Capt. Bailey P. Steele, 1st Tennessee, Maney's brigade, Cheatham's division:

"In charging up the hill . . . , Color-Sergt. Mitchell, bearing our flag, was killed, and every one of his eight Color Corporals fell about the same instant; four of them killed dead. One of the killed was Eugene 'Spludge' Wharton. . . . At the fall of the flag, . . . Sergt. Maj. John W. Carter, who was fighting in the ranks of my company sprang, for the flag, followed by Sergt. 'Ted' James, also of my company. Carter had scarcely straightened up with the colors, when his right thigh was broken by a minnie ball and as he reeled and was falling he shouted to Sergt. James, who had reached his side and had already grasped the flag, 'Here, Ted, take it. I am shot.' I was lying but a few feet distant, with my left thigh broken, and witnessed this scene, and heard Carter's words distinctly over the roar and din of battle. Sergeant James, moved forward holding aloft the colors, but had proceeded but a few steps when he fell badly wounded. Adjt. T. H. McKinney, then caught up the colors."

(CS) Watkins, 1st Tennessee, Maney's brigade, Cheatham's division:
"When the regiment recoiled under the heavy firing . . . , Billy Webster and I stopped behind a large oak tree and continued to fire at the Yankees. . . . We were not more than twenty paces from them; and here I was shot through the hat and cartridge-box. . . . Billy and I were in advance of our line, and whenever we saw a Yankee rise to shoot, we shot him."

(CS) Marcus B. Toney, 1st Tennessee, Maney's brigade, Cheatham's division:
"Our boys got so close to the battery that the smoke covered them."

(US) Sgt. Ferguson, 1st Wisconsin, Starkweather's brigade, Rousseau's division:
"The dense cloud of smoke from the rapid discharge of cannon and advancing musketry hid the enemy with an almost impenetrable veil, but they were near enough . . . (that) nearly half the regiment was swept away by the shower of bullets that poured in from the advancing column and during the brief but savage struggle that ensued for the possession of the guns. . . . A 'buck and ball' cartridge . . . interfered with my usefulness . . . (along with) a further perforation, this time of my foot."

(CS) Toney, 1st Tennessee, Maney's brigade, Cheatham's division:
"Tom Lanier was killed some thirty feet from the battery, not by the artillery, because we were under the crest of the hill, and the pieces could not be depressed so as to reach us, but the men supporting the battery were the ones that caused most of our trouble. . . . Robert (S. Hamilton) was shot through the forehead, and fell not far from where Tom Lanier and . . . Jack Goodbar fell."

(CS) Watkins, 1st Tennessee, Maney's brigade, Cheatham's division:
"Lieutenant-Colonel Patterson halloed to charge and take their guns, and we were soon in a hand-to-hand fight – every man for himself – using the butts of our guns and bayonets. One side would waver and fall back a few yards, and would rally, when the other side would fall back, leaving the four Napoleon guns; and yet the battle raged. . . . Guns were discharged so rapidly that it seemed the earth itself was in a volcanic uproar. The iron storm passed through our ranks, mangling and tearing men to pieces. . . . The . . . air seemed full of stifling smoke and fire. . . . The sun was poised above us, a great red ball sinking slowly in the west. . . . Lieutenant Joe P. Lee and Captain W.C. Flournoy (were) standing right at the muzzle of the Napoleon guns, and the next moment seemed to be enveloped in smoke and fire from the discharge of the cannon. . . . We were right among the wheels of their Napoleon guns. . . . A part of the time they would be in our hands and the enemy . . . would charge and recapture them. They would tuck their heads, rush forward and grab the coupling poles of the cannon, then we would beat them in their face with the butts of our muskets. Men were falling and dying. . . . I saw W.J. Whittorne, . . . a strippling boy of fifteen years of age, fall, shot through the neck and collar-bone. He fell apparently dead, when I saw him all at once jump up, grab his gun and commence loading and firing, and I heard him say, 'D—n 'em, I'll fight 'em as long as I live.' "

(CS) Toney, 1st Tennessee, Maney's brigade, Cheatham's division:
"Colonel Patterson was slightly wounded in the wrist, but he tied a handkerchief around it and continued to give orders until a . . . grapeshot hit his mustache, going through his head, killing him instantly."

(CS) Watkins, 1st Tennessee, Maney's brigade, Cheatham's division:
"Colonel Patterson . . . was killed standing right by my side."

(CS) Bruce, 1st Tennessee, Maney's brigade, Cheatham's division:
"I was near Col. Patterson and saw him fall from his horse. . . . Some one helped me on his horse which was being led to the rear. It was a great help to me, but I was afraid . . . that I would be shot in the back."

The 1st Tennessee drives the 1st Wisconsin from Bush's battery, but then the Confederates inexplicably fall back to the bottom of the hill:

(CS) Capt. Thomas H. Malone, staff of Maney's brigade, Cheatham's division:
"The firing upon our right ceased, and in great excitement, I galloped toward the point where it had been heard, and found the 1st Tennessee quietly marching to the rear. The first man I met was Bill Kelley, of Company A. He told me they had had a most severe fight, had lost nearly half the men and had retreated, under orders of Lieut-Col. Patterson, as he understood, when just on the point of carrying all before them. Upon inquiry I found that Lieut-Col. Patterson was dead. While urging on his men he was fatally shot, and as his horse turned, going back to the rear, it was supposed that the retreat had been ordered by him. . . . Bill Kelley . . . told me that a great number of our old company had been killed or badly wounded, and among others he mentioned a man named McLemore, and said, 'Tom, your prophecy didn't come true. You always said that the bullet had never been molded that could break his hard head; but he was shot right in the head and killed.' I was much grieved, for I had the greatest respect for McLemore. . . . Kelley also reported to me that another of our men to whom I was greatly attached, – Joe Sewell – was killed. . . . Colonel Feild, the colonel of the regiment, who had been ordered with the 9th, 6th, and 27th Tennessee and the 41st Georgia, took charge of the 1st (Tennessee)."

(CS) Col. Feild, commanding the 1st Tennessee, Maney's brigade, Cheatham's division:
"I rallied the regiment at the foot of the hill, no other regiment forming but mine, some 30 or 40 men of the other regiments falling into the ranks. In the mean time the enemy came back to the guns behind the battery, and also marched two regiments (79th Pennsylvania and 24th Illinois) on our left on a wooded hill which lay at right angles with the hill."

Gen. Terrill fears another Confederate attack will overwhelm Bush and Stone's batteries. He decides to have his infantry hold the Confederates while his batteries are pulled back to a ridge to form a new defensive position. An officer who had gotten a wounded comrade to a field hospital returns to the front just before the second attack:

(US) Capt. Taylor, Garrard's battalion, Terrill's brigade, Jackson's division:
"The guns of our (Bush's) Battery (were) posted on an eminence to the left of us about 100 yards. . . . (Gen. Terrill) ordered Col. Garrard to support it. We were moved hurriedly up the crest of the hill. . . . and nestled close in under the guns, many of the Artillerars had been killed the ground around was slippery with blood, and many a poor dark looking powder begrimed Artillery man was laying stretched out upon the ground around us, torn and mutilated."

To the right of Bush's Battery, Maney's first line and Stewart's 4th and 5th Tennessee press toward Stone's Battery:

(CS) Lt. Rennolds, 5th Tennessee, Stewart's brigade, Cheatham's division:
"To the left of the field a fence divided it from a body of woods, and the left of the regiment followed the fence. Near the top of the long ascent, another fence crossed this at right angles, and just beyond it, on the highest elevation, were placed three Federal batteries, which continually belched grape and canister. Behind the cross fence was posted the enemy's third line of battle. In front of the fence some thirty or forty yards, a force of infantry was stationed in a gully. This detachment, on our approach, opened a withering fire of small arms, but the . . Fifth pushed forward in the face of it all. . . . The occupants of the gully . . . clambered up the steep ascent and retreated across the open field beyond, (and) over the fence. . . . The advancing regiment . . . cut down many of them before they could get out of range. The gunners of the battery, seeing their support vanish, . . . seized their guns and drew then out of sight over the crest by hand. When the regiment reached the cross-fence, in front of the battery, Privates G.W. Crawford, Sam Archer and a few others, who were near the fence running east and west, found themselves face to face with the Federal line just across in the next field. Archer was fatally shot and the others retired across the gully."

(CS) Luke W. Finlay, 4th Tennessee, Stewart's brigade, Cheatham's division:
"Rucker, of the Thirty-third (Tennessee) – standing six feet and six inches – who came to our part of the fight, . . . having the center of his forehead struck by a ball, glancing upward peeling off his hair, said, as he

threw his gun to the ground: 'There! That would have killed brother George as dead as Hector!' – His brother was one inch taller."

(CS) Joseph Edward Riley, 33rd Tennessee, Steart's brigade, Cheatham's division:
"In one of our charges, . . . (a) minie-ball, coming from the left of direct front, struck . . . my pocket book . . . in my right pants pocket. I had about $600.00 of Confederate money in this ordinary sized clasp pocket book but the minie drove the pocket book and mascerated money through the muscles of the thigh just in front of the femur and barely protruded through the skin to the right and back of hip joint. As I fell I noticed that a large hickory tree had been recently cut near me, burying itself in the ground and had left a deep trough in the earth. Into this I rolled and lay flat, for the shot of both sides now was peppering the ground. Both lines surged back and forth over this ground and so much soil was upturned that it almost covered me up, lying in the trench made by the falling tree."

Charging up the hill at the left end of Starkweather's line is the 1st Tennessee, aiming for two guns Bush lacked the horses to remove:

(CS) Col. Feild, commanding the 1st Tennessee, Maney's brigade, Cheatham's division:
"I led the regiment up the hill alone, without any support, under a heavy fire of musketry, driving the enemy back and taking his guns again."

(US) Capt. William S. Mitchell, 1st Wisconsin, Starkweather's brigade, Rousseau's division:
"The Rebels were close to the Piece in front of my Co. I called for men to run it to the rear. . . . 6 of my men with myself started to run it off to the rear. 3 of the 6 were shot dead. . . . Wm E. Wechselberg . . . was the first to jump to his feet – had not fairly straightened up when a Ball whistled by me & struck him in the face passing through his Head. . . . He was close behind me . . . when he fell. . . . I heard the Ball whistle but at the same time did not know he was dead. . . . I felt something (hit) . . . my pants & looking down I saw the hole made by a Ball passing through pants & Boot but . . . did not even scratch me. . . . Billy Brown fell immediately after he had fired. . . . He was shot through the right breast, the Ball taking an angling

course, and I think touched the Heart. He fell and as he did I grasped his hand & heard his last & only words 'Capt My God.'"

(US) Capt. Taylor, Garrard's battalion, Terrill's brigade, Jackson's division:
"We were driven from the guns, and the Battery a second time fell into the hands of the enemy as we fell back from the crest of the hill, drawing the caissons with us."

(CS) Col. Feild, commanding the 1st Tennessee, Maney's brigade, Cheatham's division:
"The regiments (79th Pennsylvania and 24th Illinois) on our left then opened their fire upon us, killing and wounding a dozen officers and men at each discharge. Just then I discovered Hardee's battle-flag coming up on our left about 500 yards in rear. Expecting that the regiment that carried the flag would engage the enemy that were cross-firing upon us I determined to hold the hill at every cost."

But, the Confederate regiment, one of Cleburne's command, is almost out of ammunition and is falling back. Without support, Feild has no choice:

(CS) Col. Feild, commanding the 1st Tennessee, Maney's brigade, Cheatham's division:
"I ordered my regiment to retire, . . . leaving half their number dead and wounded on the top of the hill."

(US) Capt. Mitchell, 1st Wisconsin, Starkweather's brigade, Rousseau's division:
"Toward the close, I saw many poor fellows lying on the ground their tongues out & swollen fairly suffocating for water. I was nearly crazy myself, as I had been talking or rather yelling to the men untill I was so dry I could no swallow. Fortunately Charley Messenger found a Bottle of Brandy & gave me some. It tasted wet and that was enough. After taking a good pull I felt much revived and after giving the rebels two or three good volleys they retreated."

The 1st Wisconsin and fragments of the 21st Wisconsin move forward and reoccupy Bush's battery position:

(US) Capt. Taylor, Garrard's battalion, Terrill's brigade, Jackson's division:
"The ground (was) almost hidden from the view by the forms of the dead, wounded, and dying that lay thick upon it. Then I saw our . . . Brigadier (Terrill) with his coat off, sleeves rolled up and working one of the two guns of the battery. . . . He stood there . . . whirling the rammer of a field gun around his head . . . and with it driving his cartridge and canister far back into the barrels of the cannon."

(US) Charles K. Radcliffe, 105th Ohio, Terrill's brigade, Jackson's division:
"While standing by this battery and watching its operations . . . Terrill was struck in the breast by a piece of enemy's shell."

(US) Maj. James A. Connolly, 123rd Illinois, Terrill's brigade, Jackson's division:
"General (William R.) Terrell, commanding our brigade, was (wounded) . . . by a shell within 5 feet of me, and while he was giving me directions for rallying the men. I was the only one with him; I raised him to a sitting position and saw that nearly his entire breast was torn away by the shell. He recognized me and his first words were: 'Major

Brig. Gen. William R. Terrill

do you think it is fatal?' I knew it must be, but to encourage him I answered, 'Oh I hope not General.' He then said: 'My poor wife, my poor wife.'"

(US) Evan Davis, 21st Wisconsin, Starkweather's brigade, Rousseau's division:
"We were ordered to haul the cannons by hand to the rear. . . . The horses belonging to the battery were all shot or stampeded away. I had my blanket and coat rolled together and carried over my shoulder. Was ordered to throw away anything that interfered with our fighting, so I dropped them never thinking of retreating before the enemy, and I never saw that coat and blanket again."

To the right, the Federal line is too strong for Maney's first line and Stewart's 4th and 5th Tennessee:

(CS) Lt. Rennolds, 5th Tennessee, Stewart's brigade, Cheatham's division:
"The field officers, unaware of the exact situation, urged the men forward a second and a third time, but each time, lacking support on the left, were compelled to retire. The gunners of the battery again drew their guns forward and opened fire."

(CS) Col. George C. Porter, 6th Tennessee, Maney's brigade, Cheatham's division:
"We, together with a portion of the Fourth Tennessee, were driven from the summit of this hill in the corn field, but were again rallied in a ravine near a stone fence and ordered back by General Maney to dislodge, if possible, certain sharpshooters and to fire upon a battery that was engaged with one of ours a short distance to the front. The order was given and the summit was again reached."

(CS) Capt. John M. Taylor, 27th Tennessee, Maney's brigade, Cheatham's division:
"About sundown . . . (I) fell wounded three times – one shot crushing . . . (my) right thigh. Lieut. (Albert) Andrews was wounded in the left hip."

(CS) Lt. W.R. Moore, 5th Tennessee, Stewart's brigade, Cheatham's division:
"I had charge of the company. Late in the evening while we were at the crest of a hill my men would lie down load their guns rise up and shoot. The enemy came down in the woods to our right nearer than the line in front. I seeing the danger of an enfilading fire, ordered my men to change the fire to the right. About that time one of my men turned on his elbows to shoot. I heard a thud, saw the lint rise from his breast, he sank on his gun. In a short time one of the men came with his gun, his barrel being turned at right angles by shot or shell and said, 'I got that man's gun. He can't use it.' I stood there giving orders; had lost sight of myself. John Paisley came and held his hand torn into shreds. I ordered him to the rear. In a short time I was struck through the side of the face and neck. . . . The ball seemed to pull as it passed through my flesh. . . . I turned and fell . . . on my face. One of my men pulled me and asked if I wanted to be carried off the field. I could not answer, being paralyzed, but knew what was going on. He took hold of my left arm and pulled it over his shoulder and around his neck and started with me, my feet dragging. We met one of the . . . (infirmary) corps and he assisted me. In about a quarter of a mile I began to use my limbs. . . . The pain was not acute. It felt much like a hand or arm 'asleep' being rubbed to restore circulation."

(CS) Sgt. Maj. Louis B. McFarland, 9th Tennessee, Maney's brigade, Cheatham's division:
"(In a) ravine at the foot of another steep, hill, occupied by the enemy . . . (we) were . . . behind a rail fence, where we remained . . . until nearly night. . . . Desultory firing from the hill . . . splintered the rails, (and) caused us to change positions and play the part of many squirrels we had shot from the limbs."

(US) Capt. Taylor, Garrard's battalion, Terrill's brigade, Jackson's division:
"I . . . (fell) from the explosion of a shell within a few feet of me, knocking an Enfield rifle out of my hands which I was in the act of elevating; and throwing me violently to the ground. I lay there stunned for a few moments, and as soon as I discovered the extent of my wound ran back to the nearest hospital about one mile in the rear."

EYEWITNESSES AT THE BATTLE OF PERRYVILLE

It is clear Maney's and Stewart's regiments cannot storm the Federal position and they are ordered to pull back:

(CS) Lt. Rennolds, 5th Tennessee, Stewart's brigade, Cheatham's division:
"The line was formed and marched by the left flank into a body of woods."

(CS) Riley, 33rd Tennessee, Stewart's brigade, Cheatham's division:
"As soon as the bullets ceased to rain around the top of my trough, I emerged from my hiding place, pulled the bayonets from two Yankee guns took them for crutches and made my way back to a small creek."

(CS) Capt. Malone, staff officer, Maney's brigade, Cheatham's division:
"I rode over the field. . . . Seeing what appeared to me to be a great bundle of rags, . . . Emmett Cockrill and I got down to examine it. It proved to be a body in which , it seemed, a shell had exploded, leaving no trace of humanity except blood and bones and shattered flesh. I saw . . . (an officer) of the Federal army, lying on his back, with his feet toward the front. . . . I hesitated some time, and finally I said: 'I don't know who that man is, but he is a Federal general,' and I cut off one of his passons and kept it. . . . Emmett came up while I was looking at the body of the Federal general, and . . . said: 'Why, damn it! That's Jim Jackson!' – he and Emmett had been great friends. Then he paused a moment and said: 'Well, Jim, old boy, you ought to have had better luck!' "

Behind the Federal line, troops try to reorganize:

(US) Fitch, 21st Wisconsin, Starkweather's brigade, Rousseau's division:
"(We) rallied again . . . , under the fire of the enemy, in rear of the main Union line."

(US) Davis, 21st Wisconsin, Starkweather's brigade, Rousseau's division:
"Our regiment, or what was left of it, was formed in line again, some distance in rear, expecting any moment another attack from the enemy."

(US) Fitch, 21st Wisconsin, Starkweather's brigade, Rousseau's division:
"In a very few minutes after the rallying of the twenty-first, the other regiments of the brigade fell back to the same place. The rebels did not push farther towards our front, but kept up a continual fire."

(US) Davis, 21st Wisconsin, Starkweather's brigade, Rousseau's division:
"Col Sweet was sitting on the ground in the rear of the regiment. We were laying down. I happened to be looking at the Col. When he was hit in the arm by a . . . bullet, and he was carried off the field.. . . . While laying there a certain comrade at my right discovered that the hammer of his gun was up. Being excited and nervous accidently the hammer went down with sufficient force to explode the cap and sent the charge crashing though the legs of comrade Bingham of our company."

A soldier who helped get a wounded comrade to the field hospital stays to help:

(US) Pillar, 21st Wisconsin, Starkweather's brigade, Rousseau's division:
"I helped bind up some of our boys wounds and then was going back to the field when the doctor said I could do more good there."

A civilian who has been helping treat the wounded at a Federal field hospital can take no more:

E.L. Davison, Springfield merchant:
"It was now about 5 o'clock, being completely worn out I got on my horse. . . . I soon came to a house where there were a number of wounded lying on the ground, but no surgeon to attend them. Just inside lay the finest specimen of a man I ever saw. His eyes were closed but his lips were moving, he was breathing very rapidly, each breath causing a bubble of pale colored blood from his breast. I dismounted and went to him; putting my hand on his forehead I asked him to talk a little louder. He opened his eyes – they were large brown – and said, 'Tell my mother and sister' then stopped. I got down on my knees and put my ear to his mouth and listened a few seconds: on raising my hand I found he was dead. This impressed me more than any other incident of the day. He was so young and handsome. I then rode through thousands of soldiers at rest, lying on the ground, playing games and appearing to be a merry lot. They had not moved since I passed them that morning. . . . I soon passed Gen. Buel and he was reading the same book as when I passed him in the morning."

At the Wilkerson farm house Federal field hospital, surrounded by a greensward, or grassy area:

(US) Dr. S.K. Crawford, regimental surgeon, 50th Ohio, Webster's brigade, Jackson's division:
"Between this sward and the road was a small lot occupied by an abandoned cabin and a rank growth of wild hemp. About 5 o'clock p.m. this old cabin was full of colored servants in search of safety, in fact, the lot was filled with them, . . . and about this time it was discovered that our hospital was between the opposing lines. . . . The firing became brisk on both sides of us, the shot and shell screaming over our heads with . . . an almost deafening effect. Just before sunset, the rebel artillerymen on the hill to our left . . . (fired) three or four solid shots in rapid succession into the primitive roof of our cabin. . . . The servants decamped in the wildest disorder. . . . They did some wonderful leaping. . . . Not one of them was injured . . . , but . . . the clapboards and decaying weight poles began flying in every direction."

A captured Federal brigade commander, Col. William Lytle, arrives at a Confederate field hospital for treatment:

(CS) Dr. J.C. Hall, surgeon, 37th Tennessee, Johnson's brigade, Buckner's Division:
"Dr. W.M. Gentry, the brigade surgeon, made a careful examination of the wound . . . in the cheek, and assured the . . . (colonel) that it was not a serious injury and that he would soon recover. . . . (Col.) Lytle had a different opinion, and frankly expressed the belief that it was a penetrating wound of the skull and involved the brain. Dr. Gentry felt sure that he was correct in the opinion he himself had rendered, but was too regardful of the feelings, the fears, and hopes of a wounded man and captive to differ with him at such a moment, and informed him that he would call in consultants to examine the injury.

"My operating-table was . . . only a few feet from where this examination was made, and Dr. Gentry invited me to examine. . . . It was . . . probably as late as four or five o'clock. I walked over to the chair where . . . Lytle was seated, and was introduced to him by Dr. Gentry. The . . . (colonel) was sitting with his back toward the sun, his head turned slightly toward the right, while the strong rays of the sun played over the right side of his face, bringing out every lineament of the wound . . . a 'ragged tear in his cheek.' . . . Dr. Gentry had not informed me of the nature of his diagnosis. . . . I observed that it had been inflicted by a small missile, such as a pistol-ball or a shot from one of the buck and ball cartridges, then in use by some of our troops. The ball had grazed the side of the cheek in front of the ear for a distance of a half-inch or more, completely denuding the skin of the outer cuticle, . . . and then entered the soft parts of the cheek, ranging forward and downward.

"I remarked to Dr. Gentry that the index of the shot indicated that the ball entered from the rear, and that if it had not escaped was lodged somewhere in the anterior part of the face, probably near the chin. . . . (Col.) Lytle was so sensitive that he misconstrued the remark, and promptly replied: 'No, sir; you are wrong in your diagnosis. I was wounded from the flank while I had my sword aloft trying to rally the men, and the bullet is in the base of my brain.'

Col. William H. Lytle

"I promptly assured the . . . (colonel) that I had no thought of reflecting upon his honor or courage; that I was cognizant of the fact that . . . (an) officer occupied every attitude on the battle-field, and was as liable to be wounded in the back as in the face while discharging his duties; that I was simply tracing the course of the missile, so as to arrive at a definite opinion touching on its entrance and final lodgment. This so far reassured him that he frankly acknowledged that he had misconstrued the meaning of the remark. A few moments later the shot was located by Dr. Gentry in the soft parts near the point of the chin, when I withdrew and resumed duty at my own table."

DARKNESS ENDS THE FIGHTING

As Adams' and Cleburne's Confederate brigades push McCook's regiments back to the line forming at the Russell house, McCook realizes his corps is in danger of being driven from the battlefield. He appeals for reinforcements to Gilbert, commander of the nearest corps, and to Buell, the army commander. The request reaches Gilbert about 4 p.m., and he orders Gooding's Brigade and Pinney's Battery to McCook's aid.

(US) Alexander Pepper, 59th Illinois, Gooding's brigade, Mitchell's division:
"When the sun was less than an hour high, there came an order . . . for the . . . Brigade of Gilbert's corps. . . . Our brigade consisted of four regiments, the 74th and 75th Illinois, new regiments, and the 22nd Indiana, an old regiment and as good as the best, and the 59th Illinois."

(US) D. Lathrop, 59th Illinois, Gooding's Brigade Mitchell's division:
"Cheerfully the brigade marched out to meet the foe, The men had been held within hearing distance of the fearful carnage all day. . . . Many were the inquiries, 'Why are all these thousands of soldiers kept here idle all the day so near the battle-field?' 'Why not move them to the assistance of our brave boys on the left?' "

(US) Pepper, 59th Illinois, Gooding's brigade, Mitchell's division:
"We was the only troops that went out of all them thousands that lay there idle at that time."

(US) Lathrop, 59th Illinois, Gooding's Brigade, Mitchell's division:
"The distance to the point of danger was something less than a mile. It was now nearly sunset."

Shortly after 4 p.m. McCook's plea for help reaches Buell's headquarters. Buell's position is in the acoustic shadow that blocks sound of cannon and rifle fire, so the army commander doubts McCook is in much trouble. But, unaware that Gilbert has dispatched help, he issues orders for Gilbert to send two brigades:

(US) Maj. J. Montgomery Wright, assistant adjutant-general on Buell's staff:
"Colonel James B. Fly, our chief of staff, called me up, and sent me with an order to General Gilbert, commanding the center corps, to send at once two brigades to reinforce General McCook, commanding the left corps. . . . I did not know what was going on at the left, and Colonel Fly did not inform me. He told me what to say to General Gilbert, and to go fast, and taking one of the general's orderlies with me, I started on my errand. I found General Gilbert at the front, and as he had no staff-officer at hand at the moment, he asked me to go to General Schoepf, one of his division commanders, with the order. Schoepf promptly detached two brigades, and he told me I had better go on ahead and find out where they were to go. There was no sound to direct me, and . . . I passed outside of the Union lines and was overtaken by a cavalry officer, who gave me the . . . information that I was riding toward the enemy's pickets. . . . I had heard no sound of battle; I had heard no artillery in front of me, and no heavy infantry-firing. I rode back, and passed behind the cavalry regiment, which was deployed in the woods, and started in the direction indicated to me by the officer who called me back."

Confederate batteries are shelling the Federal position at the Russell house while Adams' brigade is moving along the south side of the Mackville Road and Cleburne's regiments are moving up through a cornfield:

63

(US) William H. McCleary, 42nd Indiana, Lytle's brigade, Rousseau's division:
"We was then ordered to fall back to a piece of woods in the rear of Loumises battery it being about 4 of a mile acrost a corn field."

(US) Maj. James M. Shanklin, 42nd Indiana, Lytle's brigade, Rousseau's division:
"We were ordered across the field by the flank, to take position in the woods, and wait the advance of the enemy, now coming up the hill in beautiful style, cheering as though the victory were won, and throwing shell and grape furiously. The screams, the wild, terrible demon yells of the bombs, and the snake-like hissing of the bullets, made that march over Peter's farm decidedly the most interesting trip I ever took. We were very near the woods when, simultaneously with the bursting of a shell over my head, I felt a stunning blow, and fell to the ground. Two of the men sprang to me, and carried me off."

(US) George M. Kirkpatrick, 42nd Indiana, Lytle's brigade, Rousseau's division:
"We formed behind a fence . . . in the edge of the timber. Dick Nash, a man of Co. 'A' was lying in the corner of the fence. Dick was known as a fellow that could outswear any soldiers in Flanders. The rest of us were hugging the ground, for the bullets were coming thick and fast. I saw Dick get up on his knees and offer up a prayer as fine as a minister could do."

As Cleburne's Confederate brigade moves up through the cornfield, it is taken under fire by the 33rd Ohio, then the 10th Ohio:

(US) Lt. Spillard F. Horrall, 42nd Indiana, Lytle's brigade, Rousseau's division:
"(Harris') Battery and . . . (Webster's brigade) on the left of the 42d engaged the enemy hotly as he advanced, the line of the (80th Indiana) regiment . . . and the 42d forming an angle; the battery . . . occupying a good position on a small knob between the two. . . . The attention of our command was directed to a strong line of the enemy approaching our front. Instantly a heavy fire was opened upon them, but they moved on as steadily . . . as if on drill in camp. Some practiced marksmen of Company G were ordered to keep the rebel flag down. Three times it, with its bearer, fell and was taken up again. The fourth time it fell within seventy-five yards of our line."

(US) Kirkpatrick, 42nd Indiana, Lytle's brigade, Rousseau's division:
"The Johnies . . . came up to the fence, where we were and . . . our whole regiment gave them a volley that stopped them until the other three regiments which were in our Brigade could get there. These were the 10th Ohio, 3rd Ohio and the 15th Kentucky, and they got back of us, and fought hard."

(US) Lt. Horrall, 42nd Indiana, Lytle's brigade, Rousseau's division:
"The 42d held its position and drove the enemy before it, . . . strewing the field with the dead and wounded."

Wood's confederate brigade moves up on Cleburne's right and hits the 42nd Indiana:

(US) Kirkpatrick, 42nd Indiana, Lytle's brigade, Rousseau's division:
"We had to retreat, shooting all the time. Other troops came up and we fell back on a hill. It was so smokey that we could not see far."

(US) Lt. Horrall, 42nd Indiana, Lytle's brigade, Rousseau's division:
"Just about . . . sun-set we received orders to charge on a rebel regiment."

(US) Kirkpatrick, 42nd Indiana, Lytle's brigade, Rousseau's division:
"Captain Olmstead of Co. A, raised his sword and called, 'Come on, Boys,' and turned to go down the hill. . . . At that moment . . . a bullet pierced his brain. My partner and I were . . . the two first in the regiment.

The bullet which killed Captain Olmstead went between us, and Captain Olmstead's brains blinded us, as he fell directly before us, and we jumped over him, with the determination to avenge his slaughter."

(US) Lt. Horrall, 42nd Indiana, Lytle's brigade, Rousseau's division:
"Lieut. Col. Denby received a shot which passed directly between his lips, cutting a part of the upper lip away. It was . . . inspiring . . . to see that brave officer, with the sanguinary tide streaming from his mouth, cheering, huzzahing, brandishing his sword, and urging and encouraging the men on. . . . He rode in front of our lines, pointing to the enemy and urging the men on. . . . Calm and collected rode Col. Jones upon his horse, cheering the men, urging them on, and sharing with us all the dangers of the field. Many of the enemy's balls were aimed at him, but . . . he escaped being hurt himself, but his horse was wounded. All the while the . . . Colonel led us on. . . . Adjutant Evans, with hat in one hand and sword in the other, rode up and down the line, waving his sword and hat, and cheering us on."

(US) Kirkpatrick, 42nd Indiana, Lytle's brigade, Rousseau's division:
"About half way down the hill two Johnies were sitting behind a rail cut log, with their guns cocked ready, and one of them shot for my head, his bullet passing right below my ear, clipping the hair; the other drew blood from Lockwood, my file leader. As soon as they shot they squatted close to the log, and threw up their old gray hats and said 'We will surrender.' . . . Two guns come down on those two Johnies' heads, and I found my gun broken. . . . The whole thing was all over in thirty seconds or less."

(US) Lt. Horrall, 42nd Indiana, Lytle's brigade, Rousseau's division:
"We . . . (drove) the enemy at least three hundred yards down the hill into a ravine. . . . As twilight was setting in, our ammunition gave out, and . . . the enemy was flanking us right and left."

The approaching enemy unit is Cleburne's brigade:

(US) Lt. Horrall, 42nd Indiana, Lytle's brigade, Rousseau's division:
"Orders came to retreat over the hill."

(US) Kirkpatrick, 42nd Indiana, Lytle's brigade, Rousseau's division:
"Colonel Denby had got shot in the mouth, and his lips were bleeding and he was mad. He was riding along the line shouting to cease firing. By this time I had picked up another gun, and it had a load in it. The smoke of battle had opened up, and we could see the Rebs and I fired right in front of the Colonel's horse. The horse jumped back and Colonel Denby struck at me for shooting. I was looking for another cartridge, so sergeant McCutcheon . . . threw his gun over my head and caught the blow of the sword. The sword . . . cut into the barrel of the gun, behind the front sight of it clean to the bore. . . . The Colonel wanted to get us out of there, for about a hundred yards distant, were five lines of Rebs coming. Denby then said, 'Right, face forward! by file, right double quick,' and as we were going up the hill, I had not had a chance to see the Rebs yet."

(US) Lt. Horrall, 42nd Indiana, Lytle's brigade, Rousseau's division:
"At the command 'Fall back!' I told my company to obey; but, being lame, I could not 'double-quick.' . . . Slowly and in good order our troops fell back, though we were fired into right and left by small arms, and from our rear by musketry, grape, and canister shot."

(US) Kirkpatrick, 42nd Indiana, Lytle's brigade, Rousseau's division:
"There being a tree about twelve inches through the butt, and forked six feet from the ground, I jumped behind it. No sooner had I looked about, than a musket ball struck me on the leather cap brim, blistering my forehead. In my fright, I thought that my brains were laid bare, because of the stinging pain, and the blood pouring down into my eyes, and as I followed the regiment, I was afraid to put my hand up there, for fear to disturb my brain, which I supposed to be exposed by the wound."

(US) Lt. Horrall, 42nd Indiana, Lytle's brigade, Rousseau's division:
"Whilst falling back, Lieut. Col. Denby's horse was shot under him, and fell, fastening the Colonel's foot under his side. Capt. McIntire assisted in getting him disengaged from his horse, and though it was in the midst of a . . . rain of missiles of death, both got away safely, the Colonel leaving his horse upon the field. Near the same time, Adjutant Evans' horse was shot under him."

(US) Kirkpatrick, 42nd Indiana, Lytle's brigade, Rousseau's division:
"I passed D. Evens, the adjutant, whose horse had been shot dead and had fallen upon one of the adjutant's legs. Two or, three men were trying to drag the horse off, and they hallowed to me to give them a hand, but for once I could not respond to a call for help, and it did seem as if I had done enough for one time, as we had shot away forty-five rounds. I had to slow up because of the shock of the wound on my forehead, and by now the regiment had gotten away from me."

(US) McCleary, 42nd Indiana, Lytle's brigade, Rousseau's division:
"Was compelled to fall back by degrees near a mile."

(US) Lt. Horrall, 42nd Indiana, Lytle's brigade, Rousseau's division:
"Water was scarce, but I had a canteen full. One of our comrades asked for water, and drank half. Passing on, I saw the upturned face of a boy not out of his teens, head against a tree, eyes fast fixing on death, and he said, 'Captain, please give me water; I am dying.' . . . The canteen passed to his lips, and he drank the last drop."

(US) Kirkpatrick, 42nd Indiana, Lytle's brigade, Rousseau's division:
"The ammunition train was coming up, or trying to get up in an old field as I went over the hill, there was a six mule team with a wagon load of cartridges. The darkey teamster was unloading the boxes, so that he could pull up farther toward the front. The wheel mule was turning his head and braying, when a solid shot went through the mule's head, striking the front end of the wagon and unloading the boxes. The shot went past the darkey. Never . . . will I forget the astonishment of that Negro. He looked up at me and started to run. . . . (A) shell went into the ground about ten feet ahead of me, and burst, throwing the yellow clay into my face."

Adams' Confederate brigade is advancing, and McCook orders Webster to block the charge. Webster has only the inexperienced 98th and 121st Ohio to stop Adams:

(US) Wesley S. Poulson, 98th Ohio, Webster's brigade, Jackson's division:
"They finally concluded to make a charge on our battery. Their sharp shooters were deployed in advance of the column some 40 to 50 yards, for the purpose, I suppose, of 'picking off' our commanding officers. . . . They sent a regiment to flank ours on the right. The flanking regiment kept behind a hill from us and we were entirely unconscious of this movement until they were opposite the right wing of our regiment. During this time we were watching the line in front of us. It was a grand sight to see. The line was composed of some of Bragg's best disciplined troops. The men kept in excellent order, and when our battery would belch forth solid shot or shell at them, the line would fall as if all the men were linked together. As soon as the shot or shell struck they would rise at a word from their commander, and march forward till they again would see the smoke and again prostrate themselves to the earth. They seemed not to notice a man killed and wounded, but boldly marched on leaving them behind, and keeping their ranks well closed. They were marching down a declivity and we could plainly see the killed and wounded left behind. One shell burst in their line that killed and wounded at least 12 men. This shell was fired just after they arose and I suppose they did not like to lie down and get up more than once in the same place. The line moved on and there on the hillside was a little lot of rebels still in death and others rolling in agony caused by their wounds. Rebels as they were, and deserving death as they did, the sight truly made me feel for them and had I not known their object in coming towards us, I should really have pitied them. . . .

"When Lt. Col. Porman first saw the regiment which was flanking us he called for attention and we instantly sprang to our feet. We were now facing eastward towards the advancing line of rebels. We were ordered to 'right face, forward march' and then to 'file right.' "

(US) Sgt. Maj. Duncan C. Milner, 98th Ohio, Webster's brigade, Jackson's division:
"Our regiment was then placed in a piece of woods to the rear of where we had been."

(US) Poulson, 98th Ohio, Webster's brigade, Jackson's division:
"This placed us with our left flank towards the advancing line – which was now ascending the hill on which our battery was placed – and I faced toward the regiment that was flanking us."

(US) Sgt. Maj. Milner, 98th Ohio, Webster's brigade, Jackson's division:
"We could see plainly the columns of rebels approaching and their hateful flags flying. I had found a musket and borrowed some ammunition, and took my place with the boys. . . . We had then our first fire. . . . Our men, tho a little confused in getting arranged, stood up to it well."

(US) Lt. Silas Emerson, 121st Ohio, Webster's brigade, Jackson's division:
"The enemy opened on us with cannon and musketry . . . , they not being over thirty yards from us. We were marching by the left flank and were not in line of battle when they first fired on us. We formed, however, as soon and well as we could and returned this fire."

(US) Poulson, 98th Ohio, Webster's brigade, Jackson's division:
"One of Company F was struck in the first fire, the ball striking him in the face just below the left eye. Seeing his face so covered with blood and hearing the mournful noise he made seemed to strengthen my nerve till I felt revengeful. We were within 80 or 90 yards, I think, of them. I shot three times from this place."

(US) Sgt. Maj. Milner, 98th Ohio, Webster's brigade, Jackson's division:
"(I) fought some, and I also did the duties of my position, namely, to aid keeping the men in order. . . . The first fire did scare me a little, but that was soon over, and when the battle was the fiercest, when men were falling all around me and the balls falling like hail, I felt perfectly calm. I knew that my life was in the hands of God."

(US) Lt. Emerson, 121st Ohio, Webster's brigade, Jackson's division:
"A cannon ball struck . . . Thomas Mass . . . and went right through his breast which killed him instantly. . . . Capt. Odor of our company was also struck by a cannon ball. . . . I was standing so close to him that our elbows touched each other. His blood and flesh flew all over me. . . . I had no time to think after the capt. fell. The command of the company devolved upon me."

(US) Sgt. Maj. Milner, 98th Ohio, Webster's brigade, Jackson's division:
"We were . . . moved a little higher up the hill."

(US) Poulson, 98th Ohio, Webster's brigade, Jackson's division:
"(I) moved to where the company had gone, which was some 50 yards. They (had) received orders for this move which was made on 'double quick.' I thought they were running from the rebels and would not go until I saw the Captain make a motion with his hand for me and three or four others to come on. On the way to them I halted long enough to take aim and shoot once and then reload my rifle and when I got to them I shot the fifth and last time. I think I was not more than 50 or 60 yards from the one I shot at last. He fell, but whether I or someone else hit him no one could tell.

"We were here formed into a line having been thrown somewhat into confusion by the excitement of the movement. Orders were given to march forward and marching as near as I can guess some 30 yards, just as I was making a step with my right leg, it was struck about three inches below the knee joint with a large rifle ball instantly shattering both bones. I set my rifle down very quick to keep me from falling and with it hopped it out of the way so as to let the rest of the regiment pass. Then I laid down, and it so happened that near where I was stood a stump. I lay down by this with my head toward it so as to bring it between me and the line of advancing rebels who were now firing rapidly at us. It was fortunate for me a rail pile between me and the regiment that had flanked ours. I heard several balls strike the stump and heard the splinters knocked from the rails but received no further injury myself.

"In less than five minutes after I was wounded the rebels were all around me shooting at the Union men. One shot several times off the stump by which I lay. His gun rested on the stump with the barrel extended over me having bayonet fixed and gleaming, and had I made signs of life he perhaps would have used his bayonet on me."

(US) Sgt. Maj. Milner, 98th Ohio, Webster's brigade, Jackson's division:
"Our men would step to the top of the bank, take aim and fire and step back under the bluff and load. Here we lost a good many of our men either killed or wounded."

(US) Poulson, 98th Ohio, Webster's brigade, Jackson's division:
"Our men – a Regiment of Illinois, I think – made (the rebels) run and then came down as far as where I lay. I told the boys to 'give them fits.' They replied they would and then wanted to carry me off, but I refused to let them, saying to them use your guns and let me alone. As soon as the rebels ran, I cut the string off my canteen and tied it around my leg so as to stop the blood from flowing so freely, and I have no doubt but some other boys might have saved their lives by the same means. I believe in a half an hour longer had I not done this I would have lost so much blood that death would have followed shortly. In a few moments our line was driven back and the dirty, greasy, rebels were again around me. This time the most of them passed me and when up near our line, and it seemed to me as if the firing was all at the same place the lines were so near to each other. Some of the rebels were afraid to go near and hid behind trees, bushes, and whatever was near. The rebel color bearer came up opposite to where I lay and within about 20 feet of me. He there placed his staff on the ground and remained, I suppose some 20 minutes in that position. He was a portly looking man and better clad than most of the rebels were. Many of them were barefooted, hatless, and without a coat, and their shirts and pants seemed considerably worse for wear and tear. . . . One large fat rebel fell near me that had a furrow made along the top of his head from front to back by a rifle ball, and the jar he received when he fell caused the brain to protrude the entire length of the furrow. I never saw him stir after he fell. His head was within a yard of my feet."

As Cleburne's Confederates close in on Webster's position, the Federal commander orders Harris' Battery to pull out, but the artillerymen have only enough horses to save two of their six guns:

(US) Joseph P. Glezen, 80th Indiana, Webster's brigade, Jackson's division:
"Harris' (two guns) . . . drove past us to the rear, . . . fast . . . , and Lt. Colonel (Lewis) Brooks was ordered to fall back and take a position at the road on the hill, about 150 yards in our rear."

(US) Lt. Emerson, 121st Ohio, Webster's brigade, Jackson's division, McCook's corps:
"We soon . . . got orders to about-face and retreat, which we did in some confusion."

(US) Glezen, 80th Indiana, Webster's brigade, Jackson's division:
"We . . . formed in line of battle and gave the rebels a few well directed rounds, but owing to the continued falling back of the Federal lines to our right and left, our position became untenable, and we were directed to fall back about 300 yards further."

(US) Sgt. Maj. Milner, 98th Ohio, Webster's brigade, Jackson's division:
"The ammunition I had borrowed gave out, and I furnished myself from the body of a dead man. Col. Webster . . . was now – about 5 o'clock – in the rear of our regiment, about 20 feet from me. I had fired and had turned around and was just in the act of loading, when I saw him fall. I dropped my gun, and was the first at his side. He told me he thought he was mortally wounded, and prayed for God to have mercy on his soul.

DARKNESS ENDS THE FIGHTING

He also said: 'Tell my dear wife and children they were last in my thoughts.' Some soldiers assisted me in carrying him down farther into the woods, and laid him behind a tree. I examined his wound, and found the ball had entered his right hip, and he was bleeding profusely. I then started to hunt the surgeons."

Webster's 98th and 121st Ohio are driven back by the veteran Confederates, who continue to push toward the Russell house. But, Cleburne's brigade is losing cohesion and running low on ammunition as it pursues the 42nd Indiana toward the Federal line.

(US) Glezen, 80th Indiana, Webster's brigade, Jackson's division:
"We again took position in support of Harris' (two guns) . . . which had already commenced thundering. . . . Here a new line was established."

Federal artillery staggers Adams' brigade, and it falls back. Federal gunners also hit Cleburne's troops. He realizes the defenders are too strong and orders his weary men to retreat. Wood's brigade, however, continues to advance as Rousseau's men withdraw across the Benton Road. In Wood's path is the 38th Indiana, which had been pulled back when it ran out of ammunition:

(US) Col. B.F. Scribner, commanding 38th Indiana, Harris' brigade, Rousseau's division:
"We lay to await the wagon with ammunition. The battle was now renewed with great fury, and to my consternation there came down upon us a fleeing mob of routed and panic-stricken raw recruits, who, rushing in a disorganized mass, with the enemy at their heels and trampling over my men, fled away like scared sheep. I was in utter despair, and thought that all was lost, expecting of course that the Thirty-eighth would be swept away with the crowd, but to my surprise and joy, there lay my brave boys; . . . and springing to their feet, with bayonets fixed and without a round of ammunition."

Behind McCook's line, the staff officer sent from Buell's headquarters with word that help is on the way cannot hear the battle and is still looking for some one or something to guide him to the front:

(US) Maj. Wright, assistant adjutant-general on Buell's staff:
"I overtook an ambulance train, urged to its best speed, and then I knew that something serious was on hand. . . . Directed by the officers in charge of the ambulances I made another detour, and pushing on at greater speed I suddenly turned into a road, and there before me, within a few hundred yards, the battle of Perryville burst into view, and the roar of the artillery and the continuous rattle of the musketry first broke upon my ear. . . . The . . . spectacle . . . was wholly unexpected, and it fixed me with astonishment. . . . At one bound my horse carried me from stillness into the uproar of battle. One turn from a lonely bridle-path through the woods brought me face to face with the bloody struggle of thousands of men. . . .

"My rapid approach excited the curiosity of a soldier, who, standing near McCook, was just capping his gun. He dropped the butt of his musket on the ground, threw his head forward and opened his mouth, as if listening intently, and at the instant dropped his gun, clapped both hands to his face, gave a wild howl, and went dancing off the road in a most absurd fashion. A buck-shot had passed between his teeth and through his cheek. . . .

"I think what I told General McCook lifted something off his mind. He looked relieved, and he told me to remain . . . and he would send a message back by me. . . . I . . . hastened to dismount to hurry off a note to the Chief of Staff."

The 59th and 75th Illinois, 22nd Indiana and Pinney's Battery, reinforcements first dispatched by Gilbert, begin arriving:

(US) Maj. Wright, assistant adjutant-general on Buell's staff:
"A fresh battery whirled past me into position and . . . infantry came cheering down the lane at the double time and ran beyond me into the position opened for them in line."

(US) Pepper, 59th Illinois, Gooding's brigade, Mitchell's division:
"We met General McCook. . . . Colonel (Gooding) of the 22nd Indiana was in command of the brigade. We was in front of the colonel, and I heard the general tell the colonel where to take us and pointed out the place where he wanted us to go – over on top of a hill by the side of a battery that stood over there but was almost silent. The bullets was passing over us pretty thick. Then I looked over there where we was ordered to go, and I saw the dead men in their blue uniforms lying around the battery and dead horses stretched out there

and on the hill where other men was lying I could also see the dust flying like a light shower of rain would strike in the dust."

(US) William H. Ball, Pinney's Battery, Gooding's brigade, Mitchell's division:
"Just ahead is Gen. McCook and staff. We hear him say to our Captain, 'We have whipped them on the right and center, and I think this brigade . . . will turn the scale on the left. You are just in the nick of time.' He showed the Captain where to plant the battery."

(US) George Q. Gardner, Pinney's Battery, Gooding's brigade, Mitchell's division:
"Our battery went into 'action front' on the brow of a slight hill in the edge of a wood.

(US) Ball, Pinney's Battery, Gooding's brigade, Mitchell's division:
"Directly in front, perhaps 300 yards, was . . . (Russell's) frame house. To its right, and further off, a ridge, where the enemy had a battery. To the right of their battery was a burning house, whence rose . . . (a) column of smoke. . . . We went into battery on the edge of a wood to the right of the lane, the enemy's shells bursting all around us. There is only room for five guns, the sixth remaining idle. It is 5:30 o'clock, and the sun an hour high. Our first shot rings out loud and clear. . . . The boys . . . load and fire with . . . rapidity, coolness and precision."

(US) Gardner, Pinney's Battery, Gooding's brigade, Mitchell's division:
"Owing to the dense smoke and lateness of the afternoon, it was at first hard to locate the enemy, . . . our Captain . . . sat on his horse and, shading his eyes with his hand, shouted, 'Where are they! Where are they! D—- 'em, where are they!' . . . At our immediate front was a heavy bank of smoke and a continual flash of flame, and from it poured forth a storm of lead and iron hail. Our boys began firing as rapidly as well-drilled artillerymen could do. . . . The infantry was ordered to advance."

(US) Pepper, 59th Illinois, Gooding's brigade, Mitchell's division:
"When we got the order to go . . . and the officers mounted their horses, our regimental surgeon also mounted his fine horse and said he would go with us this trip. . . . No money would have hired me to go up on that hill and run the risk that I did. . . . But I must go and get through with this unpleasant affair. They gave the order and we made the start."

(US) Gardner, Pinney's Battery, Gooding's brigade, Mitchell's division:
"Gen. McCook . . . sat on his horse near our left. The infantry moved forward with a shout."

(US) Pepper, 59th Illinois, Gooding's brigade, Mitchell's division:
"Long before we gained the top of the hill, every mounted officer in the brigade was killed or shot off his horse. We got our position and held it for sometime. The Rebels were in the edge of the timber while we were in the open ground."

(US) Lathrop, 59th Illinois, Gooding's Brigade, Gilbert's corps:
"The enemy opened fire with grape and cannister from their batteries, and poured volley after volley of musketry into . . . (our) ranks."

(US) Pepper, 59th Illinois, Gooding's brigade, Mitchell's division:
"We had hardly gotten into position until our color bearer fell. Another brave young man grabbed it up and went down in a minute or two. The men fell all around us fast after the second man fell with the flag. The orderly sergeant of Company K at the side of our company grabbed up the flag and knelt down on one knee, and with all the noise of the guns, I heard him say, 'Here . . . is your colors; stand by or rally around them!' The bullets whizzed passed our heads so thick that it did seem to me if a man had held his arm up straight it would have been shot off. We did not stay right on top of the hill. . . . I was standing by the side of a young man and saw a ball strike him in the forehead. He whirled around and pitched down the hill."

(US) Lathrop, 59th Illinois, Gooding's Brigade:
"The . . . men returned the fire . . . for half an hour, each one loading and firing as rapidly as possible without order or system."

(US) Col. Scribner, commanding 38th Indiana, Harris' brigade, Rousseau's division:
"The Twenty-second Indiana had moved up on my right. I dashed to the field officer on their left and pointing out the enemy's advancing line, urged him to open upon them a well directed fire, which they did, and which seemed to check their advance."

(CS) J.P. Cannon, 45th Mississippi, Wood's brigade, Buckner's division:
"Our boys were mowed down by the bullets of the Indianians on top of the hill. Almost every mounted officer in the brigade was killed or disabled in the charge, and our line was perceptively thinned before we reached the foot of the hill."

(US) Ball, Pinney's Battery, Gooding's brigade, Mitchell's division:
"The rebel battery is compelled to change position twice. . . . They attempt to take our battery by infantry charges."

(CS) Cannon, 45th Mississippi, Wood's brigade, Buckner's division:
"We pressed on and up until within 30 yards of the enemy. . . . Glancing to the right, hardly a respectable skirmish-line could I see. To the left it was the same. . . . Those who were able to run were scattered for 300 yards back, every fellow taking care of himself. . . . My attention was riveted on the bluecoats in front and so occupied with pulling up the steep hill that I had not observed what was taking place on my flanks. When I found out I was almost or quite alone I 'lit out.' . . . When I got into the field it seemed as if every Yankee within a mile concentrated his gun directly on me, and the weeds were cut off all around and under me; but . . . I escaped without a scratch. I took cover behind the first hill that offered protection from the rain of bullets, where a few other stragglers had stopped."

As fire from Gooding's regiments and artillery halts Wood's Confederates and pushes them back, McCook's troops have a chance to regroup:

(US) Maj. Wright, assistant adjutant-general on Buell's staff:
"The reinforcements brought new spirit to the jaded line of troops which held their position. . . .

"Waiting for news to carry back, I saw . . . young Forman, with the remnant of his company of the 15th Kentucky regiment, . . . and as they silently passed me they seemed to stagger and reel like men who had been beating against a great storm. Forman had the colors in his hand, and he and several of his little group of men had their hands on their chests and their lips apart as though they had difficulty breathing. They filed into a field, and without thought of shot or shell they lay down on the ground apparently in a state of exhaustion. I joined a mounted group about a young officer, and heard Rumsey Wing, one of Jackson's volunteer aides, telling of that general's death and the scattering of the raw division he commanded. . . . I asked about (Gen.) Terrill, . . . and was told that he had been carried to the rear to die. . . .

"I thought things looked pretty well, and I asked General McCook if he had any message to send. He told me to go back and tell General Buell he thought he was all right and could hold his ground. . . . As I rode back to General Buell's position on the main road, I saw the great yellow moon rising out of the tops of the hills I had left, and across its face and through the background of dark blue sky, and from opposite directions I saw the shells from opposing batteries cross and fall like meteors toward either line. It was a beautiful view."

On the battle line, Rousseau's troops continue to fall back, but the Confederate attack is running out of steam. Adams' and Cleburne's brigades are spent, and Wood's brigade has been driven back. Hardee moves Liddell's Confederate brigade up to resume the attack. An aide guides Liddell to Doctor's Creek and relays the order "go where the fire is hottest":

(CS) Brig. Gen. St. John R. Liddell, brigade commander, Buckner's division:
"The sun had just sunk behind the trees. I looked around without halting for the hottest place. It seemed to be everywhere. I crossed the creek, my comd. following; when suddenly it struck me to attempt the capture of a heavy Battery I had seen from the ridge firing over his own lines from the rear of his left wing. I now ordered the men to move rapidly, and did not call a halt to form the line for attack until I had reached nearly the extreme right of Cheatham's Divn, then fighting in my front. This done, . . . we pressed forward in line."

(CS) John M. Berry, 8th Arkansas, Liddell's brigade, Buckner's division:
"Nearly night . . . we were ordered hastily forward."

(CS) Brig. Gen. Liddell, brigade commander, Buckner's division:
"We met . . . stragglers flying from the front toward the rear."

(CS) Cannon, 45th Mississippi, Wood's brigade, Buckner's division:
"I had hardly time to catch my breath before a thrilling and welcome sight was presented – a line of gray . . . coming to reinforce us.

*Liddell's men spot the 22nd Indiana pushing the 32nd Mississippi and 33rd Alabama
back and fire into the Federals. Gooding orders the 22nd Indiana to fall back and go into
line to the left of the 75th Illinois:*

(CS) Cannon, 45th Mississippi, Wood's brigade, Buckner's division:
"We immediately began to rally the stragglers."

(CS) Brig. Gen. Liddell, brigade commander, Buckner's division:
"A young officer in violent language and manner wildly called on his men to halt and return to the fight, and having rallied a company requested permission to join my Comd. . . . I granted the permission."

(CS) Cannon, 45th Mississippi, Wood's brigade, Buckner's division:
"When . . . (Liddell's) line reached us we had 13 of the two Alabama companies together under Lieut. Andrews, and falling in with them moved forward again."

(CS) Brig. Gen. Liddell, brigade commander, Buckner's division:
"As we neared the front passing thr'o a Battery captured by Cheatham, the roar of fire arms rendered it difficult to be heard. . . . Genl. Cheatham, pipe in mouth, rode up to me, saying very excitedly and loudly 'Genl you can save the fight -!! go on and save it.' I replied to him, 'I shall try, Genl, but come and show me your line. It is now getting too late to distinguish colors clearly and I might fire by mistake upon your men.' 'No – go on and save the fight, you will find the line.' Still marching forward, I appealed to him again, but to no purpose."

(CS) C.M. McCouley, commanding 7th Arkansas, Liddell's brigade, Buckner's division:
"The Arkansas brigade moved at quick time through the darkness, smoke, and dust."

(CS) Brig. Gen. Liddell, brigade commander, Buckner's division:
"The full moon was high up and the twilight of a clear Oct. evening had rapidly emerged into a bright moonlight. Suddenly, we confronted a dark line hardly more than 25 paces off, on the crest of an elevation we were ascending, when immediately, without orders, a desultory fire issued from my line."

(CS) Berry, 8th Arkansas, Liddell's brigade, Buckner's division:
"Soon the smoke of the battle and the approach of night made it difficult to tell foe from friend. We were ordered to cease firing, as it was feared our own men were in our front."

EYEWITNESSES AT THE BATTLE OF PERRYVILLE

(CS) Brig. Gen. Liddell, brigade commander, Buckner's division:
"A sudden . . . cessation of firing had taken place on both sides, . . . , and in this momentary silent interval, except the desultory fire from my line, . . . could be heard a distressing cry from the dark line before us, 'you are firing upon friends; for God sake stop.' In an instant everything was still. Uncertain who was before me . . . , I was just about to give the order to (go) forward with Bayonets fixed when Gen. Leonidas Polk rode up alongside; . . . he quickly expressed his delight at seeing me in that place; when I interrupted him by informing him of my men having fired by mistake into Cheatham's Divn, which would not have happened had that Genl. come with me. Genl Polk seemed shocked at the accident, and said 'what a pity. I hope not. I don't think so. Let me go and see. Open your ranks.' It was done and the brave old man spurred his horse with a jump thr'o the opening."

(CS) J.T. Hamilton, 5th Arkansas, Liddell's brigade, Buckner's division:
"We (had) chanced upon the Twenty-second Indiana . . . in a dense woodland. . . . The right of our regiment was within ten paces of them."

(CS) Brig. Gen. Liddell, brigade commander, Buckner's division:
"Parleyings happened almost simultaneously along the whole line of both sides."

(CS) Berry, 8th Arkansas, Liddell's brigade, Buckner's division:
"Col. (John H.) Kelly darted forward."

(CS) Brig. Gen. Liddell, brigade commander, Buckner's division:
"Kelly . . . who was calling out to know the regt before him, was answd. 'Indiana.' Thinking it might be Louisiana, he called again – and was answd. Indiana, 'do you want us down there?' 'No,' said Kelly. 'Stay where you are.' "

About the same time:

(CS) Maj. Gen. Leonidas Polk:
"Having cantered up to the colonel of the regiment . . . , I asked him in angry tones what he meant by shooting his own friends, and I desired him to cease doing so at once. He answered with some surprise, 'I don't think there can be any mistake about it; I am sure they are the enemy.' 'Enemy!' I said; 'why, I have only just left them myself. Cease firing, sire; what is your name, sir?' 'My name is . . . (Lt. Col. S.I. Keith), of the . . . (Twenty-second) Indiana; and pray, sir, who are you?' . . . I saw, to my astonishment, that he was a Yankee, and that I was in rear of a regiment of Yankees. . . . I saw there was no hope but to brazen it out; my dark blouse and the increasing obscurity befriended me, so I approached quite close to him and shook my fist in his face, saying, 'I'll soon show you who I am, sire; cease firing, sir, at once.' I then turned my horse and cantered slowly down the line, showing in an authoritative manner to the Yankees to cease firing; at the same time I experienced a disagreeable sensation, like screwing up my back, and calculating how many bullets would be between my shoulders every moment. I was afraid to increase my pace until I got to a small copse, when I put the spurs in and galloped back to my men."

(CS) Brig. Gen. Liddell, brigade commander, Buckner's division:
"(Gen. Polk) hastily returned, exclaiming 'Genl every mothers son of them are Yankees. I saw the Col. Comdg brigade and looked closely at the dark clothing of the men and am sure of not being mistaken.' . . . The news was circulated loudly- 'Yankees!' The trumpet sounded to 'fire.' "

(CS) Berry, 8th Arkansas, Liddell's brigade, Buckner's division:
"On reaching . . . our lines . . . (Col. Kelly's) shrill voice rang out, 'It's the enemy, boys; give it to them!' "

(CS) Brig. Gen. Liddell, brigade commander, Buckner's division:
"A tremendous flash of musketry for the whole extent of the line for nearly one quarter of a mile in length, followed."

DARKNESS ENDS THE FIGHTING

(CS) McCouley, commanding 7th Arkansas, Liddell's brigade, Buckner's division:
"We poured into their ranks the most destructive volley I ever witnessed. Loading as we advanced, two other volleys were fired, the last being not over five paces from their lines."

Point-blank volleys from the 2nd, 6th and 7th Arkansas riddle the 22nd Indiana. Gooding falls wounded and Keith is killed. The shredded 22nd Indiana flees across the Benton Road.

(CS) Brig. Gen. Liddell, brigade commander, Buckner's division:
"I discovered that the return fire had ceased, and . . . directed the trumpeter to signal the cessation on our part. The smoke soon cleared up, which enabled Genl Polk to ride forward with me and see the result. The Federal force had disappeared. . . . The ground . . . was literally covered with the dead and dying. I returned to the line and announced . . . the field was ours. It was answered with repeated cheers – and then followed loud cheering far to our left, which we supposed to be from Anderson's Div. It . . . turned out to be the enemy, who had driven in our left wing, as we had their left."

The cheering Liddell hears is the arrival of Steedman's Federal brigade, the second brigade sent by Gilbert to shore up McCook's battered line. The reinforcements, however, are too far off to help Gooding's brigade. Remnants of the shattered 22nd Indiana rally at a fence, then retreat again. This reverse forces the 75th Illinois and then the 59th Illinois to fall back, too.

(US) Lathrop, 59th Illinois, Gooding's Brigade, Mitchell's division:
"The enemy at this point had massed their forces for the purpose of turning the right flank of the left wing. . . . It was useless to attempt to resist this mighty host, and the order was therefore given for each one to provide for his own safety. Major Winters, of the Fifty-Ninth, repeated the order the third time before the men ceased firing, and then they most reluctantly left the field. . . . Owing to the dusk of the evening and the favorable formation of the ground many of the rebel bullets overshot. . . . Those on horseback were in the most danger. . . . The Fifty-Ninth, on going into the trap, numbered two hundred and ninety-one men, and on coming out brought off one hundred and eighty-three – leaving one hundred and eight on the field; twenty-three of whom were killed, sixty-two wounded, and twenty-three taken prisoners."

Gooding's brigade retreats farther, leaving Pinney's Battery without support:

(US) Ball, Pinney's Battery, Gooding's brigade, Mitchell's division:
"We, . . . receiving no orders, continued to fire on the rebel battery, which responded slowly and sullenly."

75

(CS) Brig. Gen. Liddell, brigade commander, Buckner's division:
"I now directed my Battery to move forward, and had the bodies removed from its path. . . . Genl. P. seeing, asked my object. I answered that I designed taking the heavy Battery, which . . . was then in the edge of the woods in advance of the skirmish line. Gen. P. objected and said, 'I want no more night fighting; it will be a waste of ammunition. Await orders just as you are.' I ventured to remonstrate- that I now knew nothing to be before me but the panic stricken enemy, and let me go forward and secure the fruits of our success.' He was very positive in refusing and then rode off to some other part of the field.

"All I could do now was look after the wounded, removing the Federals to a hospital established by them during the day, and which was close at hand on the Mackville road. . . . The ground was strewn with small arms, which being in our way, I ordered details to stack them in large piles. We got tired of doing this after two hours work, and scarcely seemed to diminish the number. I suppose there could hardly have been less than 4000 stand lying around. The baggage ambulance of Gen. McCook was captured and sent at once to Genl Bragg."

(US) Maj. Shanklin, 42nd Indiana, Lytle's brigade, Rousseau's division:
"A little after sunset the firing ceased almost entirely."

(CS) McCouley, commanding 7th Arkansas, Liddell's brigade, Buckner's division:
"Being slightly wounded, and sickened at the groans of the wounded and the pale and powder-stained faces of the dead, I turned to the left and walked some distance toward the Bardstown and Perryville pike. . . . I heard the rapid approach of a horseman. I drew my pistol and awaited his coming. He was uniformed, and I think was a staff officer, and he cried out as he came up: 'Here is water for the . . . Indiana Regiment.' I told him his regiment was killed or captured, and noticed he must have had about a hundred canteens of water about him, some tied to his horse's neck and saddle. My first impulse was to shoot him, but I decided to take from him several of the canteens, and advised him which way to go . . . to trace the remainder of his comrades."

(US) Ball, Pinney's Battery, Gooding's brigade, Mitchell's division:
"At 8 o'clock, having been engaged about two hours and a half, and thinking it useless to work longer in the dark, we cease firing. The rebel battery discharged a single gun afterward, and then all was silent. . . . We remained in position about an hour. . . . Then an officer rides up and says that although he has no authority, he thinks we had better limber up and be ready to move back through the line to the rear, as it is reported that the enemy was in the woods. . . . We limber up quickly, but do not move. Suddenly, bang, bang, bang go three guns almost in our very faces. We were completely taken by surprise. The shots came from rebel skirmishers, who advanced out of the woods on our left front and approached us unawares. . . . The Captain shouts: 'Unlimber and give them canister. By God, I'll show them what we are.' We do so as quickly as possible and stand ready to fire; but not seeing the foe, and still being afraid we will fire on friends, the order was not given. We look and listen a few minutes longer. . . . Then we limber up and slowly move back"

Off on McCook's right, darkness ends the advance of a limited Federal counterattack:

(US) Brig. Gen. William P. Carlin, brigade commander, Mitchell's division:
"We reached the garden stone fences on the north side of Perryville, where my line was halted. I threw out a strong picket to the left of my line, which reached a road running from the town back northeasterly to the main rebel army. . . . This picket there captured two or more caissons belonging to the Washington Artillery of New Orleans (Slocomb's Battery), with an escort of nearly 100 men. The caissons were loaded with ammunition, and were going to their front, which was to our rear and left. Several surgeons were with these caissons and escort."

The Battle of Perryville is over. On the battlefield and in the field hospitals are about 890 dead Federals and 530 dead Confederates. Roughly 2,890 Federals and 2,640 Confederates are wounded. About 440 Federals and 230 Confederates have been captured or are missing.

NIGHT ON THE BATTLEFIELD

Toward sunset, as the fighting peters out, wounded stream to the rear of Confederate and Federal lines. Among the dead, dying and wounded where Maney's and Stewart's Confederate regiments fought Starkweather's Federal brigade:

(US) Sgt. Edward Ferguson, 1st Wisconsin, Starkweather's brigade, Rousseau's division:
"(I was) gathered up in a blanket by sympathizing comrades and friends, and transported as tenderly as possible in an ambulance to the deserted house taken as a field hospital."

(US) L.E. Knowles, 1st Wisconsin, Starkweather's brigade, Rousseau's division:
"I remained unconscious near the stone wall . . . until nearly sunset, when I came to, and . . . I went back to the rear, guided by the direction of shot and shell that occasionally came from the enemy."

(CS) Benjamin A. Haguewood, 5th Tennessee, Stewart's brigade, Cheatham's division:
"I was left among the dead and dying. . . . Was discovered by a comrade and started with him to rejoin my men. . . . Overcome by exhaustion. . . . Laid me down to await my fate."

(CS) William W. Turner, 41st Georgia, Maney's brigade, Cheatham's division:
"As I was returning from the battle field about dusk, I heard a shot from the direction of the enemy and turned round just in time to receive a spent ball on my right cheek, which knocked me down but did not break my skin, only gave me great pain for a few days and a black eye. . . . When I recovered sufficiently from the shock I started again for the rear in search of my command. As I recrossed the field occupied by my regiment before it was relieved, I found the flag of my regiment – bearing which, four men had been killed and three times that number wounded."

Behind the Russell house, a Federal soldier who had gone in search of a doctor for his mortally wounded brigade commander, Col. George Webster, returns with a canteen of water and some brandy:

(US) Sgt. Maj. Duncan C. Milner, 98th Ohio, Webster's brigade, Jackson's division:
"I met some soldiers carrying him, and after administering the brandy we carried him until we met an ambulance, and he was then hauled to . . . (the Wilkerson) house about a mile from the battlefield, used as a hospital. We carried him thru the crowds of wounded, who covered the ground all around the house, and got him into a corner of a room, the floor of which was lined with the wounded. Here the ball was taken out. It had entered the right side of the right hip, passed thru the lower part of his body, and had lodged on the inside of the skin on the left side of the left hip. It was easily cut out. I stayed with him about half an hour, doing all I could to make him comfortable. . . . It was a dreadful place to be in; the shrieks and groans of the wounded were awful. . . . (Lt.) Col. Poorman came in, and it was concluded best to take Col. W. from here and carry him farther back."

Behind the Confederate line:

(CS) William E.M. Preston, 33rd Alabama, Wood's brigade, Buckner's division:
"Near sunset . . . we went over the battlefield looking after our wounded boys who had not already been carried to the house at the field hospital and also getting the effects out of the pockets of our dead friends. . . . We would send the effects to their folks at home. . . . We carried wheat straw for the wounded to lie upon and water for them in their cedar canteens."

EYEWITNESSES AT THE BATTLE OF PERRYVILLE

(CS) Capt. W.W. Carnes, commanding Carnes' Battery, Donelson's brigade, Cheatham's division:
"The brigades of Cheatham's Division . . . were being drawn back for alignment with other commands to form a new line in thick woods."

(CS) John W. Headley, Austin's Sharpshooters, 14th Louisiana Battalion, Adams' brigade, Anderson's division:
"It was understood that the battle would be renewed the following morning."

(CS) J.P. Cannon, 45th Mississippi, Wood's brigade, Buckner's division:
"We had used up our ammunition, and . . . Gen. Buckner ordered the Colonels to disband their regiments 20 minutes, to supply ourselves from the cartridge-boxes of the dead. They proved to be not very full, and I had to search several before getting my 40 rounds. I also exchanged my old gun for a new Enfield rifle which was lying by the side of its late owner."

(CS) J.K. Street, 9th Texas, Smith's brigade, Cheatham's division:
"We . . . captured . . . any amount of small arms all the troops who went in to the fight with old muskets come out with enfield and Springfield rifles."

(CS) Luke W. Finlay, 4th Tennessee, Stewart's brigade, Cheatham's division:
"From the field . . . each soldier . . . (took) an extra rifle to the place of bivouac near the rock fence; . . . our boys fully equipped themselves with Enfield rifles, exchanging their old guns for these new ones taken from the foe."

(CS) H.W. Graber, 8th Texas Cavalry, Wharton's brigade:
"We were ordered to destroy the small arms left on the field, which were very thick, by breaking the stocks on the trees, which job we soon abandoned because many of the guns were loaded. The batteries captured by our people were exchanged for our own guns, as we only had horses to carry off the number captured, leaving our inferior guns spiked on the field."

(CS) Col. William Miller, 1st Florida, commanding Brown's brigade, Anderson's division:
"The deserted batteries of the enemy . . . we were powerless to carry away. So many of our battery horses were killed that with difficulty could we carry off our own guns."

(US) Wesley S. Poulson, 98th Ohio, Webster's brigade, Jackson's division:
"Shortly after sunset some of the rebels were running around to gather up arms, revolvers, watches, Bowie knifes, etc. They came to where I lay and asked me where I was from, to what regiment I belonged, how long the regiment had been service, and a great many other questions. They took my gun, carried it about 10 yards and set it up against the fence with many others. . . . One Rebel lieutenant asked me if I had a revolver. I told him 'yes.' He then asked where it was. I told him that I had given it to our wagoner the day before to haul until I called for it again, and he replied, 'I wish to God you had it with you, I would soon have had one.' I am very glad I've not got it, said I. One asked me when I had had any water to drink. Not since noon said I. He said he would give me his canteen which was full of water for mine without a strap to it. I told him I was willing and we exchanged. It was now dark. They said they would be back in a short time with a wagon to take me to a hospital. I told them just to leave me there, not bother about moving me. To this they would not assent, saying that there would be more fighting the next day and I would get hurt."

On the Federal side:

(US) Evan Davis, 21st Wisconsin, Starkweather's brigade, Rousseau's division:
"We were glad when night caused hostilities to cease."

(US) Erastus Winters, 50th Ohio, Webster's brigade, Jackson's division:
"We . . . were moved a short distance to the rear, where we received a fresh supply of ammunition and the roll was called to see how many were missing."

(US) Daniel H. Chandler, Simonson's Battery, Harris' brigade, Rousseau's division:
"We knew we had been whipped, but we knew too we had help and done our best to get ready to fight the next day."

(US) William G. Putney, bugler, Barnett's Battery, Greusel's brigade, Sheridan's division:
"The ammunition wagons are brought up from the rear to replenish the empty limber chests."

(US) D.D. Holm, Simonson's Battery, Harris' brigade, Rousseau's division:
"There having been no opportunity on account of the scarcity of water to replenish . . . canteens since quite early in the morning details were sent a distance to the rear to fill the canteens; the drivers had orders to 'stand to horse,' and the cannoneers to remain at their posts."

(US) Chandler, Simonson's Battery, Harris' brigade, Rousseau's division:
"The night came in clear and cold."

Henry Villard, Northern newspaper correspondent:
"An almost full moon had arisen and lighted up the field very brightly."

(CS) William A. Bryant, 3rd Florida, Brown's brigade, Anderson's division:
"The night was a splendid moonlight night."

(CS) Graber, 8th Texas Cavalry, Wharton's brigade:
"An armistice was had by mutual consent, for . . . taking care of the wounded and burying the dead."

(US) Lt. James M. Randall, 21st Wisconsin, Starkweather's brigade, Rousseau's division:
"Details of men were made under charge of officers to visit the battlefield and look after the killed and wounded. These parties, both union and confederate met upon the field under a flag of truce."

(US) Sgt. Mead Holmes Jr., 21st Wisconsin, Starkweather's brigade, Rousseau's division:
"The captain said, 'Who will volunteer to carry off the dead?' Four or five of us started, laying off our arms, and carrying a handkerchief tied to a stick, for flag of truce."

(US) Lt. Randall, 21st Wisconsin, Starkweather's brigade, Rousseau's division:
"Lieut. Crawford of Co 'G' went upon the field without authority and voluntarily surrendered himself to the confederates and was paroled by them."

(US) Sgt. Holmes Jr., 21st Wisconsin, Starkweather's brigade, Rousseau's division:
"We found our poor major dead and stripped. . . . What a loss to us! Others were dead, and many wounded; I helped carry off four, and . . . I helped carry off one poor fellow with his mouth and lower jaw shot off. . . . (I) gave out from exhaustion. . . . The moon shone full upon the . . . sight, — men and horses dead and wounded, wagon-wheels, army caissons scattered, and the moans and shrieks of the wounded."

(US) George M. Kirkpatrick, 42nd Indiana, Lytle's brigade, Rousseau's division:
"Peter Truckee of Evansville, and I, went back onto the field in the moonlight, and we found . . . Captain Olmstead, slain in our sight that day."

(CS) Cannon, 45th Mississippi, Wood's brigade, Buckner's division:
"The full moon beaming down on upon the pale faces of the dead made it the more ghastly and sickening. . . . While hunting for ammunition I found Capt. Price, one of our brigade staff officers, who was mortally wounded, and procuring a stretcher, with the assistance of three others, carried him to the field hospital, which we found only after a very laborious tramp of more than a mile."

(CS) Capt. Bailey P. Steele, 1st Tennessee, Maney's brigade, Cheatham's division:
"Almost under the brass guns captured by the 1st Tennessee Regiment . . . (I) was lying desperately wounded. A Federal captain of . . . the 1st Wisconsin . . . came up in search of a friend. He expressed sorrow at . . . (my) condition, moved . . . (me) into a comfortable position, and gave . . . (me) water from a canteen."

(CS) Sam Watkins, 1st Tennessee, Maney's brigade, Cheatham's division:
"John T. Tucker, Scott Stephens, A.S. Horsley and I were detailed to bring off our wounded. . . . Friend and foe were lying dead and dying side by side. . . . Now and then a cluster of dead Yankees and close by a cluster of dead Rebels. . . . We gathered up the wounded and left the dead where they fell."

(CS) W.T. Grisham, 34th Mississippi, Jones' brigade, Anderson's division:
"We were ordered to pile up our dead and build a fence around them for burial. Eighteen were killed out of the right wing of the regiment."

(CS) Preston, 33rd Alabama, Wood's brigade, Buckner's division:
"We went in squads to where our dead friends lay to make sure we had got all their effects and examine more closely where they had been shot."

(CS) Watkins, 1st Tennessee, Maney's brigade, Cheatham's division:
"We helped to bring off many a poor dying comrade – John Thompson, Billy Bond, Byron Richardson, and the two Allen boys – brothers, killed side by side. . . . We helped bring off a man by the name of Hodge, with his under jaw shot off, and his tongue lolling out. We brought off Captain Lute B. Irvine. Lute was shot through the lungs and was vomiting blood . . . and begged us to lay him down and let him die. But Lute . . . (lived). Also, Lieutenant Woldridge, with both eyes shot out. I found him rambling in a briar-patch. . . . Lieutenant Thomas H. Maney was badly wounded. . . . I helped bring off Bill (Whitthorne) . . . a mere lad of 14 or 15 years."

(CS) Stephen J. Harrod, 33rd Mississippi, Wood's brigade, Buckner's division:
"I was among those picking up the dead and wounded . . . , and as I was barefooted and a Union soldier with good boots lay near by with a coat thrown over him, I decided to take the boots; but the supposed dead soldier shouted, Leave my boots alone, and I did."

(CS) Lt. James Iredell Hall, 9th Tennessee Robert Gates, 6th Tennessee, Cheatham's division:
"I had lost a good deal of blood and consequently was very much weakened and have not a very distinct recollection of how I was taken from the field. . . . Some of the boys who knew where I was lying came back to pick me up. . . . I remember being carried for a short distance by John William Calhoun on his back. . . . I remember being carried in an ambulance down the dry bed of a creek it seemed to me for a long, long distance."

(CS) Thomas B. Ellis, 3rd Florida, Brown's brigade, Anderson's division:
"Ambulances came and took me and Frank (Saxon) and others to a small farmhouse as Field Hospital."

(US) Poulson, 98th Ohio, Webster's brigade, Jackson's division:
"The rebels came with a wagon. . . . They asked me how I was wounded, and where; if my leg would have to come off, if I thought it would get well so that I could go into service again, if I would like to be in another battle, if I had had enough of fighting, and many such questions as these. All of which I answered readily. I told them if I ever got fit for duty again I wanted to have another chance at the rebels. To this one replied very crusty like 'We're not rebels, we're Confederates you damn yankee.' I am no yankee but a Union man, said I. They concluded to take me prisoner. . . . I asked them . . . how far it was to the hospital they were going to take me to. Three quarters of a mile was the answer. Two men lifted me up so that two who were in the wagon could reach me and take me in. One of the latter sat down and told me to lean against his breast, which I did; he then held me there as warmly and tenderly as my own brother could have done. He told one of the Union boys - there were four besides myself in the wagon - to hold my foot and keep my leg straight so as to keep the pieces of bone from cutting the flesh so as not to give me pain. He seemed very sorry that so many poor fellows were killed and wounded. He sympathized with me and even shed tears, some of which fell on me. He said he was a conscript and was forced into the Army. When we had traveled, I think, two miles they stopped to see if that hospital was full. The surgeon they said had as many men and more than could be attended to that night and the next day."

At Sheridan's Federal division, which had not been heavily engaged in the fighting:

(US) Putney, bugler, Barnett's Battery, Greusel's brigade, Sheridan's division:
"Campfires are built and the men gather round them to tell the incidents of the day. Some have little to eat, which they share with their comrades."

(US) Capt. Allen L. Fahenstock, 86th Illinois, McCook's brigade, Sheridan's division:
"All we had for Supper was a Small piece of Beef and Parched Corn."

(US) Robert M. Rogers, 125th Illinois, McCook's brigade, Sheridan's division:
"We had nothing to eat since the night before, . . . and after the fight was over, and the over-strung nerves began to relax, hunger took possession of us, and all set about the hunt for food. . . . (I) came across some boys who were carrying an immense piece of beef . . . , and . . . they donated a very considerable portion of it. Returning to the command . . . (I) divided with my partner, and fastening our share to a sharpened stick thrust it into a fire which was burning near by. . . . We were hungry, and although we had no salt or seasoning of any kind for our beef, we ate it with a relish. Our scant supper being finished, we sauntered off to glean from those we might meet, an account of the battle as they had seen it. The serious part of it was over, . . . and now the more comical side came up. To hear each one relate his feelings during the time we lay there under that rain of lead and iron, to hear the jokes that passed from one to the other, and to hear how the woods echoed with the shouts and laughter of our boys, feeling in their own minds that they had done their duty, was very diverting."

(US) Putney, bugler, Barnett's Battery, Greusel's brigade, Sheridan's division:
"The joke and the laugh goes round, and so with the warm coffee the spirits rise."

(US) Brig. Gen. Philip H. Sheridan, division commander:
"General Gilbert asked me to join him at Buell's headquarters (the Dorsey house), which were a considerable distance to the rear. So after making some dispositions for the evening I proceeded there as requested. I arrived just as Buell was about to sit down to his supper, and noticing he was lame, then learned that he had been severely injured by a recent fall from his horse. He kindly invited me to join him at the table, an invitation which I accepted with alacrity, enjoying the meal with a relish known only to a very-hungry man, for I had eaten nothing since morning. Of course the events of the day were the chief topic of discussion . . . but the conversation indicated that what had occurred was not fully realized, and I returned to my troops impressed with the belief that General Buell and his staff-officers were unconscious of the magnitude of the battle that had just been fought."

On the battlefield:

(US) Albion W. Tourgee, 105th Ohio, Terrill's Brigade, Jackson's division:
"Anxious groups went up and down our lines seeking their own commands or inquiring for friends."

(US) Cpl. George W. Morris, 81st Indiana, Caldwell's brigade, Mitchell's division:
"Soon after stacking our arms a number of the regiment started out to view the field. It was beautiful night – a clear sky and full moon. It was our first view of a field of battle, and it made us feel very sad. Before we advanced very far, we came across five of the enemy lying on the hillside dead. Their faces were very pale and the light of the moon glittered on their eyes. It was fearful to behold. We came to some who were wounded, and sitting around a small fire. Our boys talked with some of them, who seemed very friendly. On a battlefield, after a fight, human nature becomes milder and soldiers will give an enemy a drink of water."

Two Confederate officers return to the scene of earlier fighting that involved their unit:

(CS) W.L. Trask, adjutant, Austin's Sharpshooters, 14th Louisiana Battalion, Adams' brigade, Anderson's division:
"There in two straight lines as they had fallen when shot lay the (enemy) dead in such numbers, I could have walked on their bodies without touching the ground for several yards. Scarcely a man could be seen out of his place in the line, and they reminded me more of a wagon road than anything else I could compare them to. A few had crawled away in their agonies to die a little out of their proper line but nearly all seemed to have fallen in their tracks as they had stood and fought. . . . They were mostly of the 10th Ohio . . . of Lytle's Brigade. . . . Some were not quite dead, but all were beyond all human aid. I turned away from them with a feeling of awe and pity and went to visit other portions of the field."

Trask and his companion arrive at the Russell house, which had been used as a Federal field hospital until the Federal line was forced back:

(CS) Trask, adjutant, Austin's Sharpshooters, 14th Louisiana Battalion, Adams' brigade, Anderson's division:
"I (went) . . . to a farm house in front of where the enemy's battery had fought so long and stubbornly and where our own battery had done such fearful execution. The enemy had withdrawn after the firing ceased and left their dead and wounded behind. . . . In the yard several of the enemy's dead were lying – in the smoke house near by several more lay dead, having crawled there during the fight. . . . Several more were still groaning in the last agonies of death. Lieutenant Martin who had accompanied me helped two out of the smoke house into the yard where we gave them water and covered them with blankets. We then turned our attention to the main building. It had been used for a hospital by the enemy early in the fight and it was afterwards badly torn by our shot and shell.

"The surgeons had left in a hurry, their tables and instruments were scattered around. . . . A dozen dead and wounded still remained there some groaning piteously. Among them was a boy of not more than twelve summers, badly wounded in the thigh. He begged us to carry him inside our lines where he might never see

Russell house: The home of John Calvin Russell is the "white house" referred to in many accounts of the battle. Federal doctors used it as a field hospital during the battle and for about two weeks afterward. According to family tradition, Russell's 17-year-old daughter, Isaphena, used a pitchfork to load the piles of amputated arms and legs into a wagon. Two loads were hauled away and plowed under on the farm. The Russell house burned in 1964.

another Yankee. He said his father was a Southern soldier in General Morgan's command, that . . . (Federals) had forced him with them, and made him fight against his will. While Martin was holding him in his arms he became sick and vomited. Martin then laid him on the grass, (and) covered him with a blanket. . . .

"We next visited other portions of the field coming to several more of the enemy's wounded. We gave them water, covered them with blankets, and passed on. We came to the 'Simonton Ohio Battery' which we had captured. We found the cannon still on the ground in the same position it had last occupied in the battle. Ammunition was scattered every where in profusion and confusion. Twenty or more dead horses lay near by. Many more wounded stood around in groups, and a number of dead artillerists lay in a row, side by side, close by.

"Noticing a man leaning on his elbow not far off, I rode up to him. . . . I asked the wounded man if he wanted water, he replied that he did and after drinking he seemed grateful. He told me he had a wife and two sweet children in 'Ohio' – that he was wounded in the bowels and knew that he could not live until morning. He complained of cold and we placed two blankets over him."

(CS) Graber, 8th Texas Cavalry, Wharton's brigade:
"After dark we tied our horses in the edge of a woods, to a rail fence which enclosed a large corn field, where the desperate fighting stopped. As the most of the corn was destroyed by the lines of battle, we had to pass over a good deal of ground to get sufficient corn for our horses. At the point where I stopped gathering, having . . . as many ears of corn as I could carry in my arms, the dead lay so thick I believe I could have stepped from one to the other within a radius of ten or fifteen feet. Among them I noticed . . . a magnificent looking man lying on his back with his eyes open, seemingly looking at the starry firmament. Noticing that he wore an officer's suit, I turned up his collar which disclosed two stars, denoting his rank as lieutenant-colonel. I afterwards learned that he commanded a Tennessee regiment in Cheatham's Division."

(CS) Marcus B. Toney, 1st Tennessee, Maney's brigade, Cheatham's division:
"After getting all the wounded off, with the reflected rays from a burning barn, . . . I sat by (Robert S. Hamilton's) . . . dead body and . . . penned the following: 'BATTLEFIELD, PERRYVILLE Ky., October 8, 1862. Mrs. W. C. Hamilton, Lexington, Ky.: Robert was killed in gallant charge this evening. Will take care of remains until you arrive. MARCUS B. TONEY.' Mrs. Hamilton was Robert's sister-in-law, and I wrote to her because his brother, W. C. Hamilton, was a Union man, and Robert never wrote a line to him; but all his correspondence was with his sister-in-law, and he always read her letters to me. . . . The blue and the gray mingled together all that night removing the wounded. I approached one of the blue and asked him if he would deliver the note to Mrs. Hamilton, and he promised me that he would."

(US) William H. McCleary, 42nd Indiana, Lytle's brigade, Rousseau's division:
"About 9 oclock PM . . . our men hauling off the wounded as fast as they could to the hospitals the men almost exhausted for want of water and food having nothing to eat all day."

(US) Wallace P. Benson, 36th Illinois, Greusel's brigade, Sheridan's division:
"Nearly two hundred wounded were at the hospital, where I was taken, with all manner of wounds."

(US) Knowles, 1st Wisconsin, Starkweather's brigade, Rousseau's division:
"My wound proved to be slight, and after washing off the blood with which I was well smeared, I felt about as good as new, except that I was a little groggy. I slept in a field hospital yard that night."

A Federal artilleryman who had taken a wounded comrade to a field hospital earlier returns to check on his friend:

(US) Ormond Hupp, Simonson's Battery, Harris' brigade, Rousseau's division:
"(Countz) stayed with me the rest of the night, telling me all he knew concerning the battle – the loss in the battery was two killed, sixteen wounded and twenty horses killed and that the rebels held the field. He thought the fight would open in the morning, as preparations were being made for the same."

Behind the Confederate line, a wagon carrying wounded Federal prisoners continues to search for a field hospital where the men can be treated:

(US) Poulson, 98th Ohio, Webster's brigade, Jackson's division:
"The driver stopped at every hospital . . . till we had gone five and a half miles, and the house and yard was full nearly of wounded rebels. This contained the only Union boys for this house. I was taken to the porch and laid on it. The rebels formed a circle around me and quizzed me for two hours I think. The surgeon tried to make me drink a half pint of whiskey but could not succeed. I was too anxious to see and know what was going on, for to get drunk. . . . I told them I was a temperance man and intended to be one until I died, be that time long or short. Most of the rebels got very drunk and such a wicked set of men I never was with before and do not desire to be again. As far as acts were concerned they had used me well, and in speaking they used very rough language, but it appeared to be natural for them."

Many Confederate wounded are brought to the Goodnight home:

(CS) Toney, 1st Tennessee, Maney's brigade, Cheatham's division:
"Dr. Buist had taken possession of a house some half a mile from the battlefield, owned by a man named Goodnight, who had deserted it on the eve of battle. . . . We turned it into a hospital."

(CS) Chaplain Joseph Cross, Donelson's Brigade, Cheatham's division:
"My hands and clothes are besmeared with blood. . . . Nothing is heard but the rumbling of the ambulances, the groans of the sufferers, the slash of the surgeon's knife, and the harsher sound of the saw."

NIGHT ON THE BATTLEFIELD

(CS) Charles Quintard, surgeon and chaplain, 1st Tennessee, Maney's brigade, Cheatham's division:
"It was a horrible night. . . . I suppose excitement kept me up."

(CS) Lt. W.R. Moore, 5th Tennessee, Stewart's brigade, Cheatham's division:
"We got to the . . . (Goodnight) hospital after dark. I laid on the yard that night, the house being full before I got there."

(CS) Toney, 1st Tennessee, Maney's brigade, Cheatham's division:
"We expected to bury W. J. Whitthorne, of the Maury Grays, Columbia, Tenn."

(CS) Quintard, surgeon and chaplain, 1st Tennessee, Maney's brigade, Cheatham's division:
"(The) stripling of fifteen years fell in the battle apparently dead, shot through the neck and collar-bone."

(CS) Toney, 1st Tennessee, Maney's brigade, Cheatham's division:
"Billy Whitthorne, as we all called him, (lived). . . . In the . . . small . . . upper room were two beds. . . . We took off the mattresses, thus making room for . . . T. H. Woldridge, B. P. Steele, T. H. Maney, M. B. Pilcher, Mac Campbell, Lute Irwin, I. H. Wheless, and Lieutenant Hammond. These eight men were my patients. Four of them were on the bedsteads and four on the floor. Comrade Woldridge lost both of his eyes and Captain Pilcher, Captain Steele, Lieutenant Maney, Mac Campbell, and Lute Irwin were all badly wounded."

(CS) Chaplain Cross, Donelson's Brigade, Cheatham's division:
"A young man of the Sixteenth (Tennessee), with his shoulder shattered, comes to have his wound dressed. He reports . . . Colonel Savage badly wounded and trying to get off the field. I mount . . . and hasten to his help. After riding about two miles, I meet a company of Yankee prisoners; and close behind them, on horseback, moving very slowly, comes the Colonel. 'Well, Doctor,' he cries with a cheerful voice, 'I have

Goodnight house: Confederates used Jacob Goodnight's home and grounds as a field hospital during the battle. Confederates who died there were buried in the Goodnight family cemetery. The house no longer stands.

got all my wounded men off the field, I believe; and now I am coming off myself.' 'Are you badly hurt, Colonel?' I ask. 'Not much, I think,' he replies; 'shot through the calf of the leg; no bones broken but poor old George has had a ball through his head, and I have to ride slowly.' I discover that his horse is bleeding profusely, and staggering beneath his burden. I propose to exchange with him but he . . . (declines) the offer. 'Old George has a good constitution,' he says; 'I think he will hold out on me.' . . . In half an hour we were at the surgeon's quarters. I helped the Colonel down; pulled off his boot; it was full of blood. The surgeon dressed his wound, and he mounted old George again. . . . We rode two miles farther, and stopped at an unoccupied house. I found a straw bed, laid the Colonel upon it, and tied old George to the fence."

A Confederate staff officer trying to find Cheatham's headquarters doesn't realize the road he is following leads into the Federal line:

(CS) Thomas Claiborne, Buckner's staff:
"I . . . soon rode into a large number of very excited soldiers who were evidently discussing the day's fight and disaster. The woods in which the road ran had not shed its leaves. The light of the moon fell through . . . their limbs. It made my uniform unrecognizable. 'What soldiers are you?' I said as I came on them. 'Buell's,' several answered. 'All right! Please let my horse move forward,' and I passed through the crowd and beyond it, turned widely to my left, and rode into General Polk's headquarters. Here I found an aid of General Bragg's in search of me. Thence we rode to Bragg's headquarters, who sharply questioned me about the report that the enemy had turned his left. I reaffirmed (it) . . . , yet he was incredulous until word was presently brought him that the Washington Artillery caissons, going to the old camp for ammunition, had fallen into the enemy's hands."

At Federal headquarters:

Villard, newspaper correspondent:
"General Buell . . . decided to make a general attack . . . at daylight. . . . The corps commanders were sent for to receive their instructions . . . Troops at the front were kept moving into proper positions for the onset in the morning."

(US) Michael H. Fitch, 21st Wisconsin, Starkweather's brigade, Rousseau's division:
"A new line of battle was selected still farther in the rear, in a rising wood."

(US) Sgt. Holmes Jr., 21st Wisconsin, Starkweather's brigade, Rousseau's division:
"Soon we were moved, and . . . we went silently."

(US) Fitch, 21st Wisconsin, Starkweather's brigade, Rousseau's division:
"The twenty-first passed in the dead stillness of night . . . through the enclosure of a country house which had been made a hospital. The yard was literally covered with the wounded, dead and dying. The dead silence was broken by the most painful groans of the wounded. A halt happened to leave the twenty-first in this yard for a few moments, where the men could look and learn the dire results of war and exposure."

(US) Davis, 21st Wisconsin, Starkweather's brigade, Rousseau's division:
"We were moved from place to place during the night in preparation for renewal of the conflict next morning."

A Federal brigade on the northern edge of Perryville gets orders to pull back:

(US) Brig. Gen. William P. Carlin, brigade commander, Mitchell's division:
"About 9 o'clock that night Gen. Mitchell came to me and ordered me to return towards my former position about a mile."

(US) L.W. Day, 101st Ohio, Carlin's brigade, Mitchell's division:
"We halted for the night near an old house used as a general hospital. . . . Surgeons of both armies were very busy. . . . Doubtless they were kind-hearted and careful, but to us it seemed like brutality. There were several piles of amputated limbs, to which accessions were being made constantly. Dead and dying men were lying promiscuously around. Others were awaiting their turn to be thrown upon the operating table, an old work-bench, while still others were being bandaged and patched up in various ways and assigned to this hospital or that. . . . Some seemed to be resigned, others were cross and snappy. Some prayed; some cursed; some were silent and grim as death; others were noisy and almost violent. . . . Deep heartrending groans now and again . . . betokened suffering beyond expression."

The strain of fighting and the sights and sounds of the battlefield have worn many soldiers out:

(US) Holm, Simonson's Battery, Harris' brigade, Rousseau's division:
"The men were greatly exhausted and . . . not having had any opportunity to eat anything since early morning . . . lay down besides their teams and were soon utterly unconscious of their surroundings."

(US) McCleary, 42nd Indiana, Lytle's brigade, Rousseau's division:
"We lay down . . . on the ground without blankets or napsacks but being so exhausted we would lay anywhere."

(US) Capt. Fahenstock, 86th Illinois, McCook's brigade, Sheridan's division:
"We Laid down on the hard Rocks with No . . . Covering. . . . Dead Men Laying by Our Sides."

Some soldiers, however, are too close to the Confederate line to rest easy:

(US) Col. John Beatty, commanding 3rd Ohio, Lytle's brigade, Rousseau's division:
"The enemy is in the woods before us, and as the sentinels occasionally exchange shots, we can see the flash of their guns and hear the whistle of bullets over our heads. The two armies are too near to sleep comfortably, or even safely, so the boys cling to their muskets and keep ready for action."

(CS) Capt. C.W. Frazer, 5th Confederate, Johnson's brigade, Buckner's Division:
"The armies rested, the picket lines in places being not a hundred yards apart."

(US) Tourgee, 105th Ohio, Terrill's Brigade, Jackson's division:
"Campfires shone . . . here and there, and watchful pickets sent a challenging shot . . . now and then. . . . Came the steady rumble of wheels and hoarse tones of command. We thought the enemy were preparing to renew the attack."

(US) Chandler, Simonson's Battery, Harris' brigade, Rousseau's division:
"All silent except the tread of men the rumble of wheels or the groans of the wounded and an occasional shot would ring out clear and sharp in the night air."

(US) Tourgee, 105th Ohio, Terrill's Brigade, Jackson's division:
"Long past midnight the detail sent out for water returned with full canteens. It was the first water we had tasted since the fight began."

(US) Winters, 50th Ohio, Webster's brigade, Jackson's division:
"All through the night I could hear the poor, wounded boys calling for water."

(US) Davis, 21st Wisconsin, Starkweather's brigade, Rousseau's division:
"I well remember the pitiful cry for water from the parched mouths of our wounded and dying comrades when we had none to give. The only time in my life I gave thanks for a mouthful of whiskey was when . . . Jack Glass, our co. teamster, brought to us some canteens full of whiskey, enough to give each comrade a mouthful, which when I took a mouthful dissolved the powder in my mouth caused from biting the cartridges and that whiskey . . . was a blessing without disguise."

(US) Tourgee, 105th Ohio, Terrill's Brigade, Jackson's division:
"Would we fight upon the morrow or not? We waited anxiously for the day to break, for the sun to rise."

(US) Rogers, 125th Illinois, McCook's brigade, Sheridan's division:
"(I was) suddenly awakened by a noise, and on rising up could see by the light of the moon that our supply train had come up, and that Sergeant Cole, who had command of it, was unloading the wagons. . . . Giving . . . (my) partner a punch, . . . (I) told him it was time for breakfast, so up we got and made for the nearest pile of hard-tack. We filled our haversacks, and taking a goodly number in our hands, beat a retreat to our blankets. Lying on the ground we munched our biscuits, and felt thankful that we were still alive."

Elsewhere on the battlefield:

(CS) Preston, 33rd Alabama, Wood's brigade, Buckner's division:
"Although we were thoroughly tired out, . . . we were up with the wounded boys and assisting the doctors nearly all night. . . . Some complained of being cold. . . . We wrapped our blankets about them."

(CS) Carroll H. Clark, 16th Tennessee, Donelson's brigade, Cheatham's division:
"The moaning and sighing of the wounded and dying that night were heart-rending."

(CS) Capt. Frazer, 5th Confederate, Johnson's brigade, Buckner's Division:
"Lying among the dead and wounded, exhausted by forty-eight hours of constant duty, I heard with the death-gurgle the words known wherever Masons are. I answered, and sent through a priest to an Ohio sister the last words of a brother. . . . – The last drop of water from my canteen was on his tongue."

(CS) Orderly Sgt. William A. Brown, Stanford's Mississippi Battery, Stewart's brigade, Cheatham's division:
"The ambulances were running all through the night, bringing off the dead and wounded. At any hour during that night we could hear the cries of pain from the wounded as they were jolted over rough roads."

A Confederate shot with a ramrod is found where he had collapsed while trying to find his way to a field hospital:

(CS) Haguewood, 5th Tennessee, Stewart's brigade, Cheatham's division:
"Was put on ordnance wagon and carried to Haroldsburg, Ky."

After visiting areas where his unit had fought during the day, a Confederate and his companion find their bivouac:

(CS) Trask, adjutant, Austin's Sharpshooters, 14th Louisiana Battalion, Adams' brigade, Anderson's division:
"It was now 11 PM and after reaching our comrades we made a cup of fresh coffee, supplied from Yankee haversacks, talked a while with some prisoners who were lying around loosely among us, apparently perfectly at home, and then we laid down to rest and sleep. The moon shone down upon us in great brilliancy and I took advantage of it to read a 'St. Louis Republican,' picked up on the field and the first newspaper I had seen for weeks, and also the first northern one, for months."

(CS) James K.P. Blackburn, 8th Texas Cavalry:
"I was without a bedfellow that night, and as the nights were frosty I looked out for some other person to get the benefit of his blanket for a covering while mine should be spread on the ground for the pallet. We only had one blanket each, hence the necessity of having a partner. ... Many dead of both armies (were) lying around. The wounded had been removed, or most of them. ... I found Sam Woodward of my company with a good blanket and no bedfellow for the night, and we soon arranged to bunk together. I said, 'Sam, you look for a place as smooth as you can find, ... and we will fix for bed.' In fifteen or twenty minutes he came to me and said, 'I have found a fairly good place, but there are two dead men on it.' I said, 'They are as dead as they will ever be, are they not?' He said, 'Yes,' and I said, 'Then we will remove them a little space and occupy their place.' He said, 'All right,' and we went to the spot selected and turned one man over one way and the other the other way — they were lying parallel with each other —, (and) made our bed between them. ... One dead was a Confederate and (the) other one a Federal soldier. ... Some of our boys, nearly barefooted, were searching around among the dead for footwear. ... Mullins of Company D found a good pair of boots on ... another ranger who was asleep among the dead. He immediately decided the boots would suit, grabbed one of them, and jerked it off Wheeler's foot. This aroused Wheeler to consciousness and he called out, 'What in the h-ll are you doing there?' 'Nothing, d—n you, I thought you were dead and I needed those boots.' "

Back at the Goodnight house field hospital:

(CS) Lt. Hall, 9th Tennessee, Maney's brigade, Cheatham's division:
"It must have been nearly midnight before we reached the (Goodnight) hospital. The surgeons on examination pronounced my wound necessarily mortal, and I was placed on the ground under an apple tree between two men whose wounds were similar to mine. A liberal dose of morphine was given to each one of us and I remember its soothing effect on me. The other two men were suffering internally from their wounds and knowing that my wound was similar to theirs kept me awake for along time by asking me such questions as 'how I felt,' and 'whether I thought I could last through the night.' I finally got to sleep."

(CS) Toney, 1st Tennessee, Maney's brigade, Cheatham's division:
"John Sullivan('s) ... wife accompanied him to the war, and was very, valuable in assisting the boys in needlework and cooking. ... She was a buxom Irish woman of 250 pounds and could march and do any kind of work. At Perryville John Sullivan had part of his skull shot off. ... (The) hole in his forehead ... exposed a part of the brain. Mrs. Sullivan was at the hospital ... when we reported after midnight that John was left on the field for dead. ... She said, 'Be Jesus, I will go to him myself,' and she did and brought John ... on her shoulder ... to the Goodnight Hospital."

While Confederate doctors tend to Sullivan, who will live despite the head wound,
Federal surgeons at the Wilkerson house field hospital finally get to a wounded officer who
has been waiting since about dark:

(US) Capt. Robert B. Taylor, Garrard's battalion, Terrill's brigade, Jackson's division:
"After remaining in the hospital until 12 o'clock ... I had my wound dressed and was discharged, ... not being allowed to leave the yard – I found in the grounds around the house many officers and men in my condition 'lightly wounded.' – The moon ... was high up ... shedding its brilliance over the scene. ... I sat down upon the steps of the hospital, and gazed up into the face of the moon in thankfulness, and gratitude to its maker for bringing me through ... that day in safety. I had been seated at the door step about half an hour ..., when a surgeon told an officer in my hearing as he came out of the house 'that General Terrill had just died.' ... I for a moment was staggered by the news, and begged the Surgeon to tell me the particulars of his death. ... He informed me that General Terrill had been struck on the breast with a shell, ... ; and that in the explosion of the shell, the entire left breast was torn from his body, that he had been brought to this hospital, and after lingering there died of his wounds but a few minutes since. ... I was detailed at 1 o'clock (a.m.) to go in command of a detachment of men and four ambulances up to the Battlefield, about 400 yards distant, to assist the wounded off the field to the various hospitals. ... There were already five or

six parties . . . on the field and every step we made toward the front we met an ambulance returning slowly . . . with its groaning brethren. We continued at this work until late the next morning."

(US) Adam S. Johnston, 79th Pennsylvania, Starkweather's brigade, Rousseau's division:
"Was hauled from off the battle-ground in an ambulance wagon at half past two in the morning for fear of the enemy opening fire on our hospital or old house in which we remained all night . . . ; having our batteries planted close by, if another engagement would ensue, they would draw the enemy's fire on our building. So we, four in number, were hauled five miles this morning to Antioch church, . . . and thrown out in a pile like wood, for they had been removing wounded off the battle-ground all night until the church was perfectly filled, and under every shade tree nigh at hand. I rolled over and over, as I was so disabled that I could not walk, until I got to a fence, and with loss of blood and pain and fatigue, became sleepy in a short time."

At the Wilkerson house field hospital:

(US) Dr. S.K. Crawford, regimental surgeon, 50th Ohio, Webster's brigade, Jackson's division:
"No medicines, no dressings, no rations, was the awful fact that had to be faced. . . . (I) was ordered . . . to remain and take care of all that were found living when morning should come."

At a Confederate field hospital on the battlefield:

(US) Poulson, 98th Ohio, Webster's brigade, Jackson's division:
"I did not sleep very much that night. I was suffering . . . all night - my leg was very painful indeed. They furnished me plenty of water and I kept it wet and cool as possible, for I knew the cooler I could keep it the better it would be for me."

Several miles from the battlefield, in Springfield, a weary businessman who had visited the battlefield is awakened by a commotion at his house:

E.L. Davison, Springfield merchant:
"About 1 o'clock (a.m.), I was aroused and looking out saw an ambulance and five or six men coming into the yard through the big gate. I was soon up and found I knew all of the men. They were friends of mine and my wife. They said in the ambulance was . . . Gen. James S. Jackson, who had been my College friend for several years. He had fallen in battle and the officers were taking his remains to Louisville.

"I went out to the cabin and aroused the servants to take and feed their horses. There I met my wife arousing the cooks and in short time they were cooking supper.

"On returning to the house I stopped at the ambulance and looked at the coffin that contained my friend and thought of the happy days we had spent together. Now he was gone never to be seen again. This made me feel very sad. Hearing loud laughing and talking, in the house, I went in and found the men around the side-board mixing toddies and guying each other about how they acted in battle. My wife soon had supper ready and I never saw men eat so much, some of them eating ten and twelve biscuits. They got off about 4 o'clock."

Earlier in the night, Bragg, the Confederate commander, concludes a second Federal corps is at hand, and it will certainly attack his weary and wounded army in the morning. Bragg orders a retreat, to begin after midnight, to the army's position before the battle. The artillery will quietly pull out first, followed by the infantry:

(CS) Cannon, 45th Mississippi, Wood's brigade, Buckner's division:
"When we had delivered our charge at the hospital it was 10 o'clock, and we hoped to rest and sleep the remainder of the night; but the army was already in motion, and we had to fall in and march till 1 a.m., when we bivouacked in a creek bottom where the timber had been cleared off and not a stick of wood left for us to make fires. We had stripped to our shirts for the fight, and sent off blankets, coats and all other baggage to the wagons that morning, not expecting to be caught out on a frosty night in such light apparel. . . . We piled together on the damp ground, shivered and slept short naps."

(CS) John Euclid Magee, Stanford's Mississippi Battery, Stewart's brigade, Cheatham's division:
"Up at 2 o'clock – expected to renew the battle."

(CS) Trask, adjutant, Austin's Sharpshooters, 14th Louisiana Battalion, Adams' brigade, Anderson's division:
"We were quietly aroused, told to make as little noise as possible and prepare to march at once. We all felt sure the object was to make a night attack on the enemy's flank."

(CS) Col. Miller, 1st Florida, Brown's brigade, Anderson's division:
"At two o'clock in the morning . . . McCook's (Federal) corps . . . (was) a quarter of a mile distant across the open ground, their camp fires burning brightly."

(CS) Orderly Sgt. Brown, Stanford's Mississippi Battery, Stewart's brigade, Cheatham's division:
"Before daylight, at 3 AM, . . . we were . . . ready to march, or fight as the case might be – we expected a fight."

(CS) Headley, Austin's Sharpshooters, 14th Louisiana Battalion, Adams' Brigade, Anderson's division:
"We reached the Harrodsburg Turnpike, a mile from Perryville, soon after daylight."

(CS) Trask, adjutant, Austin's Sharpshooters, 14th Louisiana Battalion, Adams' brigade, Anderson's division:
"We were much disappointed when we found ourselves back at the position we had left in the morning and were ordered to stack arms again. It was now 4 AM nearly daybreak."

(CS) Headley, Austin's Sharpshooters, 14th Louisiana Battalion, Adams' Brigade, Anderson's division:
"Taking leave of Major Austin and his friends I mounted my horse and made my way along the pike to rejoin my (cavalry) company."

(CS) Col. Miller, 1st Florida, Brown's brigade, Anderson's division:
"We became aware that the army had retreated, and our brigade which had received no orders was alone in front of the enemy. The men were quietly aroused, formed in line and without noise moved over the battlefield to the Perryville and Harrodsburg road."

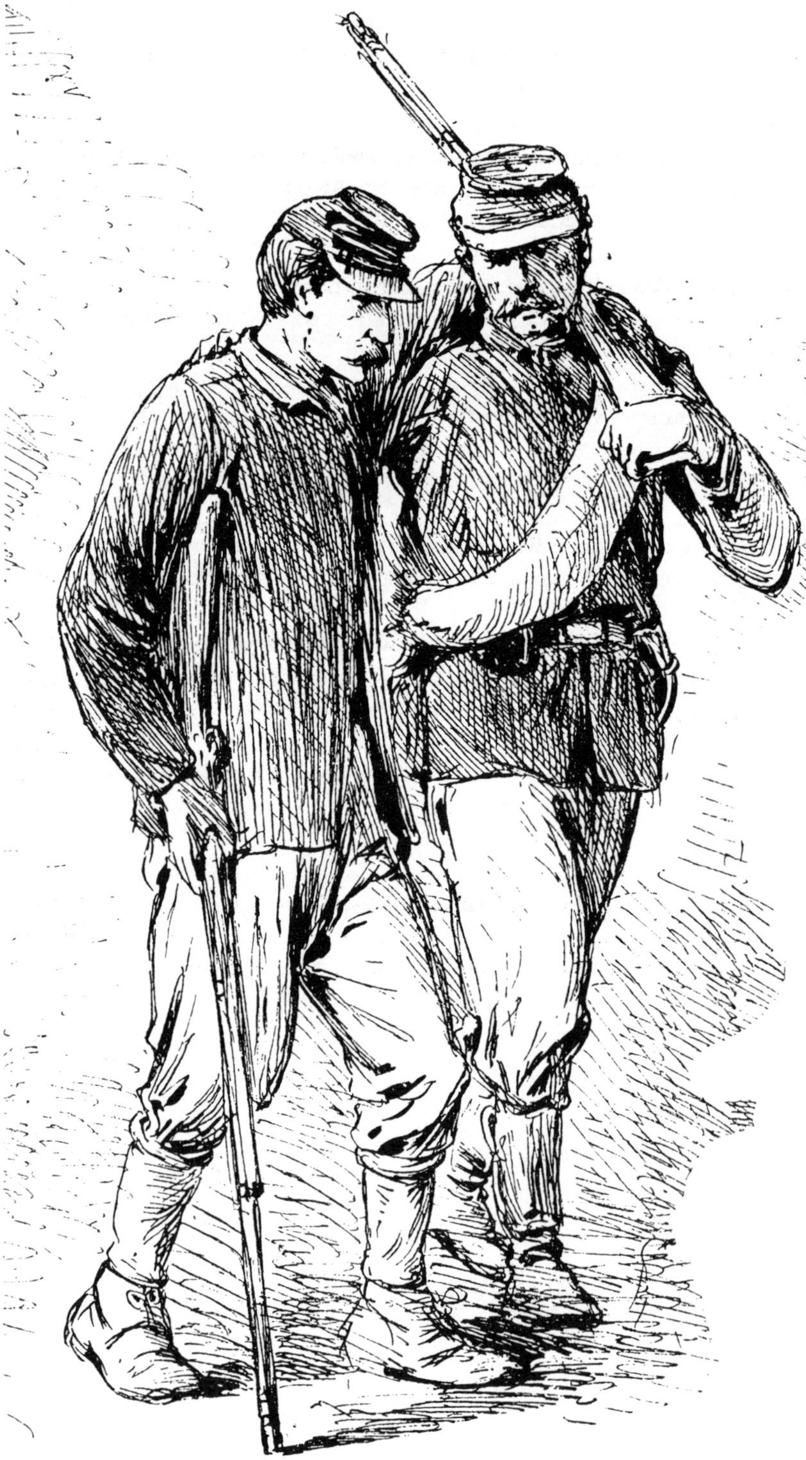

CONFEDERATES RETREAT

Buell expects the Confederates to stay and fight again, so his corps commanders have orders to unite and attack in the morning:

(US) Lars O. Dokken, 15th Wisconsin, Carlin's brigade, Mitchell's division:
"At 3 a.m. we were roused and assembled in fighting lines and marched forward."

At Buell's headquarters:

Henry Villard, newspaper correspondent:
"When I was aroused at four, I found that nobody else at headquarters had slept. A light breakfast was ready, at which I learned from the staff that, since one o'clock, several reports had come in from our picket-lines that continuous noises had been heard indicating the movement of artillery and trains and a general retreat of the enemy. . . . This was not considered satisfactory news."

To the west of Perryville, on a farm just north of Springfield:

William Caldwell McChord, 12:
"It was generally understood that the battle would continue. . . . I determined to see it, and Nat Wickliffe, a cousin from Bardstown, who was about 17 years old and was always in for any sort of excitement, had been spending several weeks at our house. When about 4 o'clock in the morning, after a hasty breakfast, we started to the scene of the battle. I was riding my faithful Flash; Nat, his horse Blucher, . . . and my brother Al, riding his gray eagle mare. Thus we started out, each with a navy revolver under his coat."

In Federal lines on the battlefield:

(US) Sgt. Mead Holmes Jr., 21st Wisconsin, Starkweather's brigade, Rousseau's division:
"We slept till sunrise; I expected to see it rise for the last time, for I supposed at daylight we should pitch in till death or victory were ours."

(US) Capt. John W. Tuttle, 3rd Kentucky, Hascall's brigade, Wood's division:
"Rose from my earthly couch this morning in a capital frame of mind and body for the desperate struggle we expected to go into."

(US) Robert M. Rogers, 125th Illinois, McCook's brigade, Sheridan's division:
"We awoke at reveille in the morning, refreshed. . . . Fires were made, and the air was soon filled with the aroma of coffee."

At a field hospital behind the Federal battle line:

(US) Ormond Hupp, Simonson's Battery, Terrill's brigade, Jackson's division:
"Orders came that all those that could must get back two miles toward Maxville to a large meeting house that had been converted into a hospital. Our company ambulance happened to come along . . . and I got in and was taken back."

At the Antioch church field hospital on the Mackville Road:

(US) Adam S. Johnston, 79th Pennsylvania, Starkweather's brigade, Rousseau's division:
"I . . . slept until after the sun was up, and on awaking I found myself completely tight against the . . . fence, on account of another wounded soldier dying while I was asleep, with his feet tight down the hill against me and his head up the hill, the ground being somewhat rolling. I called a citizen close by, that had come to see the wounded soldiers, to come to me and remove the dead man that I might help myself up by the fence. He removed the person, and threw a blanket over the body."

At the Goodnight home, being used as a Confederate field hospital:

(CS) Charles Quintard, surgeon and chaplain, 1st Tennessee, Maney's brigade, Cheatham's division:
"About half past five in the morning . . . I dropped, - I could do no more. I went out by myself and leaning against a fence, I wept like a child. And all that day I was so unnerved that if any one asked me about the regiment, I could make no reply without tears. . . . Having taken off my shirt to tear into strips to make bandages, I took a severe cold."

(CS) Lt. James Iredell Hall, 9th Tennessee, Maney's brigade, Cheatham's division:
"When I awoke . . . I had a corpse at each elbow. The men had died while I slept. Contrary to the predictions of the surgeons I was still alive."

Elsewhere in the Confederate lines:

(CS) Capt. Robert D. Smith, ordnance officer, 2nd Tennessee, Cleburne's brigade:
"I happened to pass Genl. Bragg's headquarters, and saw Generals Bragg, Polk, Hardee, Buckner, Cheatham, and Anderson holding a council of war. In a few moments we were ordered to fall back to Harrodsburg."

(CS) James K. P. Blackburn, 8th Texas Cavalry, Wharton's brigade:
"John P. Humphries . . . needed footwear and went out after daylight to see what were the chances. He found a Yankee, dead, sitting against a tree, with a good pair of shoes. John got down on his knees to take off the fellow's shoes and, just as he got one unlaced and ready to pull off, took another glance at the Yankee's face and the Yankee winked at him. He left the shoes on his dead man and came to camp and told it, and laughing that peculiar laugh, said he didn't want any shoes anyway."

(CS) Sam Watkins, 1st Tennessee, Maney's brigade, Cheatham's division:
"About daylight a wounded comrade, Sam Campbell, (had) complained of being cold, and asked me to lie down beside him. I did so, and was soon asleep; when I awoke the poor fellow was stiff and cold in death."

A Confederate chaplain calls on a wounded officer he had tended a few hours earlier and left in a home near the battlefield:

(CS) Chaplain Joseph Cross, Donelson's Brigade, Cheatham's division:
"Colonel (Savage) was comfortable, and old George was alive, though the ground where he stood was saturated with blood. The Colonel remounted, and old George carried him eight miles, to Harrodsburg."

(CS) Lt. W.R. Moore, 5th Tennessee, Stewart's brigade, Cheatam's division:
"The surgeon dressed my wound (this) . . . morning, put me in an ambulance and started to Harrodsburg,"

At a house being used as a Confederate field hospital:

(US) Wesley S. Poulson, 98th Ohio, Webster's brigade, Jackson's division:
"My leg was swollen badly and the Rebel surgeon said it would have to be taken off. He was preparing to amputate it after breakfast, but when about ready to begin the operation there was an order that came for them to be ready to march in a few minutes. They prepared for marching as soon as possible. . . . They were in a great hurry seemingly much excited. . . . There was a colonel . . . who attended to paroling us. Two besides myself were paroled on one paper and the parole was written with a lead pencil. I did not care anything about it and just told one of the boys named Henderson to keep it if it would do him any good — he was slightly wounded in the left thigh —. There were two more Union boys at this place who were not paroled on account of time I judged."

(CS) Carroll H. Clark, 16th Tennessee, Donelson's brigade, Cheatham's division:
"The severely wounded could not be carried away. . . . All the wounded who could be moved, were carried up to Harrodsburg, 10 miles from Perryville."

(CS) William E. M. Preston, 33rd Alabama, Wood's brigade, Buckner's division:
"Leaving the . . . wounded on beds of wheat straw, where we had got them together the night before, (we left) J. Seaborn Lisenby of Co. B to nurse them."

(CS) Dr. David J. Noblitt, assistant surgeon, 44th Tennessee, Johnson's brigade, Buckner's Division:
"(I) remained at the Prewitt house with the wounded that were not able to be moved."

(CS) Maj. Gen. Benjamin F. Cheatham, division commander:
"Every man of my command (had) brought from the battle-field . . . two guns – muskets – each, hoping to find transportation to haul them off . . . . As our wounded filled all our extra wagons, they were left on the ground in a line the length of the command. . . . I left . . . about sunrise, after filling all my wagons with my wounded; the balance were left in the old house and the fence-corners. Dr. Buist was left in charge of them, he built shelters over them with brush and corn-stalks to keep the sun off."

Elsewhere, the army is preparing to pull out for Harrodsburg:

(CS) W. L. Trask, adjutant, Austin's Sharpshooters, 14th Louisiana Battalion, Adams' brigade:
"At sunrise . . . our battalion was thrown forward as skirmishers."

(CS) Orderly Sgt. William A. Brown, Stanford's Mississippi Battery, Stewart's brigade, Cheatham's division:
"A little before day we moved out and fell into columns with the infantry. . . . At daylight there was some appearance of another fight; the infantry was drawn up in line, but this was only to hold the Federal at bay while our wagon trains were getting out of the way. We soon broke into columns and took the pike to Harrodsburg. . . . As soon as we broke into columns of march it became plain that there would be no fight that day. Lt. McCall requested that I go with him to the field hospital at which I had left his brother the day before.

"We soon found the place, but the ambulances, wagons, and surgeons were all gone. Only the dead, and those for whom there was no hope of life, were left. We dismounted and walked among the straightened forms. It was truly a 'bivouac of the dead,' those pale silent sleepers on that quiet October morning. The site was away from the line of march, and not even a straggling soldier disturbed the stillness of this place. Silently we passed among the dead, or paused beside those whose breathing told that they lived and must soon be as hushed as those around them. We went to the tree under which I had left the wounded man the day before. I stopped by the side of a blanket which showed the outline of a man under it. The lieutenant understood my meaning and silently drew away the blanket from the face of the sleeper. He looked on the face of his dead brother, gazed at him for a moment, and then burst into tears as he knelt on the ground by his brother's side. I left him to his dead, silently remounted my horse and rode back to the company. I could offer no further consolation. . . . Even his brother had to leave him for strangers, perhaps enemies, to consign the fallen soldier to his final resting place."

At a house where several wounded Federals have been left by the Confederates:

(US) Poulson, 98th Ohio, Webster's brigade, Jackson's division:
"About 10 o'clock not a Rebel was to be seen. . . . When all had been quiet a short time the owner of the house — who had been forced to leave it — came, and he staid there to wait on us. He brought us food the best he could get, supplied us with water, talked friendly to us and did all in his power to make us comfortable. He said he was a Union man and I believe he was. He said he owned no slaves and was opposed to the institution of slavery. I expected to lie there on that porch until mortification would take place in my leg and kill me. I was satisfied that our men were busy enough, at Perryville, attending to the wounded there and I did not think they would come out soon enough to do anything for me."

Federal troops advance warily over the quiet battlefield:

(US) Charles L. Francis, 88th Illinois, Greusel's brigade, Sheridan's division:
"We were expecting to renew the engagement and advanced."

(US) Surgeon John Tilford, 79th Indiana, Beatty's brigade, VanCleve's division:
"Moved in line of battle through woods and fields, over fences and every other obstacle one might think of."

(US) Dokken, 15th Wisconsin, Carlin's brigade, Mitchell's division:
"But we saw nothing of the enemy."

Reports of the Confederate withdrawal reach Buell's headquarters:

Villard, newspaper correspondent:
"It was confirmed between six and seven by the forward movement of the corps of Crittenden and Gilbert, which were to attack the enemy's front and left, while McCook remained in reserve. They met no resistance."

McChord, 12-year-old farm boy from Springfield:
"We arrived at the outskirts of the battle field about 8 o'clock in the morning. Inside the Federal line soldiers were everywhere; some marching, some cooking breakfast; scouts and message bearers were going in every direction as fast as their horses could carry them; signal flags were flying from every hilltop. Everything seemed to be in confusion amidst intense excitement. Everybody was expecting the battle to open at any moment."

In Confederate lines, the retreat to Harrodsburg continues:

(CS) Capt. Alfred Tyler Fielder, 12th Tennessee, Smith's brigade, Cheatham's division:
"Clear and warm and a south wind blowing. . . . About 8 oclk an order was given for the waggons all to hitch up and be ready to move immediately. . . . Our Brigade was ordered into line and marched off immediately. . . . Myself not being able to march and the sick and baggage being left at Camp."

(CS) J.K. Street, 9th Texas, Smith's brigade, Cheatham's division:
"As our Brigd was moveing off this morning the enemy ran his battery up on the hill he shelled us from yesterday evening and for about 10 minutes we were subject to a most grueling fire. We had to cross a pike in which the enemy had his battery planted and as we crossed this there were several of the most terrific showers of grape and shell fell into our ranks I ever experienced. Here Capt Lane (son of Col Lane of Bonham) commanding Co H was killed – was shot in the left side with a cannon ball which tore his intrels out. He lived about an hour and a half."

CONFEDERATES RETREAT

But no major effort is made to impede the Confederate retreat, though the Southerners expect an attack during this vulnerable movement:

(CS) Capt. Fielder, 12th Tennessee, Smith's brigade, Cheatham's division:
"By 9 oclk. a long line of waggons were moving. . . . I not being able to walk rode in Col. Bells waggon."

(CS) Trask, adjutant, 14th Louisiana Battalion (Sharpshooters), Adams' brigade, Anderson's division:
"The army marched in three columns, a column of infantry on each side while the wagons trains moved directly on the road."

(CS) John W. Headley, 14th Louisiana Battalion (Sharpshooters), Adams' brigade, Anderson's division:
"The troops were weary and disappointed, and there was no cheering when generals passed along the column. They could not understand why Bragg and Smith with about 50,000 men had marched into Kentucky and were marching out again."

(CS) Capt. Thomas H. Malone, staff of Brig. Gen. George E. Maney, Cheatham's division:
"I had occasion to ride along the column, (and) I heard a voice that seemed to me to come from the dead: 'Howdy, captain,' and there was old McLemore, hatless, with a bloody rag around his head, and Joe Sewell limping along between him and Dan Carter, who had all three of the guns. Of course, I stopped, and to hide the emotion I felt I began 'cussing' McLemore from Dan to Beersheba. Carter called out to me . . . that 'old Mac,' when he was shot, thought he was killed, but managed to say: 'Here, Dan, here's my tobacco and here's my sweetheart's picture,' and keeled over dead, as he thought. He said they then moved forward upon the enemy, and he and Joe, though much grieved about Mac, didn't have time to think very much about anything but fighting, but just in the midst of the fiercest of the battle, when they were lying within fifty yards of the enemy, he felt somebody seize his heel. He said he thought the devil had him, but he looked back and saw 'old Mac,' his face all covered with blood, saying 'Get further, Dan, and let me in.' "

(CS) John Euclid Magee, Stanford's Mississippi Battery, Stewart's brigade, Cheatham's division:
"Marched pretty fast. Got into town (Harrodsburg) at 11."

(CS) Clark, 16th Tennessee, Donelson's brigade, Cheatham's division:
"I was . . . put in the court house, with a good many wounded."

(CS) Chaplain Cross, Donelson's Brigade, Cheatham's division:
"Good Mrs. Keller took . . . Colonel (Savage) in; and, with the other ladies of the household, nursed him as if he had been a brother."

The ambulance ride to Harrodsburg is too much for one wounded Confederate:

(CS) Lt. Moore, 5th Tennessee, Stewart's brigade, Cheatham's division:
"I couldn't bear the jolt of it. They got what they said was an easy going horse, but I couldn't bear the jostle of his steps. They took me down and I started to walk. We left the pike and went through the woods, a cooler and nearer route. I was getting very weak. Two Federal prisoners were walking near by, and each had an arm amputated. I heard one of them say, 'Oh, I shall die for water!' I had them called and my canteen given to them. . . . In a short time I gave down; the men sat me down against a log. I was somewhat dazed; things looked dark about me. In a short time, Dr. Erskine, our division surgeon, came along and felt my pulse. He had some good bourbon spirits . . . and poured me out some in my cup. I protested, saying it would intoxicate me not being used to it, but he said a pint would not hurt me, being in the condition I was, and that I must drink some or I might not survive. I drank what he had poured out for me, and in a short while my natural feeling and strength began to return, and I got up and walked to the Harrodsburg hospital."

(CS) Joseph Edward Riley, 33rd Tennessee, Stewart's brigade, Cheatham's division:
"With ... (two guns as) crutches ... I made it to Harrodsburg ten miles away where my wound was dressed."

Bragg plans to halt in Harrodsburg and await Kirby Smith and his army; then, the combined Confederate forces will confront Buell. Back on the battlefield, at the Goodnight field hospital:

(CS) Marcus B. Toney, 1st Tennessee, Maney's brigade, Cheatham's division:
"Colonel Fields (had) detailed me to stay and take care of the wounded and do the best I could to bury the dead. ... (In) the morning ... while Dr. Buist was administering to the wounded, I went up to the battlefield and carried the bodies of ... twenty-seven boys of Companies A, B and C, Rock City Guards ... to ... (a) gully ... near by where they fell, and not far from the battery that they charged. ... There were no spades or shovels to be had, but I saw a breast plate upon a dead Federal, and by inverting it made a kind of scoop. With this I covered our dead. ... I buried (Lt.) Col. John S. Patterson in the orchard near the Goodnight Hospital."

The Federal army continues to spread over the battlefield, expecting to run into Confederates ready to resume fighting. Instead, they find the dead and dying from yesterday's battle:

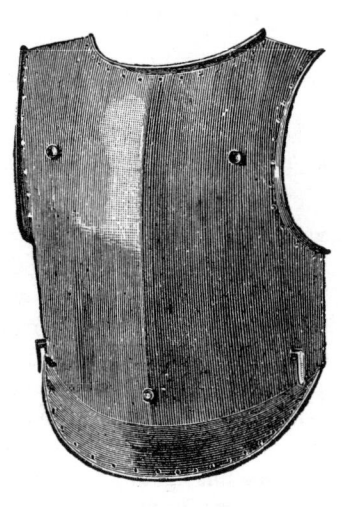

Breastplate

(US) William H. Ball, Pinney's Battery, Gooding's brigade, Mitchell's division:
"I saw one soldier with his head blown off by a shell or cannon-ball, nothing being left but a portion of his lower jaw; another was literally cut in two by the same means. We discovered a good many rebel dead behind a fence."

(US) Charles W. Keeley, 73rd Illinois, Laiboldt's brigade, Sheridan's division:
"One of our batteries was assaulted a half mile to our left. Viewing this scene on the morning of the 9th we saw blue and gray clad bodies lying very near to each other. A horse attached to a cannon lay on the body of a man which held an open knife in its hand as if attempting to free the horse from the cannon."

(US) Rogers, 125th Illinois, McCook's brigade, Sheridan's division:
"The ground was covered with the bodies of the slain. The blue and the gray promiscuously, lay around us. Here had been a party of the enemy engaged during the lull in the storm of battle in a friendly game of cards; a shell had exploded in their midst, and left them laying there dead with the cards still in their hands. Here lay a man with the top of his head shot off; yonder was one whose death must have been instantaneous, for his features were not distorted as if with pain, and he looked as if he was quietly sleeping."

(US) Dr. William Wagner, regimental surgeon, 24th Illinois, Starkweather's brigade, Rousseau's division
"The rebel dead lay in heaps, still unburied."

(US) Surgeon Tilford, 79th Indiana, Beatty's brigade, VanCleve's division:
"See some sixteen dead that had been piled together by the enemy."

Alf Burnett, newspaper correspondent:
"At one spot, in a ravine, (the Confederates) ... had piled up thirty bodies in one heap, and thrown a lot of cornstalks over them."

(US) George M. Kirkpatrick, 42nd Indiana, Lytle's brigade, Rousseau's division:
"We saw the dead bodies of . . . Confederates, piled up four feet high and fifty feet long, with a fence built around them to keep the hogs from devouring them."

(US) Francis, 88th Illinois, Greusel's brigade, Sheridan's division:
"On a rocky spot in the bed of the creek I saw four or five bodies, by their clothing, apparently officers of the enemy. These had been cared for to the extent of the building of a rail fence around them, so as to protect the remains from being attacked by the swine that prowled the woods. The disgusting sight of these animals feeding upon human gore was more than sufficient to give them immunity from . . . the hungry of our army. No one could be found sufficiently hardy to talk of eating the flesh of hogs captured near the battlefield."

(US) Henry F. Perry, 38th Indiana, Harris' brigade, Rousseau's division:
"In several places the rebels had piled their dead like cordwood, and enclosed them in pens made of fence rails, but most of them were scattered about over the field, and in many places commingled with the dead and dying of the Union Army."

(US) Sgt. Holmes Jr., 21st Wisconsin, Starkweather's brigade, Rousseau's division:
"Oh! To see the dead rebels in the woods! From one point I counted thirty-one, in a fence corner twenty-four; every where the eye rests on one, and this is not on the field proper. In our short march we passed at least two hundred, and of horses I made no count. It is a fearful sight; and to think of all these soldiers friends who would give any thing for their bloated, decaying bodies, now torn by swine and crows, — oh, it is sad!"

(US) Unidentified soldier, 15th Wisconsin, Carlin's brigade, Mitchell's division:
"In one place there were six or seven Rebels who lay in a pile, hacked to pieces. They had no clothes on; these had been burned off them, except the hand of an officer, which still had a glove on it."

As Federal troops push farther across the battlefield and reach the abandoned Confederate bivouac:

(US) William Elwood Patterson, 38th Illinois, Carlin's brigade, Mitchell's division:
"In the Chaplin Creek bottom at about the center of the lines, we passed a great number of arms which appeared to have been grounded and abandoned."

(US) Ball, Pinney's Battery, Gooding's brigade, Mitchell's division:
"I saw a good many hundred muskets thrown down in line and left by a regiment or brigade of rebels."

(US) 1st Lt. George W. Landrum, signal officer, 2nd Ohio, Harris' brigade, Jackson's division:
"One whole Brigade of the enemy stacked their arms and refused to fight. We found their arms."

(US) Surgeon Tilford, 79th Indiana, Beatty's brigade, VanCleve's division:
"It was finally found that Bragg had retreated and covered his retreat by cavalry."

(US) Evan Davis, 21st Wisconsin, Starkeweather's brigade, Rousseau's division:
"The news came . . . that the rebels had gone, and it was welcome news."

(US) Capt. Tuttle, 3rd Kentucky, Hascall's brigade, Wood's division:
"We remained in line until 2 p.m. without advancing a step. . . . Our commanders having thoroughly satisfied themselves that the enemy was certainly gone, marched us in triumph into town by the right flank and at route step to the patriotic air, 'Go to boots.'"

(US) Dokken, 15th Wisconsin, Carlin's brigade, Mitchell's division:
"When we found that they had moved away from here, we were ordered back to our camp. . . . It is near a Confederate hospital. There are many Rebels wounded and dead."

(US) Francis, 88th Illinois, Greusel's brigade, Sheridan's division:
"We wheeled around and encamped on the bed of the creek near the left of the battlefield."

(US) Kirkpatrick, 42nd Indiana, Lytle's brigade, Rousseau's division:
"We . . . found a large spring. After filling our canteens with good water, we started . . . again."

(US) William H. McCleary, 42nd Indiana, Lytle's brigade, Rousseau's division:
"The regiment . . . moved out in to the edge of the woods and camped."

(US) Sgt. Holmes Jr., 21st Wisconsin, Starkweather's brigade, Rousseau's division:
"Thank God, we have water! . . . The poor horses have had nothing all day except a little water."

(US) Cpl. George W. Morris, 81st Indiana, Caldwell's brigade, Mitchell's division:
"We marched a little farther on the field, halted and stacked arms close to an old stable, where we remained for the day. We were close to a hill which had been the scene of a bloody conflict the day before, over a battery which the enemy tried to take. It was taken and re-taken during the day. Finally, before the enemy gave it up, it was destroyed by chopping the wheels and dismantling the guns. Guns of all kinds were scattered over the ground, which were being gathered up by our soldiers.

"We bivouacked a few hundred yards from (Doctor's Creek) . . . , and now we had plenty of water to drink, which we were duly thankful for. We had suffered terribly the last few days for want of it.

"Between our regiment and the creek the enemy's wounded lay in every fence corner. Our boys . . . treated them kindly, bringing water whenever they desired it. They were mostly Tennessee troops (of Johnson's brigade). Some of them deserved no compassion, for they spoke impudently and disdainfully. Nevertheless, on account of their wounds, no notice was taken of it."

(US) Unidentified soldier, Webster's brigade, Jackson's division:
"In company with two other slightly wounded men, I went over that portion of the field where our division fought. . . . Down in the hollow, where we hammered the . . . Mississippi (regiment) hard, there were a good many dead rebs. . . . Over in the open field, where Harris' battery was posted, the ground was torn up awfully. Had we remained there with it we would have been terribly hammered. There must have been at least a dozen dead horses around there. . . . There were a good many solid shot and shell lying around, and

bullets were thick enough when one got down and looked closely for them. We met an old man and two boys, each with a basket, picking up unexploded shells. They wanted to know if the Yankees would not buy them. While we were talking about their plunder an explosion was heard down in the edge of the wood where there was a fire in a log pile. In a few minutes two men came along carrying an old citizen who had been pretty well blown up with a shell. He said he had put it in the fire to melt the lead plug out of the end of it so he could see what it looked like inside. It was not half a minute until our old citizen and his boys had their baskets emptied – and were trembling from head to foot. In their collection they had no less than half a dozen unexploded percussion shells, which would have gone off with the slightest provocation."

(US) Francis, 88th Illinois, Greusel's brigade, Sheridan's division:
"Many of our men . . . for the first time viewed . . . the body of a person killed by violence of war, and because of the dark, swollen condition of many of the bodies of the slain Southerners, a report circulated and was believed to be true by many of our men, to the effect that our enemies had been fed on gun-powder and whiskey . . . so . . . that they should become animated to fight with desperation, and that the gun-powder caused the discoloration."

The whiskey and gunpowder theory is nonsense to one Federal officer:

(US) Lt. John Robinson, 2nd Michigan Cavalry, Gay's Cavalry Brigade:
"Every officer . . . knows what care had to be exercised to keep intoxicating liquor away. Soldiers, like other men, became unmanageable under the influence of intoxicating drink. . . . (I) was assigned the disagreeable task of taking a burial party on the morning after the battle, in which our own dead lay promiscuously with the enemy's. If the faces of the enemy's dead showed greater discoloration, either from exposure to the sun or to the whisky and gunpowder, than our own men, I failed to observe it."

(US) L.W. Day, 101st Ohio, Carlin's brigade, Mitchell's division:
"Dead men lay as they fell, though the wounded had been removed. In some places the dead had been collected. I remember seeing thirty-one bodies gathered in one place. At another there were eighteen, and still at another there were twelve. The Blue and Gray were in separate heaps. In one place we saw six men dead – killed by a shell, as was evident by their position. Many dead were found near the fences where they had

sought shelter. Several charges had been made in that part of the line held by Rousseau in the vicinity of the 'Burnt Barn,' and near the haystacks. Here the dead were numerous."

(US) Col. John Beatty, commanding 3rd Ohio, Lytle's brigade, Rousseau's division:
"We go to the hill where our fight occurred. Within the compass of a few rods we find a hundred men of the Third (Ohio) and Fifteenth (Kentucky) lying stiff and cold. Beside these there are many wounded, whom we pick up tenderly, carry off and provide for. Men are already digging trenches, and in a little while the dead are gathered. . . . We have looked upon such scenes before; but then the faces were strange to us. Now they are the familiar faces of intimate personal friends. . . . We hear convulsive sobs, see eyes swollen and streaming with tears as our comrades are deposited in their narrow grave."

(US) Perry, 38th Indiana, Harris' brigade, Rousseau's division:
"The soldier's winding-sheet was a blanket, and all the dead that could be identified of each regiment were buried side by side in a long, deep trench."

(US) Lt. Silas Emerson, 121st Ohio, Terrill's brigade, Jackson's division:
"I had Jesse Adams take a squad of men . . . and bury Tom (Mass) decently by himself. They buried him under the branches of a black walnut tree on Chaplin Hill."

(US) Unidentified soldier, Webster's brigade, Jackson's division:
"Details from each regiment sent out to gather up their dead, and bury them. The four killed in my company were buried under an oak tree on the hillside near where they fell. Stout stakes were driven in the ground at the head of each grave, on which was carved the name of the occupant. The names were also carved on the oak tree, together with the number of the grave. The best we could do was to wrap the boys in their blankets closely, cover them over with leaves and then tumble in the dirt. It was not much like a funeral – it was more of a business matter. The idea was to keep the bodies in as good shape as possible, so they may be recognized if their friends come after them.

"I suppose our folks at home would think us as a hard lot if they could see how indifferently we look on a dead man. While out in the cornfield, near where Loomis' battery had such a long, hard tussle, I saw them carry a lot of dead rebels up to where a long trench had been dug. There must have been fifty bodies, and when the trench was finished they commenced putting them in. At first they were dropped down carefully, but the boys got tired, as it was a very unpleasant job, and began tumbling them in with handspikes, as they would a log. Sometimes one would tumble in face downward, and the boys would sing out: 'About face,' 'close up on the left,' 'cover your file leader,' 'if you get tired turn over,' and the like. It sounded a little rough, but these are rough men. They are from Kentucky, and they hate a rebel even after he is dead."

(US) 1st Lt. Landrum, signal officer, 2nd Ohio, Harris' brigade, Jackson's division:
"I have never hated (the enemy) . . . till now. I have now a thirst for vengeance; the sight of our men lying scattered over that field has added ten fold to my hatred for them."

(US) Michael H. Fitch, 21st Wisconsin, Starkweather's brigade, Rousseau's division:
"Burying the (regiment's) dead . . . was done by a detail of about twenty men under Captain Sessions of G Company. The officers killed were Major Schumacher, Captains Gibbs of E Company, Bently of H Company, and Lieutenant Mitchell of C Company."

(US) John H. Otto, 21st Wisconsin, Starkweather's brigade, Rousseau's division:
"The soil was so rocky we could dig not deeper than 18 inches. The corpses were wrapped in a blanket, laid in the ditch and covered with mother Earth. . . . Major Schumacher . . . was ridled bullets. One had passed clear through the head and six others had passed through chest and legs. His body was sent to Milwaukee, where his familie lived, for burial. Poor Richard Baker! . . . (A) bullet had passed nearly through his heart. He had crept up to a stump against which he leaned in a sitting posture."

(US) Sgt. Holmes Jr., 21st Wisconsin, Starkweather's brigade, Rousseau's division:
"Thirty-three of our regiment were trenched; no coffin or mark, except a rail or stone. . . . It seems hard to throw men all in together and heap earth upon them, but it is far better than to have them lie moldering in the sun. . . . Our major . . . was among the number, — no sheet nor shroud, not even a coat, for he was stripped."

(US) Perry, 38th Indiana, Harris' brigade, Rousseau's division:
"The rebels had stripped the bodies of friend and foe, of hats and shoes, and also of such articles of clothing as could be made useful."

(US) 1st Lt. Landrum, signal officer, 2nd Ohio, Harris' brigade, Jackson's division:
"By the side of every one of our dead men you would see an old pair of shoes and a greasy, filthy pile of clothes."

(US) Capt. W. O'Neill, 81st Indiana Caldwell's brigade, Mitchell's division:
"The whole of Bragg's army are dressed in butternut colored clothes, and are a dirty, poverty-stricken looking set."

A party from the 42nd Indiana searches for Capt. Olmstead's body

(US) Kirkpatrick, 42nd Indiana, Lytle's brigade, Rousseau's division:
"Five of us went . . . to bury his body, but we could not be sure, for the rebels had stolen all of his clothing except his shoes and underclothing. We hunted up the others of our dead, and the Captains body was sent back home to his family, to be laid among his family."

(US) D. Lathrop, 59th Illinois, Gooding's brigade, Mitchell's division:
"As soon as it was ascertained that the enemy had retreated, the ambulances were sent out to gather up the wounded and convey them to hospital. . . . In . . . (a) little woods-pasture lay the dead and wounded of the Third, with now and then a rebel in the midst. . . . The grounds between this and the (Russell) house, to the right and left, was strewn with dead rebels."

(US) Chesley S. Mosman, 59th Illinois, Gooding's brigade, Mitchell's division:
"It seems as though there were not ten square feet of ground on which there were not one and sometimes two or three dead men lying."

(US) Lathrop, 59th Illinois, Gooding's brigade, Mitchell's division:
"The sixty-two wounded of the Fifty-Ninth were soon collected and carefully transported to hospital, among whom was the Adjutant Samuel West. . . . Five times . . . wounded, he eventually recovered, with the loss of only one eye. . . . Another of the severely wounded was Captain Charles F. Adams, commanding Company I. . . . He . . . died in hospital."

(US) Mosman, 59th Illinois, Gooding's brigade, Mitchell's division:
"I found Lieutenant John B. Adams, of Company I, had been shot in the hip. He had lain there all night. I got him some water. . . . Lieutenant A.R. Johnson, of Company B. was killed. . . . Elias Walden was killed by a shot in the left eye, Abott in the head. . . . Surgeon Haslett was killed while dressing a man's wound, about one hundred yards back from the line of battle."

(US) Lathrop, 59th Illinois, Gooding's brigade, Mitchell's division:
"Doctor Hazlett, the Surgeon of the Regiment, . . . was shot through the neck while dressing the wound of a soldier. His remains . . . were respectably buried beneath the sheltering branches of an evergreen tree that stood close beside the spot where he was found. His boots had been stolen from his feet. A gold watch, and several hundred dollars in money, had been taken from his pockets. His hat, and a splendid case of

instruments, were also gone. The Doctor rode a very fine horse, most splendidly caparisoned, and he, too, was gone."

At a house where wounded Federals have been left by the retreating Confederates:

(US) Poulson, 98th Ohio, Webster's brigade, Jackson's division:
"The advance guard of the Union Army came along. The man who had come to us went out and told a lieutenant of the Cavalry that there were five wounded men there who needed attention. The lieutenant came in and took our names, regiment, company, etc., and sent back word for a surgeon."

Three wounded sightseers find a comrade's body:

(US) Unidentified soldier, Webster's brigade, Jackson's division:
"While coming back to the hospital we found Ike Green, of my company, hanging across the fence dead. He gave out yesterday while we were on the skirmish line, and he was not able to get into a wagon. After getting rested I suppose he started to hunt us up, and while climbing over the fence he was struck with a bullet, and there he stopped. The ball passed through his stomach and spine. . . . Several dead men have been found in hollow logs or behind logs or rocks, as though they had been wounded and crawled in there to protect themselves. One poor fellow sat beside a big tree with a Bible in his hand. He had been passed a dozen times and more during the day by ambulance drivers and burial squads, but they all thought he was alive. He had been shot in the thigh, and had gone to this tree for protection. Taking his Bible out, he thought no doubt he would find consolation in reading it; but while sitting there a ball cut him through the back of the neck deep enough to break the spinal cord. His head dropped forward a little, and there he sat."

(US) Capt. John D. Inskeep, 17th Ohio, Walker's brigade, Schoepf's division:
"I . . . visited the (field) hospitals; it was a most painful sight to see so many poor fellows in every possible state of mutilation – many suffering for want of attention; in fact the medical Dept. was sadly deficient in the means to properly care for the wounded."

At the Wilkerson house field hospital:

(US) Dr. S.K. Crawford, regimental surgeon, 50th Ohio, Webster's brigade, Jackson's division:
"By 10 a.m. . . . (I) had organized a company of 'foragers' from the straggling boys, and ordered (them) abroad to bring in sheets, bed-clothing and provisions. . . . A school for training nurses had to be organized at once. . . . The details were promptly made, the nurses were sent to search . . . for . . . neglected and wounded men."

At the Perryville Methodist Church field hospital:

Burnett, newspaper correspondent:
"(I visited) the hospital of which Dr. Muscroft was surgeon. I . . . assisted all day in bringing in the wounded from the field-hospital, in the rear of the battle-ground. The boys of the 10th and 3d Ohio were crowded into a little church, each pew answering for a private apartment for a wounded man. One of the surgeons . . . requested me to assist in holding a patient while his leg was being amputated. . . . As the knife was hastily plunged, the circle-scribe and the saw put to its use, the limb off, scarce a groan escaped the . . . fellow's lips. Another boy of the 10th had his entire right cheek cut off by a piece of shell, lacerating his tongue in the most horrible manner: this wound had to be dressed, and again my assistance was required, and I could not but notice the exhilarating effect of a few words of praise that I bestowed upon his powers of endurance had. This was invariably the case with all those whom it was my painful duty to assist. The effect of a few words of praise seemed quite magical."

Bottom house: "Squire" Henry Pierce Bottom was a farmer, cabinet maker and justice of the peace. His home and grounds were used as a field hospital. Bottom led the gathering of unburied Confederate dead on his property and their burial in a mass grave. After the war, he sought compensation from Washington, D.C., for property damage and losses from the battle. His request was denied after several area residents, including Dr. Jefferson J. Polk, testified that Bottom was a Southern sympathizer.

At the Bottom house:

McChord, 12-year-old farm boy, accompanied by a cousin and a brother:
"The Bottom residence close to the turnpike, and about two miles west of Perryville, . . . was used as the field hospital. The building was an old frame house with a long porch the full length of the building. A large hospital tent was erected in the yard with ordinary tents at different places. . . . The house, tents and yard were full of wounded Federal and Confederate soldiers."

(US) Cpl. Morris, 81st Indiana, Caldwell's brigade, Mitchell's division:
"The yard was full of wounded men, lying in rows, covered up with blankets, shrieking with pain, and some lying there dead. Close to the house was the body of a rebel major, in a corner of the fence. His face was covered. He was neatly dressed in gray cloth."

McChord, 12-year-old farm boy, accompanied by a cousin and a brother:
"I can never forget the groans, wails and moans of this hundreds of men as they lay side by side, some in the agony of death, some undergoing operations on the surgeons table in one corner of the yard."

(US) Cpl. Morris, 81st Indiana, Caldwell's brigade, Mitchell's division:
"The doctors were hard at work at a table, amputating limbs."

McChord, 12-year-old farm boy, accompanied by a cousin and a brother:
"Near the table was a pile of legs and arms; some with shoes on, some with socks, four or five feet high."

(US) Cpl. Morris, 81st Indiana, Caldwell's brigade, Mitchell's division:
"At a short distance to the left was another house used for the same purpose. . . . A battery of cannon lay dismantled near this house. . . . The yard . . . was filled with dead, laid in rows. Close to the fence were piles of arms and legs. . . . Most of the dead were black in the face, which caused them to look more frightful."

McChord, 12-year-old farm boy, accompanied by a cousin and a brother:
"In the orchard back of the house the dead were being gathered from all parts of the battle field, and were laid along side by side on their backs, in a row three hundred feet long, every one with eyes open with a vacant stare, while hundreds of soldiers were digging a trench several feet wide, in which the dead were laid close together and their faces covered with a coffee sack, after which their bodies were covered with dirt."

At other houses where the wounded and dying have been gathered:

(US) Rogers, 125th Illinois, McCook's brigade, Sheridan's division:
"Passing along we arrived at a large stone house which had been converted by the rebels into a hospital. . . . We entered the small gate, and made our way up to the front door and walked in. There, stretched upon the bare floor, in rows, lay the rebel wounded, and among the number several whose lives had just gone out. . . . Groans and shrieks rent the air. One poor wretch, who sat with his back against the wall, had had his tongue shot off . . . and was slowly dying of strangulation. The sight was too much for us, and sick at heart we hastily left the house. The yard was full of wounded men, but the character of their wounds was much slighter than those in the house. The rebel surgeons were passing around among them, and seemed to be doing all in their power for the helpless men."

(US) David B. Griffin, 2nd Minnesota, Steedman's brigade, Schoepf's division:
"I went into a Secesh hospital. . . . They were amputating legs and arms on all sides. Some were dying; others dying and calling upon absent friends and praying to die."

Burnett, newspaper correspondent:
"Accompanied by Mr. A. Seward, the special correspondent of the *Philadelphia Inquirer*, . . . I visited an improvised hospital in the woods in the rear of the battle-ground. There we found some twenty Secesh, who had strayed from their command, and were playing sick and wounded to anybody who came along. They had guards out watching, and, as I suspected they were playing sharp, . . . so I dismounted, and having on a Kentucky-jeans coat, I ventured a 'How-de, Boys?'

"They eyed us pretty severely, and ventured the remark that they needed food, and would like some coffee or sugar for the wounded boys, I went inside the log-house, telling them I would send some down; that we were farming near by there; . . . we would send them some bread. After we had gained their confidence, they wanted to know how they could get out of the State without being captured; said they had not been taken yet, although several of the Yanks had been there; but the 'd——d fools' thought they were already paroled.

"We told them that as soon as they got well we would pilot them safely out. They said they had already been promised citizens' clothing by Mrs. Thompson and some other rebel ladies. They then openly confessed that there was only one of them wounded, and that they had used his bloody rags for arm-bandages and head bandages only for the brief period when they were visited by suspicious-looking persons; but, as we were all right, they had no hesitancy in telling us they were part of Hardee's corps, and were left there by accident when the rebel forces marched.

"By a strange accident they were all taken prisoners that afternoon."

(US) Capt. Thomas McCahan, 9th Pennsylvania Cavalry, Gay's cavalry brigade:
"Our regiment was to escort Gen. McCook today, who traveled all over the battleground. . . . Some parts of the field we could not ride over, the dead rebels lay so thick. . . . They were piled up in some places, especially in front of our center battery. . . .

"A lot of us was setting on our horses and some boys told us that a general officer – rebel – was laying up in the woods. Several of us rode up, Maj. Kimmel asked me to get off and search his pockets, and the object was to find his name, I found nothing. The Major said, 'Open his shirt, may have a jacket on under.' The breast of his shirt was all bloody and thinking the Major wanted me to get my fingers in it, I remounted my horse. He got off, opened the shirt and found a gold watch and chain, which he put in his pocket, remarking that it was getting his fingers bloody.

"We were passing through where a fence had been torn away, the rails piled high. I said to the boys, – we had halted – 'Look under the rails, a wounded man may have crept under last night and was missed.' They did and saw a man. I had the rails moved. He was living and that was all. The boys understood him to say, 'Whisky.' I went to him. I had a little and gave him a few drops, shortly a few drops more. When we left he could sit up. I sent a man to the hospital to inform them and left a man with him."

Three farm boys explore the battlefield on horseback:

McChord, 12:
"To the right of the pike going toward Perryville a rail fence ran up a steep hill, and behind this . . . the Confederates had made a stand. . . . The fence was shot to pieces, and about one hundred dead soldiers were lying on each side of the fence in a perfect line.

"We then crossed to the left of the turnpike and went into the large woodland which had been occupied by the Confederate forces. . . . Scattered promiscuously throughout this woodland were hundreds of the Confederate dead. . . . A Confederate captain had been mortally wounded when the sun was on the west side. To shield himself from the blazing rays of the setting sun as he lay on the ground, he held his blanket as high as he could with his extended arm. In this position the poor fellow died. . . . When we found him, his stiffened arm still held the blanket . . . (And) the eastern sun was beaming down in his unprotected face while his wide open eyes were staring into space with an uncanny glare.

"We then . . . went across to a cornfield adjacent to the Mackville pike which had been occupied by the Federal forces. . . . The Confederate forces were lined up behind a stone fence about two hundred yards from the Federal line. . . . At this point, crossing a space a quarter of a mile wide, the Federal dead were so thick that we could not ride across the battle field without our horses stepping on the dead bodies. . . . One Federal officer was shot and fell in a fence corner which was overgrown with bushes. This poor fellow was still alive but desperately wounded. I can never forget the terrible exclamations and manifestations of intense suffering when it was attempted to remove him to the field hospital."

Villard, newspaper correspondent:
"I . . . devoted the afternoon to a ride over the entire battle-field. I could easily trace the course of the action by the ghastly lines of dead and severely wounded from the points of the first rebel attacks to where they stopped in the evening. On our side, most of the victims lay in rows along our front, where the most vigorous defense was made. Along Jackson's line, the casualties had obviously been few, showing that most of his division had sought safety in flight.

"The number of the fallen was greatest along Starkweather's brigade, while Harris's and Lytle's losses appeared to be about even. Nearly all our wounded had been removed either during the action or at night. The direction of the rebel advances was literally marked by trails of blood from a quarter to half a mile long. I counted over five hundred of their dead. Most of them appeared to have been killed instantly by bullets and artillery fire; but many showed by their distorted features that they had passed through more or less prolonged agonies. I found some two score that had been struck and mutilated by cannon-balls and shells – some with upper and lower limbs torn off, others with chest and abdomen laid open, and one with his entire and another with half his head gone.

"Our sanitary corps was at work gathering up the hundreds of wounded the enemy had . . . left on the field. These had suffered indescribably since they fell, from pain, cold, and want of food and water. The hopeless cases were left to die where they lay, and I passed dozens of them writhing in the last agony.

"The track of slaughter formed awful proof of the . . . heroism . . . with which the rebels faced . . . death. At three points I found, in spaces not over five hundred feet long and wide, successive swaths of from twenty to fifty bodies, cut down by our small arms and batteries."

While exploring the battlefield, a reporter encounters a woman who apparently is the Widow Gibson, Mary Jane Bottom Gibson, a first cousin to H.P. Bottom:

Burnett, newspaper correspondent:
"About a mile and a half to the rear of the field of battle there stands, in a large, open field, a solitary log-house containing two rooms. The house is surrounded by a fence inclosing a small patch of ground. The chimney had been partly torn away by a cannonball. A shell had struck the roof of the building, ripping open quite a gutter in the rafters. A dead horse lay in the little yard directly in front of the house, actually blocking up the doorway, while shot and shell were scattered in every direction about the field in front and rear of this solitary homestead. I dismounted, determined to see who or what was in the house. . . .

"A board had been taken from the floor, exhibiting a large hole between two solid beams or logs. An empty bedstead, a wooden cupboard, and three chairs were all the furniture the house contained. Hurrying across the field, we caught up with a long, lank, lean woman. She had two children with here: a little boy about nine, and a girl about four years of age. The woman had a table upon her head. The table, turned upside down, contained a lot of bedding. She had a bucket full of crockery-ware in one hand, and was holding on to the table with the other. The children were loaded down with household furniture. . . . As it was growing dark, I inquired the nearest road to Perryville. The woman immediately unloaded her head, and pointing the direction, set one leg on the table, and yelled to the boy – 'Whooray up Jeems; you are so slow!'

" 'How far is it, madam?'

" 'O, about a mile and a half. It ain't more nor that, no how.'

" 'Who lived in that house?' said I, pointing to the log-cabin I had just left.

" 'I did.'

" 'Were you there during the fight?'

" 'Guess I was.'

" 'Where was your husband?'

" 'He wor dead.'

" 'Was he killed in the battle?'

" 'No; he died with the measles.'

" 'Why didn't you leave when you found there was going to be a fight?'

" 'I did start to go, but I seed the Yankees comin' thick, and I hurried back t'other way; and jest as I e'enamost got to the brush yonder, I seed the "Confeds" jest a swarmin' out of the woods. So, seeing I was between two fires, I rund back to the house.'

" 'Wasn't you afraid you'd be killed?'

" 'Guess I was.'

" 'What did you do when they commenced firing.?'

" 'I cut a hole in the floor with the ax, and hid between the jists.'

" 'Did they fight long upon your ground?'

" 'It seemed to me like it wor TWO WEEKS.'

" 'You must have been pretty well scared; were you not?'

" 'Humph! skeered! Lor bless you, skeered! That aint no name for it!' "

Foragers sent out in the morning return to the Wilkerson house field hospital in the early afternoon:

(US) Dr. Crawford, regimental surgeon, 50th Ohio, Webster's brigade, Jackson's division:
"One of the most picturesque trains reported in camp . . . – wagons in variety, broodmares, lop-eared mules. . . . Old 'Blossy' and her skipping calf came behind a wagon. . . . . Many an empty stomach was surprised that evening with veal broth and fresh milk. . . . A kind Providence had sent us water, and the boys had supplied the sheeting."

At the Antioch church field hospital on the Mackville road:

(US) Hupp, Simonson's Battery, Terrill's brigade, Jackson's division:
"(I) lay under a large oak tree till 3 o'clock p. m. without anything to eat since I was wounded. . . . Countz came back and made me some coffee which revived and made quite a change in my feelings."

At the Prewitt house, being used as a Confederate field hospital:

(CS) Dr. Noblitt, assistant surgeon, 44th Tennessee, Johnson's brigade, Buckner's Division:
"About 4 o'clock . . . the Federal advance came to the hospital. Their treatment was uniformly kind. Captain Harrison, a grandson of President Harrison, was generous, . . and honorable, doing all he could to alleviate the suffering of the unfortunate. There were ten Federals and nine Confederates in this house, all badly wounded, not one being able to hand water to the other. . . . (Only I) was left in charge to wait on them. . . . (I) reported the condition to Gens. Steadman and Thomas, who visited the hospital. Gen. Steadman soon had all that was necessary for comfort and assistance."

At the Goodnight field hospital:

(CS) Lt. Hall, 9th Tennessee, Maney's brigade, Cheatham's division:
"Yankee troops came into our camp. We then realized that we were prisoners."

(US) Capt. McCahan, 9th Pennsylvania Cavalry, Gay's cavalry brigade:
"After dinner Capt. Bell and I started to visit the hospitals, a large farmhouse every room full. Many doctors amputating, a sickening sight. Rebel hospital in the yard was full, men laying in rows. They would lift one, carry him in, amputate, carry him out, and then take another. The sight was too much for me. These legs and arms were thrown out end window, down against a fence handy (to) the building. The pile was higher than the fence."

(US) Alexander Pepper, 59th Illinois, Gooding's brigade, Mitchell's division:
"We . . . bivouacked on the field, It was a sickening sight; there were a lot of Rebels lying close to where we was stopping. A man could not eat very hearty."

(US) John H. Morse, 105th Ohio, Terrill's brigade, Jackson's division:
"The boys were all fierce for a fight before they got it but now they say they never want to see another and I am sure that I do not."

At a house where several wounded Federal soldiers await medical attention after they were left behind in the Confederate retreat:

(US) Poulson, 98th Ohio, Webster's brigade, Jackson's division:
"We put in another restless night."

In Harrodsburg, Bragg changes his mind about halting and orders the army to keep moving toward Bryantsville, near his supply base of Camp Dick Robinson, while he and his staff stay to meet Kirby Smith's army. The Confederate commander worries that the Federals may get between him and Camp Dick Robinson, to the south:

(CS) Clark, 16th Tennessee, Donelson's brigade, Cheatham's division:
"The army was soon on the march. . . . John T. Haston . . . gave me some rations."

A wounded Confederate who had used two rifles as crutches to walk to Harrodsburg is given a way to stay with the army as it retreats:

(CS) Riley, 33rd Tennessee, Stewart's brigade, Cheatham's division:
"Dr. Alexander, the Brigade surgeon, was ordered to remain with the wounded. He said to me, 'Riley, take my horse and carry the baggage for these other wounded boys who can walk and return with the army.' I carried the camp outfit for four or five others."

(CS) Chaplain Cross, Donelson's Brigade, Cheatham's division:
"In the evening we are again under marching orders. I go with an ambulance for the wounded Colonel (Savage), but . . . he is already on the road."

The retreating Confederate army is leaving about 1,700 wounded in Harrodsburg. In the courthouse, being used as a field hospital:

(CS) Clark, 16th Tennessee, Donelson's brigade, Cheatham's division:
"Nine wounded in the hospital with me died that night."

The next day, October 10, rain falls after three dry weeks. Bragg and his staff wait in Harrodsburg for Kirby Smith and his Confederate troops while Buell cautiously and slowly advances. At a house on the battlefield where some wounded Federal soldiers have been waiting for aid:

(US) Poulson, 98th Ohio, Webster's brigade, Jackson's division:
"In the morning some ladies came with a nice breakfast. They staid and talked, I think, about an hour. They said they were Union folks, and would do all they could to make us comfortable. Sometime before noon three surgeons came, and I being on the porch was noticed first. They soon decided my leg must be taken off or I must die soon. They gave me chloroform, amputated my leg about an inch and a half above the knee joint. I was then taken in an ambulance back to Perryville. I was then taken to the Methodist Church, which became Hospital No.5. . . . In the hospital where I was there were for the first week about 90 wounded men. . . . There were almost every description of wounds to be found there, men struck in so many different

places, from the top of the head to the end of the toes. . . . Most of the boys in Hospital No.5 were patient, and nerved themselves to bear without complaint their pains and privations. A few were peevish, hard to please, and homesick."

Villard, newspaper correspondent:
"I devoted the 10th to visits to General Rousseau and the headquarters of General Crittenden and his division commanders. All the generals I saw expressed their great disappointment and humiliation at the unsatisfactory results, so far, of the operations of the army. . . . Several of them charged Bragg's escape without severe punishment directly to mismanagement. . . . One of the bitterest talkers was General Rousseau. He denounced General Gilbert without stint for failing to support McCook in the battle."

In Harrodsburg, a Confederate tends to a dying comrade, Capt. John C. Curtright:

(CS) J.N. Lennard, 41st Georgia, Maney's brigade, Cheatham's division:
"I . . . remained with him until his departure from this life. . . . I had several short conversations with him before his death & he told me had expected & anticipated his death & was prepared to meet it & desired that I should send his remains home if possible, but if I could not to have him decently buried. . . . During the evacuation of Corinth (Mississippi) he remarked that peace would be made on the ninth of October. . . . He . . . died about four o'clock on the ninth, a circumstance somewhat remarkable. . . . I . . . had him neatly shrouded and placed in a neat coffin. He was intered on the Tenth Inst. on the west side of Harrodsburg in a large cedar grove & grave marked so . . . (his wife) could easily find it."

The next day, October 11, a letter reporting the death of a 1st Tennessee soldier brings family members in Lexington to the Goodnight house field hospital on the battlefield:

(CS) Toney, 1st Tennessee, Maney's brigade, Cheatham's division:
"A messenger came upstairs and said that a lady was in waiting to see me. This was my first meeting with Mrs. (W.C.) Hamilton. Mr. Hamilton was with her, and they brought a hearse and casket, and a carryall with blankets and provisions for our wounded. I accompanied Mr. and Mrs. Hamilton to the battlefield. . . . When we reached the spot I raked the dirt from his face and said: 'Mrs. Hamilton, this is Robert.' 'Is it possible,' she replied, 'that these are Robert's remains?' I said: 'I will soon satisfy you.' Reaching down, I caught one of his hands, and, brushing the dirt away, I said to her: 'Do you see this?' She replied: 'I am satisfied.' Robert was a very studious young man, and in his deep studies I have seen him bite his nails to the quick. and frequently brought blood. When Mrs. Hamilton saw the hand and the condition of the finger nails, she knew they were Robert's. When the body was taken to the hospital and prepared for burial, there was no doubt in her mind."

In Harrodsburg, Bragg and his staff prepare to leave Harrodsburg and rejoin the army at Camp Dick Robinson:

(CS) Quintard, surgeon and chaplain, 1st Tennessee, Maney's brigade, Cheatham's division:
"General Polk . . . asked me to go with him to the church in Harrodsburg. I obtained the key and as we entered the holy house, I think that we both felt that we were in the presence of God. General Polk threw his arms about my neck and said: 'Oh, for the blessed days when we walked in the house of God as friends! Let us have prayer!' I vested myself with surplice and stole and entered the sanctuary. The General knelt at the altar railing. I said the Litany, used proper prayers and supplications, and then turned to the dear Bishop and General and pronounced the benediction from the office for the visitation of the sick. . . . The Bishop bowed his head upon the railing and wept like a child on its mother's breast. Shortly after this service, General Kirby-Smith begged me that he might go to the church with me, so I returned, and he too was refreshed at God's altar."

A Cavalryman visits Capt. Mark Evans, a comrade mortally wounded in the sweep over the bluff at Walker's Bend:

(CS) Lt. Frank Batchelor, 8th Texas Cavalry, Wharton's brigade:
"The morning we left Harrodsburg I called to see him for the last time, and assisted in dressing his wounds. The surgeon told me that there was hardly room for hope. . . . I found Mark entirely sensible, but so stunned by his wound that he spoke only when roused up, and then in monosyllables."

Among those leaving Harrodsburg is a soldier who had been shot with a ramrod:

(CS) Benjamin A. Haguewood, 5th Tennessee, Stewart's brigade, Cheatham's division:
"Evacuated Harrodsburg and rejoined my command at Camp Dick (Robinson)."

Buell, the Federal commander, is slow to push after the retreating Confederate army:

Villard, newspaper correspondent:
"Buell sent out three brigades from Crittenden's and Gilbert's corps, headed by my friend Colonel Edward McCook's and . . . (Capt.) Gay's mounted commands. . . . I made my way at once to McCook, who was very willing to have me accompany him again. . . . We followed the pike from Perryville to Harrodsburg, and encountered and skirmished with rebel cavalry, apparently supported by a strong infantry force. But they fell back before evening, and we entered Harrodsburg unopposed, where we found more than a thousand rebel sick and wounded."

In the courthouse, being used as a field hospital:

(CS) Clark, 16th Tennessee, Donelson's brigade, Cheatham's division:
"I was fearful that the Yanks would mistreat us Rebs in the hospital, but, I was mistaken."

THE WOUNDED AND DYING

Dr. A. N. Reed, United States Sanitary Commission inspector:
"There had been almost no preparation for the care of the wounded at Perryville, and as a consequence the suffering from want of help of all kinds, as well as proper accommodations, food, medicines, and hospital stores, was excessive."

The Federal army is not prepared to handle its own wounded and dying from the battle, and the captured Confederate field hospitals add to the burden. Doctors, nurses, medicine, food and hospital supplies are in short supply.

Dr. Jefferson J. Polk, retired physician and Perryville resident:
"All the churches and public buildings, together with most of the private houses, in Perryville, were employed as hospitals. Thousands of the wounded were brought in and made as comfortable as possible. . . . There was scarcely a house for ten miles that was not encumbered, more or less, with the sick and wounded. . . . My house was made a hospital for eight or ten of these. I was likewise appointed surgeon to a hospital containing forty wounded soldiers."

At the Antioch church field hospital for Federal soldiers:

(US) Adam S. Johnston, 79th Pennsylvania, Starkeweather's brigade, Rousseau's division:
"I lay for six days out under a white oak tree, with my wound dressed once."

Care is better at the enterprising Wilkerson house field hospital, whose doctor has organized a crash course for soldiers pressed into duty as nurses and has sent foragers out for food, bedding and supplies:

(US) Dr. S.K. Crawford, regimental surgeon, 50th Ohio, Webster's brigade, Jackson's division:
"One of the details was that of two millers, who were instructed to take possession of a small country grist-mill that had been found and reported down on the creek, at the mouth of our now babbling brook. The foragers were instructed to take a supply of cereals to the mill the first thing after daylight the next morning; and so the team moved off promptly and came back loaded with everything, including women, young and old, white and bronzed, with willing hands, needles and thread, and a supply of old domestic materials. . . .

"Having found brick and bricklayers, we soon had a fine, large brick out-oven that was wondrous in the eyes of our female help; but a brace of bakers had been one of our details. . . . Henceforth, we had the best of biscuit, Spring chicken, and roast shoat galore. . . . We had apples and apple-dumplings, peaches and peach-cobblers. Our millers, after supplying flour and cornmeal in abundance, began supplying fish to our hearts' content. Thus fed, nursed and cared for, our wounded for the most part got along fairly well. . . .

"The captured women remained with us until honorably discharged, going home of evenings in style in captured carry-alls and escorted by brace 'soger boys.' They did noble work, and several romances might have been written later of the boys who returned to the same locality. . . .

"Our dead were laid quietly and decently away."

EYEWITNESSES AT THE BATTLE OF PERRYVILLE

Though Federal military officials are slow to provide medical assistance and supplies, the United States Sanitary Commission, a civilian organization that helps wounded soldiers, quickly responds to the needs at Perryville:

Dr. Reed, United States Sanitary Commission inspector:

"Immediately on the reception of the news of the late battle, . . . I obtained at once three Government wagons, and the promise of 21 ambulances, to be ready the day following. The wagons were loaded with stores from the Louisville (Sanitary) Commission, and started the same evening for Perryville . . . .

"We found the first hospital for the wounded at (Mackville). This was a tavern, with sixteen rooms, containing 150 wounded and 30 sick, mostly from a Wisconsin regiment. Twenty-five were on cots; some on straw; the others on the floor, with blankets. The surgeon in charge – P.P. White of the 101st Indiana – had authority to purchase all things necessary. Flour was very scarce; cornmeal, beef, mutton, and chickens, plenty. There was no coffee, tea, or sugar, to be had. The cooking was all done at a fireplace, with two camp kettles and a few stew pans. The ladies of the town, however, were taking articles home and cooking them there, thus giving great assistance.

"From this place to Perryville, some ten miles, nearly every house was a hospital. At one log cabin we found 20 of the 10th Ohio, including the Major and two Captains. At another house were several of the 92nd Ohio; and the occupants were very poor, but doing all in their power for those in their charge. The mother of the family promised to continue to do so, but said, with tears in her eyes, she feared that she and her children must starve when the winter came. As at the other houses on this road, the sick had no regular medical attendance. . . .

"We reached Perryville after dark (on October 11). . . . We learned that we were the first to bring relief where help was needed. . . .

"Instead of 700, as first reported, at least 2,500 Union and rebel soldiers were . . . lying in great suffering and destitution about Perryville and Harrodsburg. In addition to these, many had already been removed, and we had met numbers of those whose wounds were less severe walking and begging their way to Louisville, 85 miles distant. To these we frequently gave help and comfort by sharing with them the slender stock of food and spirits we had taken with us. . . .

"There were, at this time, some 1,800 wounded in and about Perryville. They were all very dirty, few had straw or other bedding, some were without blankets, others had no shirts, and . . . some were being brought in from temporary places of shelter whose wounds had not yet been dressed. Every house was a hospital, all crowded, with very little to eat.

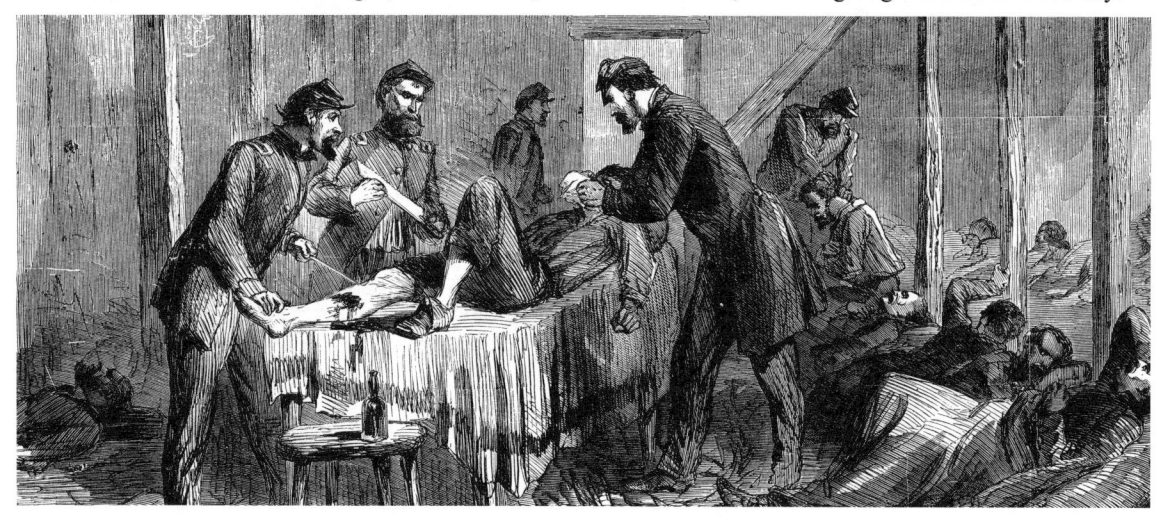

"At the Seminary building there was some fresh mutton, and a large kettle in which soup was being made. I left at this house a box of bandages, comfortables, shirts and drawers, and a keg of good butter. Three days after, at this hospital, I found that the surgeons had improvised bedsteads, and had provided comfortable beds for all their patients from the stores of the Sanitary Commission. Leaving Dr. Goddard to superintend the further distribution of supplies, on the 12th I went with Mr. Thomasson to Danville.

"We here found the wants of the sick as urgent as those of the wounded at Perryville. The Court-House was literally packed; many had eaten nothing during the day, most of them nothing since morning. . . .

"As there were many (of the sick) who were without shelter, I looked around to find some building where they might be carried, and, at last, have a roof over their heads. After some search, a carriage shop was found which would answer the purpose. This belonged to a Mr. J. W. Welch. At my solicitation he opened it, had the carriages removed, and placed it at my disposal. I then procured two loads of straw, which was spread upon the floor, and two hundred men were brought in and laid upon it

"Returning to Perryville, I had the satisfaction of seeing the condition of the wounded considerably improved, thanks to the untiring executions of the surgeons in charge, and the stores we had placed at their disposal . . . . They are still, however, far too crowded, and their condition, in many respects, is susceptible of improvement.

"At the Seminary Hospital, the best of the series, there were seventy-nine wounded . . . These were all badly wounded."

At the Methodist Church, Hospital No. 5, in Perryville:

(US) Wesley S. Poulson, 98th Ohio, Webster's brigade, Jackson's division:
"(On October 11) we were provided with some straw and in two days we had bed ticks and bunks and then we thought we were quite comfortable as far as bedding was concerned. Our fare was at first very coarse and rather scarce also, but when 'Uncle Sam' got things rightly arranged we fared as well as could be expected knowing that Uncle has so many to feed."

At the Prewitt house Confederate field hospital:

(CS) Dr. David J. Noblitt, assistant surgeon, 44th Tennessee, Buckner's Division:
"On Sunday evening (October 12) about 3 o'clock, (Ivy S. 'Parson' Markham) . . . called me and said that he felt chilly and was suffering very much from his wounds . . . in the right arm and abdomen. . . . I went to him and found him helpless. I observed that I would give him some brandy and morphine which I thought would warm him and allay his suffering.

" 'Oh Doctor,' said he, 'you can never warm me again in this life.' Said I, 'Parson we must hope for better things': and having much to do, I turned to leave the room. . . . He then observed, 'Come as soon as you can, I want to talk to you.' Soon as I could I went back to his room, it was evident that his late predictions were too true. He then asked me what I thought of his case, I told him . . . that my opinion was that he had but a short time to live. Said he, 'That is my opinion. . . . I expect to die very soon. I have a request or two to make of you, after I am gone, that is if you live to get home.' I told him it would afford me a great deal of pleasure to serve him in anyway that I could after his death. He then said, 'I am not afraid to die.' I then said to him, 'I believe that.' . . .

" 'When you get home, go,' said he, 'to see my wife and children, and tell her not to grieve for me, tell my children to be kind and obey their mother. . . .

" 'Doctor,' said he, 'My light is almost out, I want you to stay near me and wet my lips when I can no longer speak.' He asked me to tell him when I thought he was dying and to sit near him so that he could rest his head on my bosom. I did so. Soon I saw the tide of life was fast ebbing away. 'Parson,' I said, 'are you aware of your condition?' He said, 'I am.' I gave him some water, his eyes once more brightened, it was the last flicker of the taper, they closed as one going in to a sweet sleep. He was dead."

Though wounded Confederate prisoners are given what medical attention is available, Federal officers and men feel little responsibilty for dead Southerners on the battlefield. One catches the attention of a Federal cavalryman crossing the battlefield on October 12:

(US) Henry A. Potter, 4th Michigan Cavalry:
"One lay close by the side of the road. He was shot through the breast – his pockets inside out, boots stolen. He had lain there since Wednesday. About a dozen lay upon the hillside."

Alf Burnett, newspaper correspondent:
"On the Springfield road, to the right, as you entered the town of Perryville, a regular line of (Confederate) skirmishers lay dead, each one about ten feet from the other; they had evidently been shot instantly dead, and had fallen in their tracks; and there they laid for four days. One, a fine-looking man, with large, black bushy whiskers, was within a few yards of the toll-gate keeper's house, – himself and family residing there, – who, apparently, was too lazy to dig a grave for . . . the rebel's body. . . . These people seemed to pay no attention to either dead or wounded. And it was not until a peremptory order from . . . Colonel (William P. Reid of the 121st Ohio) . . . , who was in command at Perryville, . . . was issued, that the rebel-sympathizing citizens condescended to go out and bury their Confederate friends; and this was accomplished by digging a deep hole beside the corpse, and the diggers, taking a couple of fence rails, would pry the body over and let it fall to the bottom."

Dr. Polk, retired physician and Perryville resident:
"For more than ten days after the battle the field hospitals, except Antioch Church (on Mackville Road) and Mr. Goodnight's farm, were being cleared of the wounded; the two above excepted contained about three hundred of the wounded."

Among the Federal wounded being shifted to Perryville are those moved October 13 from the Sulpher Spring field hospital:

(US) William T. Clark, 79th Pennsylvania, Starkweather's brigade, Rousseau's division:
"This morning we went to the Tucker House turned into a hospital. All our Regt. is to be here that are not fit to move to Louisville. Spring-wagons of every description are being sent here for the wounded . . . from Louisville to carry the wounded thither. The chimneys are knocked off some of the houses, some of them having 4 & 5 cannon balls through them. The wagons did not come to take us & we are quartered in a house close to the river bank & near a hospital occupied by rebels. Strange how soon circumstances alters the feelings of men toward one another. Only a few days ago we were engaged in deadly conflict with each other (loyal against Rebel). Now we are doing all we can to alleviate their sufferings."

Two days later, on October 15, transportation arrives for some of the wounded:

(US) Clark, 79th Pennsylvania, Starkweather's brigade, Rousseau's division
"This morning wagons are in the street waiting for us. . . . We left at 7 o'clock. 20 teams with 150 men passed through a fine grass country & arrived at Lebanon at 3 o'clock p.m. with our wounds jolted very much. Those whose wounds are worst are put in the hospital. We are in the barracks, formerly an African Church."

On October 17 at the Goodnight hospital, a premonition of death before the battle is fulfilled:

(CS) Capt. John M. Taylor, 27th Tennessee, Maney's brigade, Cheatham's division:
"Nine days after the fight Lieut. (Albert) Andrews died . . . (beside me), his bosom friend and boy companion."

THE WOUNDED AND DYING

The next day, death claims an 8th Texas Cavalry officer wounded in the sweep across the bluff at Walkers Bend:

Mrs. B. Mills, Harrodsburg resident:
"Capt. (Mark) Evans . . . (had) received a fatal wound in the head by a Minie ball. . . . He was brought to my home. . . . He lay in a drowsy state all the time, and never opened his eyes; he talked very little, and his talk was like a man who is very drowsy. . . . The Indian boy – Capt. Evans's body servant – attended him most faithfully. . . . His brother and some friends remained with him for three days, when the enemy came they left him in my charge. . . . He had good attention until the 18th . . . , when at forty minutes past six he expired. . . . His Masonic brothers helped to get his coffin and bury him. He and Col. McDaniel, of Georgia, were buried at the same time. Their bodies now lie in the Masonic grounds."

On October 19, at the Prewitt house field hospital:

(CS) Dr. Noblitt, assistant surgeon, 44th Tennessee, Johnson's brigade, Buckner's Division:
"Feeling lonely this morning, I was led for the third time to stroll alone over the battlefield. . . . All the dead were buried, many partially. Soon I came to the spot where poor (Capt. Joel L.) Jones and his comrades . . . fell, their blood is still fresh on the grass, a few steps to the left and in my advance was still to be seen the blood of Parson Markham, where he lay for a short time after receiving his mortal wound of which he died on Sunday evening the 12th."

At the Wilkerson house Federal field hospital:

(US) Dr. Crawford, regimental surgeon, 50th Ohio, Webster's brigade, Jackson's division:
"The 20th of October, 1862, . . . the 'critters' were returned to their owners, the women sent to their own homes, the blankets and coverings returned, as far as possible to their rightful owners, and camp was broken."

While Federal wounded are steadily transferred to hospitals in Lebanon, New Haven, Louisville and New Albany, Indiana, most of the Confederate wounded remain in the Perryville area. At the Goodnight home, a Confederate field hospital:

(CS) Capt. Taylor, 27th Tennessee, Maney's brigade, Cheatham's division:
"For weeks many of us were in the (Goodnight) horse lot."

A wounded Confederate officer and some comrades on the Goodnight grounds are fortunate to have cover under some old boards hastily put together as a rough shelter:

(CS) Lt. James I. Hall, 9th Tennessee, Maney's brigade, Cheatham's division:
"Our men were very destitute of clothing. Most of them having no clothing except what they were wearing. Many of the wounded (had) had their clothes cut off them by the surgeons, who dressed their wounds, and in this way lost a great part of the little clothing they had. Rations of good quality were furnished to us in abundance by the Federals, but we were not supplied with clothing or shelter. . . .

"After a few days the good women of Ky. Came into our camp and supplied us as far as they could with such things as we need. Among others I remember particularly the good Mrs. Hogue, the wife of the Pres minister at Lebanon, Ky. who was untiring in her efforts to add to the comfort of our boys. . . .

"The people from the country around were in our hospital every day. One day a man came along whom I recognized as 'Big Jim Harlan' whom I had known as a boy fifteen years before at Danville. I had concealed under my blanket a Maynard rifle, which I had bought for Will Carnes at Chattanooga, the regular army musket being too heavy for a boy of his age and size to carry. As he was wounded in this battle and captured he had sent me the rifle to take care of. After renewing my acquaintance with Harlan and finding him to be a good Rebel, I asked him to take charge of the gun until I should call for it. He kindly consented to do this and secreted it in the voluminous folds of his big Yankee overcoat that he was wearing. . . .

"Archie Baird who had a broken thigh and Tom Melton who had a comparatively slight flesh wound died. . . . . Jas. P. Holmes, Geo. McDill who was shot through the lungs and pronounced mortally wounded and I . . . lived. . . . John Green Hall, Robert Lemmon & Willie Holmes remained to nurse the wounded. . . .

"After I had remained in the hospital about two weeks my kind friend, Col. Joshua Barbee of Danville, who was a Union man, sent his carriage for me and took me to his house. There I was placed in the room which I had occupied fifteen years (earlier) when I was a student at Centre College, and was treated with unremitting kindness by Col. Barbee and his family. . . .

"A large number of our men . . . were taken to the homes of the good people in the country and in Harrodsburg and in Danville. Willie Holmes and James Peter were cared for at the house of Mr. Messick in Danville."

In a Confederate hospital in Harrodsburg:

(CS) Lt. W.R. Moore, 5th Tennessee, Stewart's brigade:
"In about fifteen days I went out to Dr. Moore's on the Lexington Pike. He claimed kin with me, and of course I did not object. John Tolley, of Lincoln County, was there shot through the leg. We stayed for a long time. He could eat solid food, while I could only have liquid diet. My wound healed up. His did not. When Bragg's army passed over the mountains into East Tennessee, the Federals sent a lot of us to Lexington."

At the Methodist Church, Hospital No. 5, in Perryville:

(US) Poulson, 98th Ohio, Webster's brigade, Jackson's division:
"The ladies of Perryville visited us daily and not infrequently brought us something nice to eat and papers, books, and magazines to read. At first three surgeons were kept in Hospital #5 and had plenty to do. . . . We had kind and attentive nurses who were ready and willing to do all they could for us. To Nelson Bierney, John L. Erwin, James L. Rogers, Joseph Breed of Wisconsin, and William Sandusky of Kentucky I owe much respect for their kindness to me while in the hospital. . . . Notwithstanding all that could be done I saw 22 carried out of that house lifeless. Some of these died of wounds and others had sickness and wounds both."

Care of so many wounded Confederate and Federal soldiers is soon complicated by the appearance of typhoid, pneumonia, measles and dysentery, which also afflict civilians:

Fannie Bell, resident of Danville:
"We have three thousand five hundred Federal soldiers and something over a hundred Confederates sick in town. . . . The courthouse, seminary buildings, every church and unoccupied house, private dwellings and all are full to overflowing. The sickness is not now confined to the . . . soldiers. Almost every family has some, not all dangerous, but complaining of the dreadful camp disease."

At the Methodist Church, Hospital No. 5, in Perryville:

(US) Poulson, 98th Ohio, Webster's brigade, Jackson's division:
"I remained until February 17, 1863. . . . I then left Perryville for home."

THE WOUNDED AND DYING

Some wounded Confederates and Federals slip away from the hospitals and houses where they are being cared for and make their ways home or back to their regiments. But most of the wounded who survive are discharged from the hospitals as they sufficiently recover. Federals return to duty or are released from the army; Confederates are shipped to prisoner of war camps or are exchanged. Perryville's hospitals close in March 1863, but in hospitals elsewhere, wounds from the battle continue to claim lives. About 1,420 Confederates and Federals were killed at Perryville, but the toll will eventually near 2,380 as the fatally wounded succumb in the months to come.

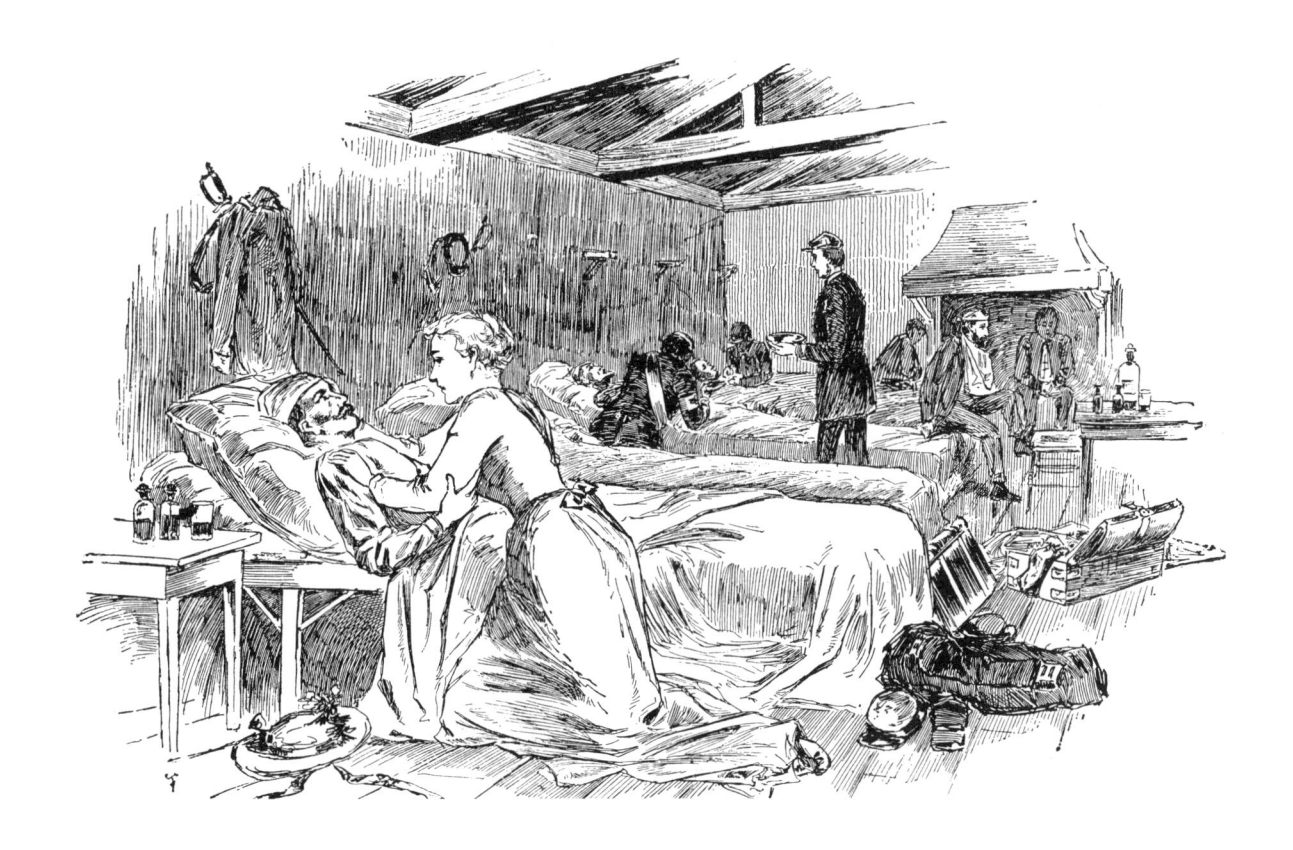

EPILOG

Perryville was not satisfactory to either side. A Confederate officer sums up the disappointment of many in the army:

(CS) Brig. Gen. Seth M. Barton, brigade commander, Stevenson's division, Kirby Smith's army:
"Bragg is either a madman or a coward & if he is not removed from his command great disasters must inevitable ensue. After a series of mistakes, which fortunately the men did not perceive, he wound his operation by abandoning the campaign and fleeing from the country he had just assured he would never forsake. . . . This . . . little operation has lost Kentucky to us beyond redemption. . . . The same wisdom has now directed a movement which seems to indicate a winter campaign in middle Tenn. before the army can prepare for it."

Resentment of the Federal commander is even stronger:

(US) D. Lathrop, 59th Illinois, Gooding's Brigade, Gilbert's corps:
"Thus ends Don Carlos Buell's campaign in Kentucky. A campaign which should have resulted in the capture or annihilation of the rebel hordes, but which will hereafter be regarded as one of the most miserable failures in the military history of the country. True, the State of Kentucky is now rid of the insolent, thieving foe, but this was not the task assigned the commander of the army of the Ohio. He was expected to utterly destroy them, and he had the men and the opportunities to do so, but instead he permitted the enemy to fall upon, in force, and almost destroy a wing of his army, when fifty thousand men were in easy supporting distance, and then, as if to complete his work of imbecility or treachery, allowed them to escape, when their retreat might still have been cut off."

(US) George M. Kirkpatrick, 42nd Indiana, Lytle's brigade, Rousseau's division:
"All the army knew that General Bragg of the Confederates and General Buell, were brothers-in-law, and had supper together the evening before, and that General Buell had promised General Bragg that he would let him get back South without a battle. Be that as it may, our general never showed himself to us, or we would have wasted a lot of bullets to revenge ourselves. He rode in an old ambulance to prevent his army from seeing him."

(US) Maj. James M. Shanklin, 42nd Indiana, Lytle's brigade, Rousseau's division:
"The whole battle was disastrous. Buell is the most stupendous failure on record."

(US) James A. Price, 10th Indiana, Fry's brigade, Schoepf's division:
"Buel the old son of a bitch. . . . I believe him to be a damed traitor."

(US) Aaron V. Nostrand, chaplain, 105 Ohio, Terrill's brigade, Jackson's division:
"That terrible damned traitor Don Carlos Buell."

Buell is relieved of command and is never again entrusted with an army. Many of Buell's Perryville veterans, however, will confront Bragg and his troops again, in late December, at the Battle of Stones River, Tennessee.

BIBLIOGRAPHY

PBA – Perryville Battlefield State Historic Site archives
PBPA – Perryville Battlefield Preservation Association archives
CV – *Confederate Veteran* magazine

Allen, Thomas: Letter dated November 12, 1862; PBPA.
Ayre, Josiah: diary; Perryville Walking Tour Web site (www.kycivilwar.org).

Ball, William H.: "AT PERRYVILLE. What an Artilleryman Saw of that Battle," by Ball; *National Tribune*, Dec. 15, 1897.
Barton, Grig. Gen. Seth M.: Letter dated Oct. 27, 1862; Seth Barton Papers, 1862; The Pearce Civil War Collection, Navarro College.
Batchelor, Lt. Frank: CV Vol. 13 (1905), pages 61-64, "A Woman's Memories of the Sixties. Some Interesting Letters not Heretofore Published," By Mrs. Maria Evans Claiborne, St. Louis, month
Beatty, John: *The Citizen-Soldier; or, Memoirs of a Volunteer*, by Beatty; 1879.
Bell, Fanny: PBPA files.
Benson, Wallace P.: *A Soldier's Diary*, by Benson; 1919.
Berkshire, Mrs. J.B.: PBPA
Berry, John M.: "Reminiscences from Missouri," by Berry in CV 8/1900; page 73.
Bevens, William E.: *Reminiscences of a Private, Company 'G.' First Arkansas Regiment Infantry May, 1861 to 1865*, by William E. Bevens; 1914. Reprinted in 1977 and 1992 as *Reminiscences of a Private. William E. Bevens of the First Arkansas Infantry, C.S.A.*; edited by Daniel E. Sutherland.
Blackburn, James K. P.: "Reminiscences of the Terry Rangers," *Southwest Historical Quarterly*, Vol. 22, 1918-1919. pgs. 38-77, 143-179. [At The Handbook of Texas online Web site, Blackburn's book is also cited as: James Knox Polk Blackburn, Reminiscences of Terry's Texas Rangers (Austin: Littlefield Fund for Southern History, University of Texas, 1919; rpt., Austin: Ranger Press, 1979).]
Blakemore, Capt. William T.: CV Vol. 5 (1897), page 249.
Bliss, Jesse C.: *Letters from a Veteran of Pea Ridge*, edited by Paul R. Cooper and Ted R. Worley; *The Arkansas Historical Quarterly*, Vol. 6, pages 462-471; 1947.
Briscoe, A.B.: *Terry's Texas Rangers*, by L.B. Giles; 1911. Reprinted
Brown, William A.: *The Civil War Travels of William A. Brown*, edited by W.T. Dixon III; 1979
Bruce, John A. Bruce: CV Vol. 10 (1902), page 177
Bryant, William A.: PBPA; Letter written Oct. 11, 1862, Byrantsville, Ky.
Burnett, Alf: *Humorous, Pathetic, and Descriptive Incidents of the War*, by Alf Burnett; 1864.

Campbell, Alex W.: "Thirty-Third Tennessee Infantry," by Alex W. Campbell; *Military Annals of Tennessee. Confederate*, edited by John B. Lindsley; 1886.
Cannon, J.P.: *Inside of Rebeldom: The Daily Life of a Private in the Confederate Army*, by Cannon; 1900.
Carlin, Brig. General. William P.: *National Tribune,* March 5, 1885.
Carden, Robert C.: "Civil War Memories of Robert C. Carden," Web site. (Originally published April 5, 1912, in *The Indpendent* of Boone, Iowa.)
Carnes, Capt. W.W.: "Artillery at the Battle of Perryville, Ky.," by Capt. W.W. Carnes; CV Vol 33 (1925), page 8-9; letter dated Feb. 13, 1895, Special Collections Library, Duke University.
Carr, Charles W.: Letter written Oct. 10,1862,"Civil War Letters of Charles W. Carr of the 21st Wisconsin Volunteers, edited by Leo M. Kaiser. *Wisconsin Magazine of History*, 43 (Summer 1960), pages 264-72. PB. Original letters in the manuscript collection of the Chicago Historical Society.
Carroll, John W.: *Autobiography and Reminiscenes*, by John W. Carroll; 1898.
Chandler, Daniel H.: diary, PB.
Cheatham, Maj. Gen. Benjamin F.: "The Battle of Perryville," by B.F. Cheatham, *Southern Bivouac*, April 1886, pages 704-705.
Cheeves, Jesse T.: "War Time Notes," by Jesse T. Cheeves, *Corinth Herald* (Corinth, Miss.) March 27, 1902. (Web page for CrossRoads Access, Inc. Corinth History).
Claiborne, Thomas: "Battle of Perryville, Ky," CV Vol. 16 (1908), pages 225-227.
Clark, Carroll H.: Series of articles published in *The Spencer* (Tennessee) *Times*, starting June 1, 1911. Articles reprinted by the *Times* in 1918 and by *The Sparta Expositor*, in Tennessee.Also in booklet *My Grandfather's Diary of the Civil War*, posted at www.rootsweb.
Clark, William T.: *The Diaries of William T. Clark*, transcribed by William G. Davis and Janet B. Davis for the Lancaster County Historical Society, Lancaster, Pennsylvania.

Cleaver, A.D.: Letter dated October 11, 1862; PBA.
Connolly, James A.: *Three Years in the Army of the Cumberland. The Letters and Diary of Major James A. Connolly,* edited by Paul M. Angle; 1959.
Crawford, Dr. S.K.: "BATTLE OF PERRYVILLE. How It Looked to a Surgeon at the Rear of the Army," by Crawford; *National Tribune*, April 2, 1893.
Cross, Joseph: *Camp and Field. Papers from the Portfolio of an Army Chaplain*, by The Rev. Jos. Cross, D.D.; 1864.
Cumings, Henry Harrison: *In Memoriam: Henry Harrison Cumings, Charlotte J. Cumings*, by Reb. J.N. Fradenburgh; 1913.

Davis, Evan: speech given 1910, transcript from Polk Library, University of Wisconsin-Oshkosh.
Davis, W.H.: CV Vol. 4 (1916), page 554.
Davison, E.L.: *Autobiography of E.L.Davison*, by Davison: 1901.
Day, L.W.: *Story of the One Hundred and First Ohio Infantry*, by Day; 1894.
Dokken, Lars O.: "Two Immigrants for the Union: Their Civil War Letters," by Lars and Knud Olsen Dokken, translated by Della Kittleson Catuna; edited by Carol Lynn H. Knight and Gerald S. Cowden. Published in *Norwegian-American Studies*, Vol. 28, 1979; pages 109ff.

Ellis, Thomas B.: memoir, Florida Historical Society.
Emerson, Edward Silas: Letter courtesy of Edward Scott Whalen, editor of *One Hundred and Twenty-First Ohio. Letters of the Civil War.*
Englis, John L.: see under Inglis.

Fahnestock, Allen L.: Journal of Colonel Allen L. Fahnestock, 86th Illinois Volunteer Infantry, Courtesy, Peoria Public Library.
Feild, Col. H.R.: *Official Records*, Volume XVI, Series I, Part I
Ferguson, Edward: "The Army of the Cumberland Under Buell," by Lieut. Edward Ferguson, U.S.V. (read December 5, 1888); *Military Order of the Loyal Legion of the United States, Wisconsin Commandery*, Vol. 1.
Fielder, Alfred Tyler: Fielder Diaries, 1861-1865; 4 vols. (one reel) Tennessee State Library and Archives.
Finlay, Luke W.: "Fourth Tennessee Infantry," by Finlay, *Military Annals of Tennessee. Confederate*, edited by John B. Lindsley; 1886.
Fitch, Michael H.: *Echoes of the Civil War as I Hear Them*, by Fitch; 1905.
Francis, Charles L.: *Narrative of a Private Soldier in the Volunteer Army of the United States*, by Francis; 1879.
Frazer, Capt. C.W.: *The Military Annals of Tennessee. Confederate*, Volume 1, edited by John Berrien Lindsley; 1886.

Gardner, George Q.: *The National Tribune*, April 23, 1885.
Gates, Robert: "Sixth Tennessee Infantry," by Gates, *Military Annals of Tennessee. Confederate*, edited by John B. Lindsley; 1886.
Gierhart, A.L.: Gierhart Papers, reminiscences; Ohio Historical Society, Call No. VFM 3004.
Gipson, W.C. "About the Battle of Perryville, Ky." by Gipson, CV Vol 9 (1901), page 163.
Glezen, Joseph P.: "Abstract from the Diary of Private Joseph P. Glezen from Company 'H,' 80th Indiana Infantry, Webster's Brigade, Jackson's Division, McCook's Corps"; genealogy collection of the Pike County (Ohio) Public Library; PBA.
Graber, H.W.: *The Life Record of H.W. Graber. A Terry Texas Ranger. 1861-1865*, by Graber; 1916.
Gribble, Martin V.: *Reminiscences of the Boys in Gray 1861-1865*, compiled by Mamie Yeary; 1912.
Griffin, David B.: Letter dated Oct. 13, 1862; *Letters Home to Minnesota, 2nd Minnesota Volunteers*, Joan W. Albertson, editor; 1992; PBPA copy
Grisham, W.T.: *Reminiscences of the Boys in Gray 1861-1865*, compiled by Mamie Yeary; 1912.

Haguewood, Benjamin A.: *The Tennessee Civil War Veterans Questionnaires*, Volume Three, compiled by Gustavus W. Dyer and John Trotwood Moore; 1985.
Hall, J.C.: CV Vol. V (1897), page 466
Hall, James I.: James Iredell Hall Papers, Manuscript Volume No. 1, Southern Historical Collection, M-302; University of North Carolina Library.
Hamilton, J.T.: *Reminiscences of the Boys in Gray 1861-1865*, compiled by Mamie Yeary; 1912.
Harlan, Col. John M.: letter dated July 4, 1911, PBA.
Harrod S.J.: Dec. 14, 1908, *Galveston Semi-Weekly News*. (Web site hosted by the Historic Templeton McCanless District in Texas).
Hartzell, John C.: *Ohio Volunteer, The childhood & Civil Memoir of Captain John Calvin Hartzell, OVI*, edited by Charles I. Switzer; Ohio University Press, Athens, Ohio; 2005.
Haywood, Benjamin A.: see under Haguewood.

Head, Thomas A.: *Campaigns and Battles of the Sixteenth Regiment, Tennessee volunteers*, by Head; 1885 (reprinted in 1961); and "The Battle of Perryville," by Head, photocopy of unidentified, undated newspaper clipping from David Fraley Files.

Headley, John W.: *Confederate Operations in Canada and New York,* by Headley; 1906.

Hearn, W.C.: "Forty-First Mississippi Regiment – A lost Sword," by Hearn; CV Vol 6 (1898), page 152.

Hoffman, Martin: Letter dated Jan. 6, 1863; PBA.

Holm, D.D.: *History of the Fifth Indiana Battery*, by Holm; no date; David Fraley files.

Holmes Jr., Mead: Letter dated Oct. 9, 1862*; A Soldier of the Cumberland: Memoir of Mead Holmes, Jr.*, by his father; 1864

Hooper, Thomas R.: PBPA copy of diary in Stones River National Battlefield archives.

Hoover, Elias H.: *The National Tribune,* June 20, 1889.

Horrall, Spillard F.: *History of the Forty-Second Indiana Volunteer Infantry*, by Horrall; 1892. CV Vol. XV (1907), page 556. "Rebels Badly Whipped; The Forty-Second Indiana Reg.," by Q.K. Juniper Wiggins (believed to be Horrall's pen name) *Daily Evansville Journal*, Oct. 21, 1862.

Hunt, William T.: "Civil War Memories of William T. Hunt," by Wealtha Etta Hunt Goben; 1966; transcribed and contributed to *Illinois Trails* by Steve Lawyer.

Hupp, Ormond: *In the Defense of This Flag. The Civil War Diary of Pvt. Ormond Hupp, 5 th Indiana Light Artillery*; John L. Berkley, editor; 1992.

Hutchinson, Stephen J.: Letter written Oct. 15, 1862; Ca. No. Microfilm Mss F-13, Clarke Historical Library; Central Michigan University.

Inglis, John L.: diary, Special Collection, Robert Manning Strozier Library, Florida State University, and "Ancient City Defenders: The St. Augustine Blues," by David J. Coles, *Civil War Times in St. Augustine*, Jacqueline K. Fretwell, editor; 1988 (Originally published as Volume 23 of *El Escribano, The St. Augustine Journal of History*, The St. Augustine Historical Society; 1986)

Inskeep, John D.: VFM 3187 John D. Inskeep Diary: Ohio Historical Society.

Irion, John T.: "Fifth Tennessee Infantry," *The Military Annals of Tennessee. Confederate*, edited by J.B. Lindsley; 1886.

Johnston, Adam S.: *The Soldier Boy Diary Book; or, Memorandums of the Alphabetical First Lessons of Military Tactics. Kept by Adam S. Johnson. From September 14, 1861, to October 2, 1864*; Pittsburgh; 1867.

Jones, George W.: diary (a transcription of a series of articles published in *The Grenada Sentinel* from June 11, 1898, to January 21, 1899), Elizabeth Jones Library, Grenada, Mississippi.

Jordan, James D.: *Reminiscences of the Boys in Gray 1861-1865*, compiled by Mamie Yeary; 1912.

Keeley, Charles W.: *Diary Record of the Seventy-Third Illinois Volunteers in the Civil War*, by Charles W. Keeley; 1925

Kirkpatrick, George M.: *Experiences of a Private Soldier of the Civil War*, by Kirkpatrick; 1924 (reprinted 1973 by the Hoosier Bookshop).

Knowles, L.E.: *The National Tribune*; May 9, 1889.

Kohlsdorf, Robert J.: Letter dated Oct. 13, 1862 (transcribed by Catherine Anne [Pelt] Hiemer), *Home League Newspapers*, Hartford, Wisconsin, Nov. 1, 1862

Landrum, George W.: The George W. Landrum Letters Mss. 543, Western Reserve Historical Society Library, Cleveland, Ohio.

Lathrop, D.: *The History of the Fifty-Ninth Regiment Illinois Volunteers*, by Lathrop; 1865.

Lennard, J.N.: (sometimes spelled Leonard) letter; Hutchinson Family Papers, Special Collections Department, Mitchell Memorial Library, Mississippi State University Libraries. (Printout from the Troup County (Georgia) Archives refers to the letter as part of the Mary Charles Evans Papers, Manuscript Collection No. 19, in the Hutchinson Papers.)

Liddell, St. John R.: St. John Richardson Liddell's "Record of the Civil War," Daniel C. Govan papers, #1000, Southern Historical Collection at the University of North Carolina Library, Chapel Hill, North Carolina.

Little, George: *Memoirs of George Little*, by Little; 1924. Also, *A History of Lumsden's Battery C.S.A.*, by Dr. George Little and James R. Maxwell; 1905.

Macmurphy, Gilbert L.: diary, Terry's Texas Rangers Web site.

Magee, John E.: diary, Duke University manuscript collection, special collections, William R. Perkins Library. (Also in Broadfoot Supplement No. 3, *Army Official Records*, Volume 3, Addendum [Reports], Vol. 16 (Serial No. 22), page 218.)

Malone, Thomas H.: *Memoir of Thomas H. Malone: An Autobiography Written for His Children*, by Malone; 1928.

McCahan, Thomas S.: diary, 1862-1864 (entries for Oct. 8, 9 and 10, 1862), Collection No. 1995, The Historical Society of Pennsylvania.

McChord, Caldwell: *Washington County, Kentucky Bicentennial History, 1792-1972*; also "Broken in Spirit," by Stuart W. Sanders, *Kentucky Humanities* magazine; year 2000, No. 1 issue. Permission courtesy of Helen Dedman, Beaumont Inn, Harrodsburg, Ky.

McCleary, William H.: diaries, transcribed by great-granddaughter, Ann Cott; Web site for the 42nd Indiana Volunteer Infantry.

McCouley, C.M.: "Who Was the Officer?" by McCouley, CV 7 (1899), page 406.

McDill, W.J. : letter in 41st Georgia folder, David Fraley files.

McDowell, William P.: "The History of the Fifteenth Kentucky Volunteer Infantry," by McDowell; *Southern Bivouac*, 1886-87.

McFarland, L.B.: "Maney's Brigade at the Battle of Perryville," by McFarland; CV Vol. 30 (1922), pages 467-469.

Miller, Silas: *History of the Thirty-Sixth Regiment Illinois Volunteers*, by L.G. Bennett and William M. Haigh; 1876.

Miller, William: "Report of General Miller to Anna Jackson Chapter United Daughters of the Confederacy," UDC Anna Jackson Chapter No. 224 Records, copy from Florida State Archives (PBPA).

Mills, B.: CV Vol. 13 (1905), pages 61-64; "A Woman's Memories of the Sixties. Some Interesting Letters not Heretofore Published," by Mrs. Maria Evans Claiborne.

Milner, Duncan C.: Letter dated Oct. 10, 1862, "A Human Document. A Letter Written by a Young Divinity Student After Perryville," *National Tribune*, Sept. 27, 1906, page 6.

Mitchell, William S.: Transcripts of Original Civil War Letters of Captain William S. Mitchell, Volume I, M76-131, Carton 1, Golda Meir Library, University of Wisconsin-Milwaukee (Noe files, PBPA).

Moore, W.R.: "Reminiscence," by Moore, *Historic Maury*, Volume 6-7, 1970-71, published by Maury County (Tennessee) Historical Society. (Series of letters written by Moore to the Pulaski, Tennessee newspaper about his experiences.)

Morris, George W.: *History of the Eighty-First Regiment of Indiana Volunteer Infantry in the Great War of the Rebellion 1861 to 1865*, by Morris; 1901.

Morrow, Mathew L.: *The History of Tuscarawas County, Ohio*; 1884.

Morse, Bliss: *Civil War Diaries & Letters of Bliss Morse*, compiled and edited by Loren J. Morse; 1985.

Morse, John H.: Letter dated Oct. 16, 1862, *Civil War, The Letters of John Holbrook Morse, 1861-1865*, edited by Bianca Morse Federico and Betty Louise Wright; 1975.

Mosman, Chesley A.: *The Rough Side of War, The Civil War Journal of Chesley A. Mosman, 1st Lieutenant, Company D, 59th Illinois Volunteer Infantry Regiment*; edited by Arnold Gates; 1987.

Nichols, John H.: *Proof of the Pudding. Autobiography of John Harmon Nichols*, by Nichols; 1913.

Noblitt, D.J.: letter, *Mount Carmel Baptist Church*, by Haskell Roden, pages 138-140. (Book located in LCT Genealogical Society, Fayetteville, Tennessee. Book also referred to as "Haskell Roden's Red Oak Book, TN.")

Nostrand, Aaron V.: Letter dated Dec. 4, 1862; "Civil War Letter Tells Of Personal Experiences at Perryville," *The Kentucky Explorer*, May 1992. (Originally published in the Dec. 18, 1862, *Painesville* (Ohio) *Telegraph*.)

O'Neill, Edmund E.: *The Tennessee Civil War Veterans Questionnaires*, Volume Four, compiled by Gustavus W. Dyer and John Trotwood Moore; 1985.

O'Neill, W.: *The Cannelton* (Indiana) *Reporter*, Oct. 31, 1862; PBA.

Otto John H.: *Memoirs of a Dutch Mudsill, The "War Memories" of John Henry Otto*, edited by David H. Gould and James B. Kennedy; Kent State University Press; 2004.

Palmer, Joseph: transcript of letter dated Oct. 28, 1862, apparently published Nov. 18, 1862, in the *Macon* (Georgia) *Daily Telegraph*; PBPA. (Also in *Supplement to the Official Records of the Union and Confederate Armies*, edited by Janet B. Hewett; Part III – Correspondence, Volume 2, Serial No. 94; Broadfoot Publishing Co.; 1999.)

Patterson, William E.: *Campaigns of the 38th Regiment of the Illinois Volunteer Infantry, Company K, 1861-1863. The Diary of William Elwood Patterson*, edited by Lowell Wayne Patterson; Heritage Books; 1992.

Pepper, Alexander: *Memoirs of the Civil War, by Alexander Campbell Pepper,* Dean C. Anderson, editor; 1987.

Perry, Henry R.: *History of the Thirty-Eighth Regiment Indiana Volunteer Infantry*, by Perry; 1906.

Pillar, James: Letter dated Oct. 13, 1862; PBA.

Polk, J.J.: *Autobiography of Dr. J.J. Polk*, 1867.

Polk, Leonidas: *Three Months in the Southern States: April – June, 1863*, by Lieut.-Col. Fremantle; 1864. (For identity of Lt. Col. Tanner of the 22nd Indiana, see "Organizing a Signal Corps," by W.N. Mercer; CV 7 [1899], page 549.)

Pope, Curran: Letter dated Oct. 10, 1862; "Col. Pope's Account of the Battle of Perryville," *Louisville Journal*, Oct. 21, 1862

Porter, George C.: Volume XVI, Series I, Part I, *Official Records of the War of the Rebellion.*

Potter, Henry A.: Letter dated Oct. 12, 1862; PBA.

Poulson, Wesley S.: Letters to the *Cadiz Republican*, spring 1863, reprinted in *Wesley Smith Poulson and His Civil War. His Letters and Comments by His Grandson George Wesley Poulson*, by George W. Poulson; no date.
Preston, William E.M.: diary and history of the 33rd Alabama, SPR393, Alabama Department of Archives and History.
Price, James A.: Letter dated Oct. 16, 1862; Price-Moore Family papers ca. 1850-1956, Indiana Historical Society.
Putney, William G.: Memoir transcript; William L. Clements Library, The University of Michigan.

Quintard, Charles T.: *Doctor Quintard Chaplain C.S.A. and Second Bishop of Tennessee, Being His Story of the War (1861-1865)*, edited by the Rev. Arthur H. Noll; 1905.

Radcliffe, Charles K.: "Terrill's Brigade at Perryville," *National Tribune*, June 14, 1906.
Randall, James M.: *The James M. Randall Diary,* eHistory Web site (http:www.ehistory.com/) and Ohio State University.
Reed, A.N.: "The Battle of Perryville, Sanitary Commission, No.55, Reports from the Western Department."
Rennolds, Edwin H.: *A History of the Henry County Commands*, by Rennolds; 1904. Reprinted in 1961.
Riggs, Alfred: Letter dated Oct. 10, 1862; PBA.
Riley, Joseph E.: *The Tennessee Civil War Veterans Questionnaires,* Volume 5, compiled by Gustavus W. Dyer and John Trotwood Moore; 1985.
Robinson, John: "PERRYVILLE. A 1st Mich. Cavalryman Tells About the Fight," *National Tribune*, July 15, 1886.
Rogers, Robert M.: *The 125th Regiment Illinois Volunteer Infantry*, by Rogers; 1882.

Savage. John H.: *The Life of John H. Savage Citizen, Soldier, Lawyer, Congressman*, by Savage; 1903.
Scribner, B.F.: *How Soldiers Were Made; or The War as I saw It*, by Scribner; 1887.
Searcy, James T.: letter, dated Oct. 25, 1862; LPR 78, Box 3, Folders 14 and 15; Alabama Department of Archives and History.
Shanklin, James M.: "Account of the Battle of Perryville Ky., October 8, 1862," by Lt. Col. James M. Shanklin, 42nd Indiana; *The Soldier of Indiana in the War for the Union, Vol. 1;* 1866. (The 42nd Indiana Volunteer Infantry Web site; see also, *"Dearest Lizzie," The Civil War Letters of Lieutenant Colonel James Maynard Shanklin*, Kenneth P. McCutchan, editor; 1986))
Sheridan, Philip H.: *Personal Memoirs of P.H. Sheridan. General United States Army*, Vol. I; 1888.
Simonson, George T.: undated letter, *Princeton* (Indiana) *Clarion*, Oct. 25, 1862. (Web site for 80th Indiana)
Smith, Robert D.: *Confederate Diary of Robert D. Smith*, transcribed by Jill K. Garrett, Capt. James Madison Sparkman Chapter United Daughters of the Confederacy; 1975.
Steele, B.P. Steele: CV 17 (1909), page 163. Letter dated Sept. 17, 1905, published in *The Nashville American* newspaper, clipping in Mary Nichols Britt scrapbook, Nichols-Britt Collection, Reel 6, Box 11 (MSS microfilm 1322), Tennessee State Library and Archives.
Street, J.K.: letters written Oct. 3-10, 1862; Street Papers, #4180, The Southern Historical Collection, Wilson Library, The University of North Carolina at Chapel Hill.

Talley, William R.: *An Autobiography of Rev. William Ralston Talley with a Condensed History of The Talley Family*. Microfilm, Box No. 41, Drawer No. 283, Civil War Miscellany Files, Georgia Department of Archives and History.
Taylor, John M.: "Twenty-Seventh Tennessee Infantry," by Taylor, *Military Annals of Tennessee. Confederate*, edited by John B. Lindsley; 1886.
Taylor, Lester Dewitt: PBPA
Taylor, Robert B.: "The Battle Of Perryville, October 8, 1862 As Described In The Diary of Captain Robert B. Taylor," edited by Hambleton Tapp; *The Register of the Kentucky Historical Society*, October 1962, Vol. 60, No. 4.
Thompson, James R.: *Hear the Wax Fry*, Nellie Boyd, editor; 1966.
Tilford, John H.: Diaries, 1862-1866. A\T572; The Filson Historical Society.
Toney, Marcus B.: *The Privations of a Private*, by Toney: 1905.
Tourgee, Albion W.: *The Story of a Thousand, Being a history of the Service of the 105th Ohio Volunteer Infantry, in the War for the Union from August 21, 1862 to June 6, 1865*, by Tourgee; 1896.
Trask, W.L.: War Journal of W.L. Trask, "Adams's Louisiana Brigade at the Battle of Perryville, Kentucky," W.L. Trask Papers #380, 1861-1865; Special Collections Department, Robert W. Woodruff Library, Emory University.
Turner, William W.: William Weaver Turner Collection, Troup County (Georgia) Archives.
Tuttle, John W.: Diary, Perryville Battlefield State Historic Site archives.

Unidentified (Webster's brigade): the *Pittsburg Dispatch*, page 4, October 9, 1884. Also in "Perryville-Notes from a Civil War Soldiers Dairy", *The Kentucky Explorer*, June, 1991

Unidentified (15th Wisconsin): *The Fifteenth Wisconsin*, by O.A. Buslett; 1894 (translated by Barbara Scott; 1999).

Villard. Henry: *Memoirs of Henry Villard*; 1904.

Wagner, William: Letter published in the ethnic German *Illinois Staats Zeitung,* in Chicago; translated and reprinted Oct. 18, 1862, in the *Chicago Daily Tribune.* (Found on the Web site www.battleofperryville.com/24thilvi.html)

Watkins, Sam R.: *'Co. Aytch,' Maury Grays, First Tennessee Regiment, or, A Side Show of the Big Show*, by Watkins; 1882. And, *The Civil War in Maury County, Tennessee*, by Jill K. Garrett and Marise P. Lightfoot; 1966; *Columbia (*Tennessee) *Journal,* May 30, 1900).

West, A.J.: copy of unidentified newspaper article dated October 16, 1892; PBA.

Winters, Erastus: *In the 50th Ohio Serving Uncle Sam*, by Winters; 1905.

Womack, J.J.: *The Civil War Diary of Capt. J.J. Womack, Co. E., Sixteenth Regiment, Tennessee Volunteers*; 1961.

Wright, J. Montgomery: "Notes of a Staff-Officer at Perryville," by Wright, *Battles and Leaders of the Civil War*, Vol. 3.

Y.S.: *Cincinnati Gazette*, Oct. 9, 1862, (copy found on Web site: http://facweb.furman.edu/~bensonlloyd/hst49/CincinnatiPerryvilleReport.htm).

Yeatman, W.E.; memoir in the Tennessee State Library and Archives, Civil War Section, Box 14 and 16.

General References:

Perryville. This Grand Havoc of Battle, by Kenneth W. Noe; 2001.
Perryville. Battle for Kentucky, by Kenneth A. Hafendorfer; 1991.
Staff Ride Handbook for the Battle of Perryville, 8 October 1862, by Robert S. Cameron; 2005.
"Last Stand Ridge. The Other High Water Mark," by Kenneth Noe; *North & South*, September 2001, Vol. 4, No. 7.
"The Battle of Perryville," by Luke W. Finley; *Southern Historical Society Papers*, Vol. XXX, January-December, 1902.
The Battle of Perryville 2002. A National Civil War Reenactment, Commemorative Program, October 4-6, 2002, published by Perryville Enhancement Project.

Sources found on the Internet:

"A History of the 1st Tennessee Regiment Through the Eyes of Company D 'Williamson Grays,'" by Mike Hoover.
"An Eyewitness History of the 16th Regiment, Tennessee Volunteers, May 1861-May 1865*,"* by Jamie Gillum.
"Artillery and Terrain in the American Civil War: The Battle of Perryville, October 8, 1862," by Judy Ehlen, Robert J. Abrahart and William Andrews.
"Broken in Spirit," by Stuart W. Sanders; Kentucky Humanities Council Web site.
"Complete History of the Rock City Guards," http://www.first-tennsssee.co.uk/articles.rockcityguards.htm).
Chronology of the 16th Tennessee, "The Mountain Regiment," by Jamie Gillum.
"Confederate Heartland Offensive: June-October 1862: Perryville, Kentucky, Boyle County, October 8, 1862," by Paul Hawke; Civil War Guide.
"Danville Kentucky Weather, 8-9 October 1862, During the Battle of Perryville," The Kentucky Climate Center at Western Kentucky University.
"History of the Battle of Perryville," Perryville Enhancement Project.
"Owners of the Battlefield,"by Kurt Holman; Perryville Battlefield Special Collections.
"Perryville, Kentucky," History and Classroom, The Civil War Preservation Trust.
"Perryville's Bloody Cornfield," by Stuart W. Sanders; TheHistoryNet. Com Web site. Originally published in September 2002 issue of *America's Civil War*.
"Remembering Perryville: History and Memory at a Civil War Battlefield," by Kenneth W. Noe, Popular Culture Association and American Culture Association Conference, April 14, 2001.
"16th Tennessee Volunteer Infantry Regiment 1862," http:house.freeuk.co
"Stats and Facts about the Battle of Perryville," Centre College Web site.
"The Aftermath of the Battle of Perryville," Centre College Web site.
"The Battle of Perryville," by Thomas L. Breiner.
"The Battle of Perryville," by Michael Ragsdale; Web site for 47th Tennessee Infantry Regiment.27th Alabama Infantry Regiment Web site
"The Battle of Perryville, October 8, 1862," (a chronology) by Dave Smith.
"The Road to Perryville: The Kentucky Campaign of 1862," by Robert S. Cameron.
"The Retreat After the Battle of Perryville," by Thomas L. Breiner.

EYEWITNESSES INDEX

(' times quoted on same page)

Ayre, Josiah: 25'', 41'''', 43

Ball, William H.: 71'', 72, 75, 76, 98, 100
Barton, Brig. Gen. Seth M.: 120
Batchelor, Lt. Frank: 18, 27, 112
Beatty, Col. John: 9, 10, 30, 31'''''', 48, 87
Bell, Fannie: 118
Benson, Wallace P.: 84
Berkshire, Mrs. J.B.: 2, 3
Berry, John M.: 73'', 74''
Bevens, William E.: 6
Blackburn, James K.P.: 89, 94
Briscoe, A.B.: 17'''
Brown, Orderly Sgt. William A.: 5, 6'', 8, 14'', 15'', 88, 91, 95
Bruce, John A.: 54'', 55
Bryant, William A.: 47, 79
Burnett, Alf: 98, 104, 106, 108, 116

Cannon, J.P.: 72'', 73'''', 78, 79, 91
Carden, Robert C.: 21
Carlin, Brig. Gen. William P.: 2, 4'', 26'', 50, 76, 86
Carnes, Capt. W.W.: 5, 7, 9, 12, 13, 78
Carroll, Capt. John W.: 22
Chandler, Daniel H.: 10, 13, 16, 79'', 87
Cheatham, Maj. Gen. Benjamin F.: 95
Claiborne, Thomas: 86
Clark, Carroll H.: 8, 19, 20, 21, 35, 88, 95, 97, 110'', 112
Clark, William T.: 116''
Cleaver, A.D.: 10, 23
Connolly, Maj. James A.: 24, 58
Crawford, Dr. S.K.: 27, 61, 90, 104, 109, 113, 117
Cross, Chaplain Joseph: 26, 84, 85, 94, 97, 110
Cumings, Lt. Henry Harrison: 17, 23, 24'', 36''

Davis, Evan: 59, 60'', 78, 86, 88, 100
Davis, W.H.: 4, 8
Davison, E.L.: 1, 26'', 27, 61, 90
Day, L.W.: 87, 101
Dokken, Lars O.: 93, 96, 100

Ellis, Thomas B.: 8, 44, 49, 81
Emerson, Lt. Silas: 67''', 68, 102

Fahnestock, Capt. Allen L.: 4, 81, 87
Feild, Col. Hume R.: 52, 56, 57, 58''
Ferguson, Sgt. Edward: 54, 55, 77
Fielder, Capt. Alfred Tyler: 96, 97
Finlay, Luke W.: 6, 7, 56, 78
Fitch, Michael H.: 52, 53'''', 60'', 86'', 102
Frances, Charles L.: 96, 99, 100, 101
Frazer, Capt. C.W.: 30, 31''''', 43, 49, 87, 88

Gardner, George Q.: 71''''
Gates, Robert: 40
Gierhart, Sgt. A. Lanson: 27

Gipson, Sgt. W.C.: 1, 29, 30, 31'''', 32, 49
Glezen, Joseph P.: 20, 33, 34, 68'', 69
Graber, H.W.: 78, 79, 83
Gribble, Martin V.: 39
Griffin, David B.: 106
Grisham, W.T.: 80

Haguewood, Benjamin A.: 53, 77, 88, 112
Hall, Dr. J.C.: 61
Hall, Lt. James Iredell: 23, 25, 36, 40'', 52, 81, 89, 94, 109, 117
Hamilton, J.T.: 74
Harlan, Col. John M.: 51
Harrod, Stephen J.: 80
Hartzell, Lt. John Calvin: 24, 41, 42'', 43
Head, Thomas A.: 19
Headley, John W.: 47, 48'', 78, 91'', 97
Hearn, Lt. Col. W.C.: 44'', 45, 46, 49''
Holm, D.D.: 10, 13, 14, 79, 87
Holmes Jr., Sgt. Mead: 8, 79'', 86, 93, 99, 100, 103
Hooper, Thomas R.: 5'''', 33
Hoover, Sgt. Elias H.: 54''
Horrall, Lt. Spillard F.: 9, 11, 14, 28'', 29''', 64'''', 65''''', 66''
Hunt, William T.: 23'''
Hupp, Ormond: 3'', 10, 16, 23, 37, 38, 45, 51, 84, 93, 109
Hutchinson, Stephen J.: 24'', 25, 41, 42''

Inglis, Lt. John L.: 44, 45, 46, 47, 49
Inskeep, Capt. John D.: 104
Irion, Capt. John T.: 53''

Johnston, Adam S.: 90, 94, 113
Jones, George W.: 5''', 6, 14, 15, 16
Jordan, James D.: 39

Keeley, Charles W.: 98,
Kirkpatrick, George M.: 7, 8'', 11, 30, 64'''', 65'''', 66'', 79, 99, 100, 103, 120
Knowles, L.E.: 7'', 54, 77, 84
Kohlsdorf, Capt. Robert J.: 47''

Landrum, Lt. George W.: 9, 10, 11, 12, 13'', 14, 16, 20, 21'', 22, 100, 102, 103
Lathrop, D.: 63'', 71, 72, 75, 103'', 120
Lennard, J.N.: 25, 111
Liddell, Brig. Gen. St. John R.: 1, 73'''''', 74'''''', 75, 76
Little, Orderly Sgt. George: 13, 15, 50

Macmurphy, Gilbert L.: 17
Magee, John Euclid: 14'''', 91, 97
Malone, Capt. Thomas H.: 37'', 38, 39''', 40, 41, 56, 60, 97
McCahan, Capt. Thomas: 106, 109
McChord, William Caldwell: 93, 96, 105''', 106, 107

McCleary, William H.: 29, 30'', 64, 66, 84, 87, 100
McCouley, C.M.: 73, 75, 76
McDill, W.J.: 40
McDowell, Adjt. William P.: 32'''
McFarland, Sgt. Maj. Louis B.: 39, 40'', 59
Miller, Col. William: 43, 46, 49'', 78, 91''
Mills, Mrs. B.: 117
Milner, Sgt. Maj. Duncan C.: 34, 67'''', 68'', 77
Mitchell, Capt. William S.: 57, 58
Moore, Lt. W.R.: 59, 85, 94, 97, 118
Morris, Cpl. George W.: 82, 100, 105'', 106
Morse, Bliss: 25
Morse, John H.: 110
Mosman, Chesley S.: 103''

Nichols, John H.: 35
Noblitt, Dr. David J.: 95, 109, 115, 117
Nostrand, Aaron V.: 120

O'Neill, Lt. Edmund E.: 48
O'Neill, Capt. W.: 103
Otto, John H.: 102

Palmer, Capt. Joseph: 44'', 45
Patterson, William Elwood: 99
Pepper, Alexander: 63'', 70, 71'''', 109
Perry, Henry F.: 37, 44, 45, 99, 102, 103
Pillar, James: 53'', 54, 60
Polk, Dr. Jefferson J.: 4, 113, 116
Polk, Maj. Gen. Leonidas: 74
Pope, Col. Curran: 30, 32'''', 48
Porter, Col. George C.: 25, 26, 36, 39, 40, 59
Potter, Henry A.: 116
Poulson, Wesley S.: 21'', 34'', 66, 67'''', 68, 78, 81, 84, 90, 95, 96, 104, 110'', 115, 118''
Preston, William E.M.: 77, 80, 88, 95
Price, James A.: 120
Putney, William G.: 2, 4, 5, 7'', 79, 81''

Quintard, Chaplain/surgeon Charles: 26, 85'', 94, 111

Radcliffe, Charles K.: 24, 25, 42, 43, 58
Randall, Lt. James M.: 52, 79''
Reed, Dr. A.N.: 113, 114
Rennolds, Lt. Edwin H.: 19, 42, 43, 52, 53'', 56, 59, 60

Riggs, Cpl. Alfred: 5, 7
Riley, Joseph Edward: 57, 60, 98, 110
Robinson, Lt. John: 101
Rogers, Robert M.: 3, 81, 88, 93, 98, 106

Savage, Col. John H.: 18'', 19, 21, 22'''', 33'', 35''
Scribner, Col. B.F.: 37, 38, 45, 47'', 49, 69, 72
Searcy, James T.: 13, 16
Shanklin, Maj. James M.: 11'', 14, 16, 28, 29'''', 30, 64, 76, 120
Sheridan, Brig. Gen. Philip H.: 50, 82
Simonson, Maj. George T.: 22, 33
Smith, Capt. Robert D.: 94
Steele, Capt. Bailey P.: 54, 80
Street, J.K.: 78, 96

Talley, William R.: 8, 44''''', 45
Taylor, John M.: 8, 40, 59, 116, 117
Taylor, Lester D.: 24, 25, 42'', 43
Taylor, Capt. Robert B.: 36'', 40, 41, 42, 56, 58'', 59, 89
Thompson, James R.: 18, 19'', 21, 22'''', 35
Tilford, Dr. John: 2, 3, 96, 98, 100
Toney, Marcus B.: 55'''', 84'', 85'', 89, 98, 111
Tourgee, Albion W.: 9, 17, 24'''', 25'''', 36'''', 41'''', 43, 52'', 82, 87'', 88
Trask, W.L.: 28, 82'', 88, 91'', 95, 97
Turner, William W.: 77
Tuttle, Capt. John W.: 93, 100

Unidentified (15th Wisconsin): 99
Unidentified (Webster's brigade): 100, 102, 104

Villard, Henry: 79, 86, 93, 96, 107, 111, 112

Wagner, Dr. William: 98
Watkins, Sam: 6, 54'''', 55'''', 80'', 94
West, A.J.: 39'''''
Winters, Erastus: 9, 34, 78, 87
Womack, Capt. J.J.: 18
Wright, Maj. J. Montgomery: 2, 5, 63, 70'', 72

Yeatman, Lt. W.E.: 43, 47
YS: 10'', 11, 12, 13

GENERAL INDEX

Abott: 103
Adams, Capt. Charles F.: 102
Adams, Gen.: 28, 48
Adams, Jesse: 102
Adams, Lt. John B.: 102
Adams' brigade: 28, 47, 48, 49, 63, 66, 69, 72
Alabama, 33rd: 73
Alexander, Dr.: 110
Allen, Tip: 53
Allen brothers: 80
Ambulance train: 70
Anderson, Gen.: 94
Anderson's division: 9
Andrews, Lt. Albert: 8, 59, 116
Andrews, John: 39
Army of the Mississippi: 1
Army of the Ohio: 1
Arnold, Dr.: 6
Animals stampeded: 35
Antioch church field hospital: 90, 94, 109, 113, 116
Archer, Sam: 56
Arkansas, 2nd: 75
Arkansas, 6th: 75
Arkansas, 7th: 75
Austin, Maj.: 47, 48, 91
Ayres, John: 37

Baird, Archie: 118
Baker, Richard: 102
Ball, Maj. Grover: 46
Barbee, Col. Joshua: 118
Barn burns: 31, 48, 84, 102
Beatty, Col.: 48
Beehive robbed: 6
Bell, Capt.: 109
Bell, Col.: 97
Bently, Capt.: 102
Bierney, Nelson: 118
Blucher (Nat Wickliffe's horse): 93
Bond, Billy: 80
Bottom, "Squire" Henry Pierce: 105 (photo caption), 108
Bottom house field hospital: 11, 16, 28, 30, 43, 49, 52, 105 (photo caption)
Bottom, Mary Jane: 108
Bragg, 1, 2, 9, 86, 90, 94, 98, 110, 111, 120
Bragg's headquarters: 94
Breastplate: 98
Breed, Joseph: 118
Brooks, Lt. Col. Lewis: 68
Brown, Billy: 57
Brown, Gen.: 44, 46
Brown's brigade: 38, 43, 47, 49
Bryant, Capt.: 16, 28
Buckner, Gen.: 49, 78, 94
Buckner's division: 9
Buell, Gen.: 1, 4, 5, 26, 50, 51, 63, 82, 86, 93, 112, 120

Buell doesn't hear battle: 26, 63
Buell's headquarters: 26, 63, 82, 93, 96
Buford, Col.: 36
Buist, Dr.: 84, 98
Bush's Battery: 52, 54, 55, 56, 57, 58
Byrd, Capt. Capen: 46

Caldwell, Capt. A.W.: 53
Calhoun, John William: 52, 81
Calvert's Battery: 49
Camp, Lt. G.C.: 42
Camp Robinson: 110, 111, 112
Campbell, Mac: 85
Campbell, Maj.: 32
Campbell, Sam: 94
Canfield, Capt.: 42
Carnes, Capt: 14
Carnes, Will: 40, 117
Carnes' Battery: 14
Carter, Dan: 97
Carter, Sgt. Maj. John W.: 54
Casualties, Battle: 76
Centre College: 118
Chaplin Fork: 2, 26
Chaplin Creek: 99
Chaplin River: 9, 17
Chaplin's Hill: 7, 102
Chatham Hill: 43
Cheatham, Gen.: 14, 21, 73, 94
Cheatham's division: 5, 9, 11, 17, 18, 73, 74, 78, 83
Civilians gather unexploded ordnance: 101
Clark, Lt. F.M.: 53
Cleburne's brigade: 38, 43, 47, 48, 49, 63, 64, 65, 68, 69, 72
Cockrill, Emmett: 60
Cole, Sgt.: 88
Confederate, 5th: 1, 30, 49
Cornfield, the: 52
Countz, J.: 51, 84, 109
Crawford, G.W.: 56
Crawford, Lt.: 79
Crawford house: 9
Crittenden, Maj. Gen. Thomas L.: 1, 2, 111
Crittenden's corps: 4, 5, 50, 96, 112
Crutchfield, J.W.: 53
Cumings (Parsons' Battery): 36
Cummins, Sainty: 15
Curtright, Capt. John C.: 25, 39, 111

Danville: 1, 115, 117, 118
Danville courthouse: 115, 118
Danville seminary: 118
Darden's battery: 44, 49
Davis, Maj. J.R.: 4
Dead, buried: 98, 102, 103, 106, 107
Dead, described: 98, 101, 104, 106
Dead, hogs eating: 99

129

Dead, unburied: 98, 99, 101, 116
Deaths from the battle: 119
Denby, Lt. Col.: 29, 65, 66
"Devil's Lane": 24
Dinwiddie, A.A.: 53
Doctor's Creek: 11, 12, 14, 16, 28, 43, 47, 72, 100
Doctor's Fork: 4, 42
Donelson, Gen.: 18, 19, 21, 35
Donelson's brigade: 17, 19, 21, 22, 39
Donnell, Lt. Col. David M.: 35
Dorsey house: 82
Drunk: See also Liquor, Whiskey
Drunk Confederates: 84
Drunk officer: 46
Duglas, Bob: 31
Duncan, Lt.: 45
Dysentery: 118

Edwards, Capt.: 43
Eigenman, Capt.: 29
Erick, F.: 45
Erskine, Dr.: 97
Erwin, John L.: 118
Evans, Adjutant: 65, 66
Evans, Clay: 27
Evans, Capt. Mark: 17, 27, 112, 117

Feild, Col. Hume: 37, 56, 58, 98
Flash (William McChord's horse): 93
Florida, 3rd: 44
Flournoy, Capt. W.C.: 55
Fly, Col. James B.: 63
Foragers: 104, 109, 113
Forman, Capt. James B.: 32, 72
French, Capt.: 29

Garrard, Col.: 36, 40, 56
Garrard's battalion: 36
Gay, Capt. Ebenezer: 4, 11, 112
Geltz: 42
Gentry, Dr. W.M.: 61, 62
George (Capt. Malone's horse): 39, 40
George (Col. Savage's horse): 86, 94
Georgia, 41st: 22, 36, 37, 38, 39, 40, 52, 56
Gibbs, Capt.: 102
Gibson cornfield, Widow: 22
Gibson farm, Widow: 33
Gibson, Jeems: 108
Gibson, Widow (Mary Jane Bottom): 108
Gilbert, Acting Maj. Gen. Charles C.: 2, 50, 63, 75, 82, 111
Gilbert's corps: 4, 5, 7, 50, 96, 112
Giles, Sgt. Sam: 45
Gillett, Capt.: 53
Glass, Jack: 88
"Go to Boots": 100
Goddard, Dr.: 115
Goodbar, Jack: 55
Gooding, Col.: 70, 73
Gooding's brigade: 63, 72, 75
Goodnight house field hospital: 84, 85, 89, 94, 98, 109, 111, 116, 117

Graver, Lt.: 48
Green, Ike: 104
Grover, Capt.: 13
Guns, Confederates gather from battlefield: 78
Guns, defective: 33
Guns, left by Confederates: 95, 99, 100

Hall, Col.: 41
Hall, Lt.: 40
Hall, John Green: 118
Hamilton, Robert S.: 55, 84, 111
Hamilton, Mrs. W.C.: 84, 111
Hamilton, W.C.: 84, 111
Hammond, Lt.: 85
Hardee, Gen.: 1, 5, 9, 72, 94
"Harlan, Big Jim": 117
Harris, Capt. John W.: 53
Harris, Cpl. Bob: 42
Harris' Battery: 18, 19, 20, 21, 33, 34, 64, 68, 69, 100
Harris' brigade: 19, 22, 44, 47, 48, 107
Harrison, Capt.: 37, 109
Harrodsburg: 1, 5, 9, 94, 95, 97, 98, 110, 111, 112, 114, 118,
Harrodsburg courthouse: 97, 112
Harrodsburg turnpike: 91
Haslett, Dr.: 103
Haston, John T.: 110
Hathaway, Orderly Sgt.: 42
Hazlett, Dr.: 103
Henderson: 95
Hitchcock, Charlie: 43,
Hodge: 80,
Hogs eating corpses: 99
Hogue, Mrs.: 117
Holmes, James P.: 118
Holmes, Willie: 118
Horsley, A.S.: 80
Hospital No. 5: see under Methodist Church field hospital
Hospitals, field: 26, 27, 51, 59, 60, 61, 76, 113
Humphries, John P.: 94
Hutchinson, Lt. Thomas: 41, 42

Illinois, 24th: 56, 58
Illinois, 59th: 70, 75, 103
Illinois, 75th: 70, 73, 75
Illinois, 80th: 36, 41
Illinois, 123rd: 17, 23,
Indiana, 22nd: 70, 72, 73, 74, 75
Indiana, 38th: 37, 44, 47, 69
Indiana, 42nd: 28, 64, 69
Indiana, 80th: 20, 34, 64
Irby, Capt.: 40
Irion, Capt. John T.: 53
Irvine/Irwin, Capt. Lute B.: 80, 85

Jackson, Gen. James S.: 11, 17, 24, 25, 40, 60, 72, 90
Jackson's division: 10
James, Sgt. 'Ted': 54
Johnson, Gen.: 30
Johnson, Lt. A.R.: 102
Johnson's brigade: 28, 30, 31, 33, 38, 43, 47, 49, 100

130

Jones, Col.: 11, 29, 65
Jones, Ens. J.B.: 53
Jones, Jack: 30
Jones, Capt. Joel L.: 117
Jones' brigade: 22, 23, 28, 37, 38
Jordan, Samuel: 39
Jouett, Lt. Col.: 32

Keith, Lt. Col. S.I.: 74
Keller, Mrs.: 97
Kelley, Bill: 56
Kelly, Col. John H.: 74
Kelso, Maj.: 36
Kennerly, Sgt.: 42
Kentucky, 15th (U.S.): 30, 31, 32, 48, 49, 64, 72, 102
Kimmel, Maj.: 107

Lamb, Maj.: 53,
Lane, Capt.: 96,
Lane, Col.: 96,
Lanier, Tom: 55,
Lanneau: 13,
Lebanon: 116, 117,
Lee, Lt. Joe P.: 55,
Lemmon, Jas.: 52,
Lemmon, Robert: 118,
Lester, Capt. J.R.: 4,
Lice: 8,
Liddell's brigade: 72,
Lisenby, J. Seaborn: 95,
Liquor (see also Drunk, Whiskey): 46, 58, 97, 101, 107,
Lockwood: 65,
Loomis, Capt.: 10, 13, 16,
Loomis' Battery: 10, 11, 12, 13, 14, 16, 64,
Louisville: 116, 117,
Lytle, Col.: 10, 11, 13, 29, 48, 61,
Lytle's brigade: 22, 30, 38, 49, 52, 82, 107,

Mackville tavern: 114
Malone, Capt.: 39
Maney, Gen.: 36, 37, 59
Maney, Lt. Thomas H.: 80, 85
Maney's brigade: 17, 21, 33, 39, 77
Maney's first line: 23, 28, 35, 42, 52, 56, 58, 60
Maney's second line: 36, 37
Markham, Ivy S. "Parson": 115, 117
Marks, Col. A.S.: 30
Marshall, Tom: 45
Martin, Lt.: 82, 83
Mass, Thomas/Tom: 67, 102
Matheney, Nath: 30
Mathes, Harvey: 43
Maury Grays: 85
McCall, Lt.: 95
McCall, Calvin P.: 15,
McCook, Maj. Gen. Alexander M.: 2, 16, 26, 63, 66, 70, 71, 72, 76, 106, 111, 1112
McCook, Col. Edward: 112
McCook's corps: 4, 7, 9, 17, 50, 51, 63, 96
McCreight, Gladney: 40

McCutcheon, Sgt.: 65
McDaniel, Col.: 117
McDill, George: 118
McGrath, Lt.: 32
McIntire, Capt.: 66
McKinney, Adjt. T.H.: 54
McLemore: 56, 97
McMeans, surgeon: 27
McWhorter, Frank: 39
Measles: 118
Melton, Tom: 118
Mercer, Andrew Dow: 33
Messenger, Charlie: 58
Messick: 118
Methodist Church field hospital: 104, 110, 115, 118
Milam, Lt. J.B.: 53
Miller, C.: 45
Mills, Mrs.: 27
Mississippi, 32nd: 73
Mitchell, Color Sgt.: 54
Mitchell, Gen.: 50
Mitchell, Lt.: 102
Mitchell's division: 10
Moon, the: 72, 73, 79, 82, 88, 89
Moore, Dr.: 118
Mullins: 89
Muscroft, Dr: 104
Myler, Capt.: 25

Nash, Dick: 64
New Albany: 117
New Haven: 117

Odor, Capt.: 67
Ohio, 2nd: 22
Ohio, 3rd: 27, 30, 32, 48, 49, 102, 104
Ohio, 10th: 10, 16, 22, 29, 30, 35, 48, 49, 64, 82, 104, 114
Ohio, 33rd: 17, 20, 22, 64
Ohio, 92nd: 114
Ohio, 98th: 66, 69
Ohio, 105th: 23, 24, 35, 41
Ohio, 121st: 66, 69, 116
Olmstead, Capt.: 64, 65, 79, 103
Open Hill: 17, 35, 38, 52
Open Knob: 17

Padlock, Widow: 2
Paisley, John: 59
Palmer, Capt.: 45
Palmer's Battery: 44
Parsons' Battery: 9, 17, 19, 21, 23, 24, 28, 35, 36, 37, 38, 40, 42
Patterson, Lt. Col. John S.: 37, 55, 56, 83 (?), 98
Peeples, John R.: 53
Pegues, A.M.: 40
Pennsylvania, 79th: 56, 58
Perryville: 5, 6, 113, 114, 115, 116
Perryville, Federals enter: 100
Peter's farm: 64
Pettit, A.: 45

131

Philadelphia Inquirer: 106
Pilcher, Capt. M.B.: 85
Pinney's Battery: 63, 70, 75
Plant, Lt.: 7
Pneumonia: 118
Polk, Dr. Jefferson J.: 105 (text and photo caption)
Polk, Gen. Leonidas: 2, 5, 9, 16, 37, 74, 75, 76, 94, 111
Poole, Capt. William T.: 46
Poorman, Lt. Col.: 77
Pope, Col. Curran: 31, 48
Porman, Lt. Col.: 67
Premonition: 8
Prewitt house field hospital: 95, 109, 115
Price, Capt.: 79

Quinn, Ed.: 40

Rains, Capt. Thomas B.: 39
Ramrod, Haguewood shot with: 53, 88, 112
Reid, Col. William P.: 116
Rice, Nelson: 53, 54
Richardson, Byron: 80
Road, Benton: 69, 75
Road, Mackville: 2, 63, 76
Road, Springfield: 2, 4, 116
Rogers, James L.: 118
Rousseau, Gen.: 10, 11, 111
Roycroft, J.C.: 15
Rucker: 56
Rucker, George: 57
Russell house: 9, 16, 63, 69, 71, 76, 77, 82, 103

Sanders, Rev. Miles: 28
Sandusky, William: 118
Sanitary Commission, U.S.: 114, 115
Savage, Col.: 19, 21, 22, 35, 85, 94, 97, 110
Saxon, Capt.: 49
Saxon, Frank: 49, 81
Schoepf, Gen.: 63
Schumacher, Maj.: 102
Scribner, Col. B.F.: 37
Seabrook, Lt. Ed.: 39
Seminary hospital: 114, 115
Sessions, Capt.: 102
Seward, A.; 106
Sewell, Joe: 56, 97
Sheridan's division: 10, 16, 81
Shivers: 16
Signal corp 9, 11
Simonson, Capt.: 10, 12
Simonson's Battery: 11, 13, 19, 21, 22, 28, 37, 38, 43, 45
"Simonton's Ohio Battery": 83
Skinner, Tom: 45
Slocomb, Capt.: 28
Slocomb's Battery (also Washington Artillery): 29, 49, 76
Smith, Col.: 43
Smith, Gen. Kirby: 1, 98, 110, 111
Sound of battle uncovered: 70
Springfield: 1, 90

Stanford, Capt.: 15
Starkweather, Col.: 11
Starkweather's brigade: 77, 107
Steadman, Gen.: 109
Steedman's brigade: 75
Steele, Capt. B.P.: 85
Stephens, Scott: 80
Stewart's brigade: 17, 21, 77
Stewart's regiments: 56
Stone's Battery: 52, 56
Stones River, Battle of: 120
Sullivan, John: 89
Sullivan, Mrs. John: 89
Sulpher Spring field hospital: 116
Sweet, Col.: 60
Swor, Lt. Col.: 53
Swor, G. Wash.: 53

Tennessee, 1st: 22, 37, 52, 54, 55, 56, 57
Tennessee, 6th: 22
Tennessee, 4th Cav. Bn.: 4
Tennessee, 4th: 42, 52, 56, 59, 60
Tennessee, 5th: 42, 52, 56, 59, 60
Tennessee, 6th: 37, 38, 40, 56
Tennessee, 9th: 22, 36, 37, 38, 40, 52, 56
Tennessee, 15th: 18, 19, 21, 22
Tennessee, 16th: 18, 19, 20, 21, 22
Tennessee, 17th: 30
Tennessee, 23rd: 30, 49
Tennessee, 25th: 30
Tennessee, 27th: 22, 36, 37, 38, 39, 52, 56
Tennessee, 33rd: 56
Tennessee, 37th: 28, 30, 43, 49
Tennessee, 38th: 19, 21, 35
Tennessee, 44th: 30
Terrill, Brig. Gen. William R.: 23, 24, 36, 37, 41, 42, 43, 52, 56, 58, 72, 89
Terrill's brigade: 17, 19, 36, 38, 42, 52
Thomas, Maj. Gen. George H.: 4, 109
Thomasson: 115
Thompson, Andrew: 53
Thompson, John: 80
Thompson, Mrs.: 106
Tolley, John: 118
Truckee, Peter: 79
Tucker, John T.: 80
Tucker house field hospital: 116
Turner's Battery: 36, 37
Typhoid: 118

Venable, Col.: 53

Walden, Elias: 103,
Washington Artillery: see Slocomb's Battery
Waire, Bob: 39,
Wakefield, John W.: 15,
Walker, David C.: 31,
Walker's Bend: 17,
Washington Artillery (also Slocomb's Battery): 28, 86,
Water: 1, 2, 3, 4, 5, 11,
Webster, Billy; 55,

Webster, Col.: 66, 68, 77,
Webster's brigade: 19, 33, 64, 68,
Wechselberg, Wm. E.: 57,
Welch, J.W.: 115,
West, Adjt. Samuel: 103
Wharton, Eugene "Spludge": 54
Wheeler: 89
Wheless, I.H.: 85
Whiskey (see also Drunk, Liquor): 1, 51, 88
White, Moses: 43
White, Dr. P.P.: 114
"white house," The: 27
Whitthorne, W.J. "Bill/Billy": 55, 80, 85
Wickliffe, Nat: 93

Wilkerson house field hospital: 27, 61, 77, 89, 90, 104, 109, 113, 117
Wing, Rumsey: 72
Wisconsin, 1st: 54, 55, 58
Wisconsin, 10th: 11, 21, 22, 44, 47
Wisconsin: 21st: 52, 53, 54, 58
Woldridge, Lt. T.H.: 80, 85
Wood, Gen,: 9
Wood's brigade: 64, 69, 72
Woodward, Sam: 89